India's Constitutional Identity

An analysis of selective aspects of India's constitutional identity, this book provides an analytical account of the changing and changed texture of India's constitutional identity bearing in mind the historical context in which it is articulated.

The book conceptualizes the gradual evolution of an idea by tracing the history of India's constitutionalism with reference to its conceptual roots, historical antecedents and the landmark judicial pronouncements in which the concern for its retention and protection is always privileged. The author examines specific constitutional designs that the 1950 Constitution of India put in place and argues that constitutional identity, despite being drawn on specific constitutional provisions, is also changeable in view of the rapidly transforming socio-economic milieu. He demonstrates that there are numerous instances where India's constitutional identity has undergone a metamorphosis in circumstances where newer politico-ideological values and norms are privileged.

A valuable addition to the literature on constitutionalism and constitutional practices in general and their manifestation in India's democratic experiences, in particular, this book will be of interest to academics in the fields of Government, Political Science, Law and Jurisprudence, Constitutional and Legal History and Asian Studies.

Bidyut Chakrabarty is Vice Chancellor of Visva Bharati University, Santiniketan, West Bengal, India. He is the author of numerous books on Indian Politics and Gandhi. His most recent monograph is *Localizing Governance in India*, also published by Routledge (2017). His research interests include Public Administration, Indian Politics, Indian Political Thought and Movement and the Indian Nationalist Movement.

Routledge Studies in South Asian Politics

11 **Government and Politics in Sri Lanka**
Biopolitics and Security
A. R. Sriskanda Rajah

12 **Politics and Governance in Bangladesh**
Uncertain Landscapes
Edited by Ipshita Basu, Joe Devine and Geoffrey Wood

13 **Constitutional Democracy in India**
Bidyut Chakrabarty

14 **Radical Politics and Governance in India's North East**
The Case of Tripura
Harihar Bhattacharyya

15 **The Security State in Pakistan**
Legal Foundations
Syed Raza

16 **The Socio-political Ideas of BR Ambedkar**
Liberal constitutionalism in a creative mould
Bidyut Chakrabarty

17 **The Politics of US Aid to Pakistan**
Aid Allocation and Delivery from Truman to Trump
Murad Ali

18 **India's Constitutional Identity**
Ideological Beliefs and Preferences
Bidyut Chakrabarty

For more information about this series, please visit: https://www.routledge.com/asianstudies/series/RSSAP

India's Constitutional Identity

Ideological Beliefs and Preferences

Bidyut Chakrabarty

Routledge
Taylor & Francis Group
LONDON AND NEW YORK

First published 2019
by Routledge

2 Park Square, Milton Park, Abingdon, Oxfordshire OX14 4RN
52 Vanderbilt Avenue, New York, NY 10017

Routledge is an imprint of the Taylor & Francis Group, an informa business

First issued in paperback 2020

British Library Cataloguing-in-Publication Data
A catalogue record for this book is available from the British Library

Library of Congress Cataloging-in-Publication Data
Names: Chakrabarty, Bidyut, 1958– author.
Title: India, democracy and constitutional identity : ideological beliefs and preferences / Bidyut Chakrabarty.
Description: Abingdon, Oxon ; New York, NY : Routledge, 2019. |
Series: Routledge studies in South Asian politics ; 18 |
Includes bibliographical references and index.
Identifiers: LCCN 2018054387 (print) | LCCN 2019004722 (ebook) |
ISBN 9780429507175 (ebook) | ISBN 9780429016530 (adobe reader) |
ISBN 9780429016516 (mobipocket) | ISBN 9780429016523 (epub) |
ISBN 9781138580701 (hbk) | ISBN 9780429507175 (ebk)
Subjects: LCSH: Constitutional history—India. | India—Politics and government—1947– | Democracy—India.
Classification: LCC KNS1760 (ebook) |
LCC KNS1760 .C435 2019 (print) | DDC 342.5402/9—dc23
LC record available at https://lccn.loc.gov/2018054387

ISBN: 978-1-138-58070-1 (hbk)
ISBN: 978-0-367-66065-9 (pbk)

Typeset in Times New Roman
by codeMantra

Dedicated to those fighting for justice amidst adversaries

Contents

Preface

India's Constitutional Identity: ideological beliefs and preferences is a sequel to other books that I have recently published. There are three books which can be said to have provoked me to write the present one, namely *Constitutional Democracy in India* (Routledge, Oxford, 2018), *Constitutionalizing India: An Ideational Project* (Oxford University Press, New Delhi, 2018) and *The Socio-Political Ideas of BR Ambedkar: Liberal Constitutionalism in a Creative Mould* (Routledge, Oxford, 2019). Needless to say, I have drawn on them, rather liberally, because I believe that building one argument over another helps one to develop a mega-argument, which is useful to explore mega social processes and formations. My academic exercises, undertaken so far, have convinced me that one of the most persuasive ways of meaningful explorations is to approach themes from the conceptual point of view. One needs to be little careful here because concepts by themselves may not be always helpful since they are also context-driven. Hence, they may not have, for obvious reasons, universal applications; nonetheless, they provide useful inputs to comprehend themes which are intertwined in social, economic and political processes in similar circumstances. India is a good example. Given the long duration of colonial rule, it is conceptually apt to argue that colonial system of constitutionalism cannot be ignored while theoretically grasping India's constitutional identity. It is equally true that the nationalist interventions also remained a significant source of conceptualization. A persuasive explanation is thus possible only by comprehending the dialectical interconnections between these multiple influences stemming from the prevalent socio-economic and political milieu. I have endeavoured to analytically dissect the processes that finally led to the rise and consolidation of a specific kind of constitutional democracy in India which is, simultaneously, both derivative and indigenous.

There is a further caution: despite being thematically more or less similar, my books on constitutionalism seek to capture the multifaceted character of its growth and strengthening in India. It is true that BR Ambedkar along with his colleagues who held identical views contributed significantly to the creation of a liberal democratic polity in India. Equally true is the contention that he, despite being opposed to Gandhi's widely hyped notion of village swaraj, had to accommodate the demands of the Gandhians for including panchayati raj governance in the 1950 Constitution; furthermore, he had to step down and was forced to give up his demand for gender equality when his friends championing liberal values did not back him when he was in favour of adopting the 1951 Hindu code Bill. These descriptive details are indicative of the complex processes contributing to India's constitutional identity, which cannot be conceptualized in a neat theoretical format as it is enmeshed in the equally far more complex social, economic and political realities. Similarly, the argument that India's constitutional identity is derivative of the philosophy of Enlightenment gains credence in view of the contribution that the British liberals made in creating circumstances in favour of liberal democracy. This is the theme of my *Constitutionalizing India* book which, on the basis of a thorough analysis of both the derivative and indigenous conceptual roots of Enlightenment ideas, establishes the point that constitutionalizing India is a dialectical intermingling of processes rooted in the perennial battle between the colonizers and their *bete noir*, the colonized.

A book is written by an author; but in the completion of such an exercise, help from multiple sources is required. In other words, though the author gets the credit, he/she cannot solely claim the credit given the fact that without help from others the exercise can never reach fruition. This book is not an exception. I fondly remember Dorothea and Alex of Routledge for their constant support to my academic endeavour. Two of my colleagues, Prof. Amrit Sen of Visva Bharati and Dr. Prakash Chand of Dyal Singh College, Delhi University, have also their share in improving the text. I express my gratitude to them. My students in various campuses across many continents have helped me articulate my thoughts by raising pertinent questions. Without their engagement with me, it would not have been possible for me to meaningfully deal with such a complex theme as constitutional identity. By being supportive, my family – my wife, Sanchtia and two kids, Barbie and Pablo – remains a constant source of inspiration even in adverse circumstances which I had to confront for reasons which were beyond my comprehension. Mini and Tinku, my Kolkata-based sisters and their daughters, Sreeja and Debiparna made my trip to the city of joy always self-satisfying. My colleagues in Delhi University and in departments in various parts of the globe where I taught inspired me by being both appreciative and vehemently opposed to me, again for reasons which I have failed to fathom so far. Nonetheless, I express my heartfelt gratitude to my friends and opponents for their sustained interests in me and my career confirming the assumption that 'nobody kicks a dead horse'. I must mention that in my long academic stint, I am also fortunate to have had support from so many of my 'unknown' friends who always stood by me and helped me understand life in a completely new perspective. Mere expression of being grateful to them may not be enough. I therefore bow down, with heartfelt gratitude, before them.

The preface shall remain incomplete without remembering my teachers who had unconditional faith in my ability, which was always a source of inspiration. It is perhaps the most befitting occasion for me to remember my parents who, being always generous in showering love and care, also taught me the art of being resilient amidst adversaries; my brother who is no more also instilled in me, in a very short stint of his life, the capacity to remain firm and strong in circumstances which were not exactly in my favour because battle for justice instantaneously creates enemies and is always a long-drawn one.

Bidyut Chakrabarty
Asian-Africa Institute
Hamburg University
Hamburg, Germany

Introduction

Constitution is a design of governance. It is a design that draws on chosen ideational principles which receive endorsement presumably because they help the Constitution to articulate and also translate them into practice. The idea is very simple: Constitution is based on certain fundamental principles, those principles which are critical in shaping a specific kind of governance. An example will suffice here. Broadly speaking, in so far as constitutional principles are concerned, there are two major politico-ideological perspectives: one is derived from liberal constitutionalism, and the other is drawn on the Marxist ideological paradigm. The 1977 Constitution of the erstwhile Soviet Union had its ideological roots in Marxism-Leninism, which means that it was modelled after the politico-ideological format of governance that the latter had preferred. So, in terms of its identity, it was Marxist-Leninist in character and also texture. In a similar vein, the 1789 US Constitution has a clear liberal imprint since it draws its ideological sustenance from the fundamental ideational principles of the philosophy of Enlightenment upholding toleration, compassion and empathy. Accepting individual as the focal point of the polity, liberal constitutionalism privileges the former, while the Marxist-Leninist design of constitutional governance cares more for the collectivity of the majority, proletariat in its ideological lexicon. Implicit here is the argument that for conceptualizing constitutional identity, one needs to be attentive to the ideological foundation of a Constitution for it lays out not only the structure of governance but also its vocabulary. What is thus argued here is the point that constitutional identity is intrinsically ideological since it is derivative of the core social, economic and political values, which are critical to its articulation in a particular fashion.

Important here is also the point that Constitution is also a structure because it contains a design in which the constitutional principles need to be translated into practice by specific policy designs. In other words, a Constitution remains a mere compilation of rules and regulations, however novel they are, unless they contribute to the unfolding and also consolidation in a way which conforms to the basic principles providing ideological sustenance. In two ways, this is sought to be accomplished, as the global experiences of constitutional governance inform: on the one hand, it is a matter of common sense that constitutional values help develop policy priorities in a particular fashion; it is also, on the other, imperative that the prevalent constitutional design is also adequately equipped to create an ambience in which those policy options are preferred and heartily accepted by those for whom they were adopted. What is implied here is the critical importance of specific politico-ideological processes, which make them happen and are upheld as axiomatic under the present socio-economic and political milieu. Here is another significant idea which needs reiteration. The structure of a Constitution is certainly important, but their importance is linked with the ideological character of the Constitution: if it is a liberal Constitution, the responses shall be articulated in a fashion which is radically different from that of a Marxist-Leninist Constitution.

One, however, has to add a caveat here because in practice one may not come across ideal types of either a liberal or a Marxist-Leninist Constitution. Hence, one has to couch one's conceptualization of constitutional identity accordingly. The point being made here is about the need to provide a contextual understanding of constitutional identity. It is true that the fundamental identity is derived from the basic values of an ideological predisposition; it is also true that in specific circumstances, one also confronts deviation of serious nature. In order to grasp constitutional identity of a Constitution in a milieu, one needs to be sensitive to the contextual compulsions and priorities; otherwise, the analysis of constitutional identity leads us nowhere. What is implied here is the argument that it is incumbent on the analyst to be aware of (a) the fundamental principles, or the core values, of the preferred ideological predisposition, and (b) the contextual inputs which may, on the surface, stand in contradiction with the former. Constitutional identity is thus neither static nor inflexible, but directional because it helps us understand the principal values and mores on which a particular Constitution evolves and gains acceptability.

Besides helping us grasp the character of a Constitution, constitutional identity is indicative of the power-relationships in which a specific constitutional design flourishes. In other words, in conceptualizing constitutional identity, the importance of politico-ideological processes supportive of a Constitution cannot be underplayed. By drawing on the same examples, one can illustrate the point: the 1977 Constitution of the dismantled Soviet Union drew its inspiration from the Marxist teaching that a true revolution was possible only with the liquidation of the bourgeoisie, which means that to conceptualize a new power-relationship, the extermination of a section of society was inevitable. The Constitution left no stone unturned in translating the conceptual idea into practice by including supportive provisions in the text. This was never a point of discussion among the framers of the Constitution nor was it a bone of contention at least at the initial stages of the evolution of the Soviet model of governance. For the 1789 US Constitution, the same argument holds water. Once the arguments for a confederal US lost their steam, the Federalists, Alexander Hamilton, James Madison and John Jay, succeeded in creating an environment in which the idea of a liberal US polity gained an easy acceptance. Constitutional liberalism was privileged presumably because it was both an outcome of an ideological commitment to the values of Enlightenment by the founding fathers and also their endorsement of specific ideological priorities which they espoused in their mission to make the US a liberal polity. Basic to the argument is the idea that constitutional identity represents a specific ideological texture which is largely, if not exclusively, derivative of the primary ideational value preferences. What is also clear now is the fact that constitutional identity, despite being drawn on fundamental ideological predispositions, does not seem to be static given the constantly changing socio-economic and political milieu in which the former are being reinvented.

II

Constitutional identity is also about a set of moral codes which are considered to be guiding principles for governance. A polity is meant to serve public well-being as it is governed by the prevalent moral codes which, if undermined, shall destroy the foundational values on which it is based. As argued above, Constitution upholds those moral codes which are also determinant precepts in so far as policymaking is concerned. So, conceptually, constitutional identity is a decisive mode of shaping how constitutional governance of a specific polity is articulated. Drawn on certain fundamental values and principles, Lawrence Tribe thus argues that the very identity of a Constitution,

> the body of textual and historical materials from which [fundamental constitutional] norms are to be extracted and by which their application is to be guided – is … a matter that cannot be objectively deduced or passively discerned in a viewpoint-free way.[1]

An analytical scan of the definition reveals that it is a three-dimensional definition. First, it is impossible to conceptualize a Constitution without reference to certain 'fundamental norms' in its defence which means that the former is without substance independent of the latter. Second, these fundamental norms are adhered to while devising specific designs for governance. This also entails that they cannot be undermined under any circumstances since it means the total abrogation of the values on which specific constitutional acts are justified. Third, the most critical aspect of constitutional identity is that it is neither absolutely 'objective' nor bereft of subjective preference of those engaged in the making of a Constitution. Implicit here are two important conceptual ideas: on the one hand, it is forcefully argued that constitutional identity is not given, but is built on deliberate interventions by those who act critically in shaping a Constitution; this means, on the other, that it upholds specific viewpoints which are guided, if not determined, by those involved in framing a Constitution. What is striking and also persuasive in this conceptualization is the idea that constitutional identity is deliberately chosen to opt for a specific politico-ideological course. This is a valid assessment because constitutional identity is also about the aspirational deeds of a nation which defends a particular kind of Constitution to fulfil what it deems appropriate for its distinctive politico-ideological mission.

There is another aspect which needs equal attention. The above argument that constitutional identity entails national aspiration also draws our attention to its contextual character. It is a matter of common sense that universally aspired moral codes may not always be decisive unless they are couched in local languages, mores and sentiments. For instance, liberalism had hardly had a constituency in India's nationalist offensive against the British so long as it was conceptualized in typical Western vocabulary; it became a force to reckon with once it was articulated as an instrument for building fraternity, or *Bhaichara/Hamdardi* in Indian parlance, among the socioculturally divided Indian communities. It was thus easier for BR Ambedkar and his colleagues in the Constituent Assembly to evolve a consensus for constitutional democracy in the liberal mould because it was hailed as perhaps the most appropriate system for evolving a well-knit collectivity. There were, of course, opponents who failed to muster enough support in their favour in circumstances in which constitutional liberalism appeared to have prevailed over other politico-ideological priorities.[2] What is being argued here is the point that the constitutional discourse, despite having certain generic attributes, is reduced to a mere elaboration of certain diktats unless that is linked with 'the particularistic commitments' of those being engaged in constitutionally articulating appropriate values and principles for specific nationalist purposes. This is most eloquently stated by Jacobsohn when he argued that

> fixed [constitutional] norms need to be reconciled with the particularistic commitments of local traditions and practices; the substance of a nation's constitutional identity will to a large extent reflect how the essentials of constitutionalism combine and interact with the attributes of a constitution that are expressive of unique histories and circumstances.[3]

Constitutional identity is not therefore about those universal principles, but is a creative blending of these principles with the particularistic articulation of values and mores, stemming from local traditions and practices. For a clearer understanding of what it means, an analytical dissection of the term, identity, shall be of help here: in simple terms, identity is about a particularistic self-understanding of an individual or a collectivity which is usually couched in an explanation highlighting the shared socio-economic and politically distinctive characteristics or attributes. This is also a tool for articulating self-interests of a collectivity based on a kind of sameness among those constituting the collectivity. Understood both objectively (by being together within a nation state) and subjectively (by evolving a set of distinctive individual/collective psychological traits), sameness is both a felt and internalized phenomenon which is expressed in solidarity, in shared dispositions or consciousness or in collective action. Identity thus denotes an urge to be one for a collectivity by instilling in the constituents the idea that it comprises, regardless of the internal differences, a bounded compact vis-à-vis the rest. The purpose here is to develop a consolidated self for fulfilling specific politico-ideological objectives, as history has amply shown. In other words, fundamental here is the concern for generating sameness with a view to attaining a goal, appreciated, if not shared, by those belonging putatively to the collectivity in question. An example shall illustrate the point. This is amply clear that the 1789 US Constitution is based on the 1776 famous declaration of independence that

> all men are created equal, that they are endowed by their Creator with certain unalienable rights, that among these are Life, Liberty and the Pursuit of Happiness, [and] that to secure these rights, Governments are instituted among Men, deriving their just powers from the consent of the governed.[4]

By laying out the objectives, the Declaration also set out specific goals that were complementary to the mission that was considered supreme by the signatories. Designed with a clearly spelt-out ideological goal, the Declaration further stated that

> these united Colonies are, and of Right ought to be Free and Independent States, that they are Absolved from Allegiance to the British Crown, and that all political connection between them and the State of Great Britain, is and ought to be totally dissolved; and that as Free and Independent States, they have full Power to levy War, conclude Peace, contract Alliances, establish Commerce, and to do all other Acts and Things, which Independent States may of right do.[5]

The Declaration was not just a declaration for independence but also contained certain foundational politico-ideological values that the 1789 US Constitution epitomized. That the Constitution was to be a liberal one drawn on the core values of the philosophy of Enlightenment was a foregone conclusion for the Constitution-framers who sat to draft the Constitution in the 1776 Philadelphia Convention. One may thus put forward the point that in conceptualizing the US Constitution's constitutional identity, one should not gloss over this aspect of the Declaration which, in unambiguous terms, curves out a specific ideological path for future governance. So, the Declaration was critical to constitutional identity in this regard though efforts were regularly made to translate the values that it had set out for the US citizens by adding newer measures to meaningfully address their newer concerns. For instance, the 1863 Emancipation Proclamation complemented the aspirational desire of the founding fathers to translate the idea of 'all men created equal', which was vacuous so long as slavery was maintained in the US. By proclaiming that

> all persons held as slaves within the designated State, and part of States, are and henceforward shall be free, and that the Executive government of the United States, including the military and naval authorities thereof, will recognize and maintain the freedom of said persons.[6]

The Thirteenth Amendment to the US Constitution (1865) reinforced the values of Enlightenment by abolishing slavery, which stood in contradiction with the fundamental Declaration that the US Constitution-makers so assiduously upheld.[7] Example are abound to show how constitutional identity evolves; this also demonstrates the conceptual limitations of the argument defending the point that constitutional identity is sacrosanct and this cannot be fiddled with. This is partly true because the fundamental values on which an identity is built remain inviolable. The 1863 Emancipation Proclamation and the consequent 1865 Thirteenth Amendment was an endorsement of the Jeffersonian ideological concern, which made no sense so long as slavery existed. This is true of any Constitution which, unless receptive to the prevalent politico-ideological needs of the day, shall just become a document without life. There was hardly a far more powerful elucidation of this argument than the first Inaugural Address (1861) of the newly elected Abraham Lincoln as the sixteenth US President in which he forcefully argued that

> the country, with its institutions, belongs to the people who inhabit it. Whenever they shall grow weary of the existing Government, they can exercise their constitutional right of amending it or their revolutionary right to dismember or overthrow it. I cannot be ignorant of the fact that many worthy and patriotic citizens are desirous of having the National Constitution amended. While I make no recommendation of amendments, I fully recognize the rightful authority of the people over the whole subject, to be exercised in with the modes prescribed in the instrument itself; and I should, under existing circumstances, favour rather than oppose a fair opportunity being afforded to the people to act upon it. I will venture to add that to me the convention mode seems preferable, in that it allows amendments to originate with the people themselves, instead of only permitting them to take or reject propositions originated by other, not especially chosen for the purpose, and which might not be precisely such as they would wish to either accept or refuse.[8]

Lincoln's statement is an endorsement of the fundamental attributes of the US constitutional identity and also directional for future in the sense that it charted out a specific course of steps to attain the ideological mission which the Constitution was meant to achieve. There are two interlinked concerns that the sixteenth US President expressed: on the one hand, he proclaimed that he was, out an out, a democrat and being a democrat, he held the view that demos reigned supreme which he articulated by saying that 'they had the constitutional right' of changing the Constitution, and they had 'the revolutionary right' to rescind it. This is supplemented in no unequivocal ways, on the other, when he preferred the conventional mode of amending the Constitution. The fundamental point that comes out is the idea that Constitution ceases to be an organic document unless it absorbs the existent concerns as an aid to the policymakers for translating them into specific policy designs. What is emphasized here is the fact that 'constitutional identity', argues Rosenfeld, 'can take many different forms and evolve over time because it is often immersed in an ongoing process marked by substantial changes'.[9] So, one needs to be extra-careful while conceptualizing constitutional identity since it also unfolds in response to stimuli emerging out of the complex battles being constantly waged in particular socio-economic and political circumstances.

Lincoln's preference for convention as a probable source of constitutional transformation is a significant conceptual intervention in the sense that it helps us capture the critical role that political campaigns play in bringing about changes in constitutional identity. The example from the recent US political history will suffice. The 1964 Civil Rights Act that outlawed discrimination based on race, colour, religion, sex or national origin had upheld the concern for liberty, equality and fraternity. Further to this Act was the 1965 Voting Rights Act repealing the Fifteenth Amendment Act of 1870 that prevented the African American from exercising their right to vote. These two acts had their ideological roots in the massive civil rights movement that Martin Luther King Jr. and his colleagues had spearheaded since the first quarter of the twentieth century.[10] History has also shown that the US Constitution which, despite being drawn on the Enlightenment philosophy, failed to articulate racial parity till the civil rights campaign was crystalized in the early 1960s. The promulgation of the 1965 Voting Rights Act was a significant step towards realizing the Jefferson's Declaration of all men being equal. A new ideological perspective had emerged and the US Constitution, by being adaptive, accordingly refashioned its identity. In other words, the Constitution, which was prejudiced to a section of the US population, instantaneously created a space for the disenfranchised African Americans, since it was drawn on the core Enlightenment values supportive of discrimination-free human existence. There are two critical points with significant theoretical import that need reiteration here: on the one hand, the historical trajectory of the US polity confirms that it is conceptually restrictive if constitutional identity is articulated as static or inflexible; as the above examples demonstrate it undergoes regular metamorphosis, of course, by keeping the fundamentals as axiomatic. Since constitutional identity is not inflexible, these instances also substantiate, on the other, the argument that it is an ongoing process which, if conceptualized in a predetermined format, will lead us nowhere. And thus, it will be theoretically misleading if a Constitution is conceptualized as a mere document of rules and regulations, since constitutional identity, as the above illustrations reveal, is being regularly reinvented.

III

The 1950 Constitution of India established constitutional democracy in India. It did not happen all of a sudden; the Constituent Assembly members deliberated on each and every provision for months together before they finally accepted the Constitution. The objective was to develop a protocol for coexistence with a specific grammar and tags to annotate some of the critical ideas that figure in the text. This apart, the liberal inputs from colonialism also remained critical in the evolution and also consolidation of constitutional democracy in India. Hence, an argument which does not seem to be overstretched is made by saying that underneath the liberal rhetoric of the 1950 Constitution of India remained the formidable impact of the British liberal discourse, being supported by the structure of governance, constituted by the Raj and affirmed during the course of the nationalist movement.[11] This is a fair argument since India's colonial experience confirms that constitutional democracy in independent India was a unique experiment in the global history of democracy showing how a typical foreign conceptualization of liberalism had acquired new features which were not there in its original form. What it entails is also the claim that a conceptual category gets transformed in response to the contextual inputs. This can be substantiated by reference to the historical processes shaping British colonialism in India, which hardly remained the same as days passed on, as the following discussion shows.

The impeachment trial of Warren Hastings that had begun in 1788 was a watershed in so far the colonial policies towards India were concerned: the phase before 1788 was identified as the colonial phase of British colonialism and what followed the impeachment had ushered in an era, known as the imperial phase. There was a specific historical context, as Mukherjee informs, which brought about radical changes in the British policy designs.[12] The rise of America as an independent polity following the defeat of the British in the American War of Independence and the failure of the 1773 Regulating Act to contain a corrupt administration that flourished at the aegis of the East India Company were important reasons for the imperial discourse to strike roots. While the former established that colony could not be maintained by force alone, the latter proved that a mere adoption of a law was not always adequate to ensure justice unless it was complemented by a supportive mindset, especially among the rulers. This was the context in which Edmund Burke articulated the imperial discourse while defending the impeachment motion against Warren Hastings in the House of Lords for being involved in corruption, bribery, high crime and misdemeanours which ran counter to the fundamental ethos of the Philosophy of Enlightenment on which the British suzerainty was based. Under no circumstances, these foundational values, argued Burke, could not be sacrificed because he strongly believed that

> as long as you have the wisdom to keep the sovereign authority of this country as the sanctuary of liberty, the sacred temple consecrated to our common faith, wherever the chosen race and sons of England worship freedom, they will turn their faces towards you. The more they multiply, the more friends you will have; the more ardently they love liberty, the more perfect will be their obedience.[13]

The concern here was to evolve a mode of collectivity which was not hierarchically structured between the colonizers and colonized, but to develop a sociopolitical compact drawn on those fundamental ideas, clustered around the values, norms and principles of Enlightenment. Contrary to the colonial discourse, which privileged brute force over principles, the imperial discourse upheld a set of ideas which, despite being rooted in a historical context, had universal application and validity. Burke's argument had operated at two levels: at a rather simple level, the impeachment was justified since Warren Hastings deviated from the well-established liberal values which needed to be protected against attempts to the contrary. At another, far more, complex level, the effort was directed to substantiate the claim that these values were universal in character and application. In the imperial discourse, instead of subordinating one collectivity to another, Empire was meant to inculcate the ideas of justice, fair play and humanism in colonies which were socially 'backward' and politically 'less advanced'. By making an argument that these ideas were universal, Burke set in motion processes whereby they were 'deterritorialized', which means that notwithstanding their origin in Britain, they remained valid to the humanity as a whole, and hence they could never be bypassed so long as humanity existed. The impeachment trial and Burke's defence upheld that the notion of justice that was instinctively connected with the Empire was 'inalienable' which further confirms, as Mukherjee succinctly presents, that 'the empire became the site of a deterritorialized universal justice that would rise above the national interests of Britain and serve as an impartial arbiter between the English colonial state in India and the colonized Indian society'.[14] The idea was soon to be reversed with the articulation of a new defence for the Empire by James Mill following the publication of *The History of British India* in 1858, where colonialism was defended for its civilizing mission in the colonies.

Unlike Burke who couched his arguments in the universal juridical terms, Mill gave salience to the colonial discourse by insisting on the hierarchy of civilizations, a conceptualization defending the civilizational superiority of the colonizers over the colonized. These contrasting arguments, drawn on contrasting ideological preferences, are useful in understanding the trajectory of constitutional democracy in India since the major policy designs that the British government undertook had their conceptual roots in how colonialism had unfolded in India. What is critical here is the point that the colonial design of governance that finally struck roots in India had put the colonizers in constant interaction with the colonized which paid dividends to the former since it (a) created a space for dialogue with the oppositional nationalists and (b) also allowed the constitutional means as an acceptable device to resolve differences. In other words, the constitutional designs, besides providing a structure of governance, also acted favourably in creating an environment for constitutional democracy to grow and be stronger in India which, the classical liberals strongly felt, was not, at all, conducive for liberal governance due to well-entrenched social, economic and political schisms defying commonality.[15]

IV

Constitutionally, India is a democratic republic as per the 1950 Constitution of India. A cursory look at the provisions of the Constitution confirms the description. The Constitution stipulates that the government is to be elected democratically, which means that franchise is universal, and not restricted; furthermore, the Head of the State, the President of India, is also to be chosen by votes of those elected representatives forming the electoral college. There is thus no difficulty in conceptualizing India being a democratic polity which is also republican in contrast with the Canadian or Australian polity, where the British Queen continues to remain the Head of the State, despite being clearly titular in character. So, there are two features that need to be taken into account while conceptualizing India's constitutional identity, namely the constitutional governance that the Constitution prefers is democratic and also republican. A perusal of the Constitution substantiates the claim. What is being argued here is the point that the language of the Constitution is also as critical as the values that inform its making and also operation. Implicit here is also the point that Constitution also forges an identity on the basis of the values, mores and principles which are privileged at a particular juncture of history. For instance, the Indian nationalist struggle, being couched largely in Western liberal terms, was drawn to constitutional liberalism as perhaps a preferred mode of governance. This is thus not surprising that the liberal constitutionalism was accepted once India became free. Here is a point that needs reiteration: that the 1950 Constitution was to be liberal in character and texture appears to have been preordained presumably because the dominant nationalist voice was liberal.

In terms of constitutional values, the liberal voice gained momentum and seems to have shaped the processes leading to the making of the 1950 Constitution of India. There is a caveat here: the text of the Constitution articulated liberal values as they were desired by those involved in its making. Is the text enough to forge and sustain a collective national identity? There cannot be a conclusive answer because the text appears vacuous unless it is complemented by the prevalent socio-economic and political processes. Hence, an argument is made which is also valid, suggesting that India's liberal Constitution is not exactly adequate to maintain India's collective existence unless endorsed by a well-entrenched liberal mindset. There is thus substance when Andras Sajo cautions by saying that 'the text itself has only limited potential for forging identity'.[16] One can make a larger argument which Jacobsohn makes by emphasizing the importance of practices which are critical to articulate the values that a Constitution stipulates. As he argues,

> a constitution's language may indicate a commitment on the part of its authors, and conceivably its subsequent interpreters, to establish a constitutional identity, but until corroborated in the accumulated practice of a constitutional community, the goal, however noble, will remain unfulfilled.[17]

Constitutional identity is therefore not merely textual, but also contextual, which means that an idea despite being revolutionary is hardly effective unless it is espoused by deeds. In other words, a text is vacuous unless it is translated into practice by complementary acts and designs of governance. For instance, a simplistic comparison between the constitutions of British India and the 1950 Constitution of independent India reveals that there are elements of democratic governance, which the latter incorporated in its text though, by any stretch of imagination, the former cannot be said to be democratic since they were voices of colonialism. This is not unusual and also confirms the fundamental point, made at the outset, that constitutional identity is constituted more by contextual inputs and less by the codified text; its manifestation differs from one age of history to another though the core content remains as sacrosanct as ever.

The argument, however, remains incomplete unless it is supplemented by the fact the constitutional identity is reinvented by subsequent interpretations. There are mainly two major sources of interpretations: the judiciary and the political campaigns. As is now well-established, the Indian judiciary contributed to India's constitutional identity as a democratic polity by interpreting and also reinterpreting constitutional provisions and practices. The most common example is the conceptualization of the idea of basic structure of the Constitution which, if violated, would harm the India's constitutional identity as a democratic republic. Similarly, the sustained political campaigns for Dalit empowerment and gender parity set in processes for substantial legal/constitutional changes to make India far more democratic by being inclusive in the real sense of the term. It is true that the founding fathers left enough space in the constitutional design that they favoured for the marginalized sections, including women, which helped fulfil the contemporary politico-ideological mission of making India an inclusive society in all respects. This was possible because, as argued above, of the presence of a powerful and also well-articulated mindset that stood by the endeavour. It is now clear that constitutional identity is dialectically constituted, which means that it is an offshoot of a dialectical interconnection between text and context supportive of those core principles from which the Constitution derives its sustenance. India's democratic constitutional identity is therefore as much text-driven as it is drawn on the context endorsing supportive mindset.

India's rise as a constitutional democracy is a wonder because it evolves in circumstances which do not seem to be exactly in its favour. Colonialism developed a system which is anything but democratic for obvious reasons. The nationalist struggle was led by those who were largely inclined towards Western liberal democracy presumably by being politically baptized in liberal dispensation during their formative years either as students in Britain or later. Nonetheless, the environment was not propitious for a democratic polity to strike roots, let alone flourish. And yet, India emerged as a largest democracy which is not only constitutionally guarded but also assiduously nurtured despite adversaries. It is a wonder which is very clearly captured by Shulman when he attributed the growth of India as a robust democratic polity to 'bold imagining' which he articulated by saying that 'all the great civilizations, and probably all human societies, have known that human being are capable of imagining; India merely cultivated this art or faculty, more boldly than most'.[18] So, the democratic constitutional identity was rooted in such bold thinking or imagining, to use Shulman's lexicon. As the context in which India being imagined as a democratic policy was not, at all, favourable, it was clearly a significant deviation; it was a deviation which contributed to the concern for making India democratic and bound by the rule of law. Ideas for constitutional democracy were there, but the circumstances were not conducive for, obvious reasons, in a colonial context. And yet, constitutional democracy evolved as a natural choice once India became politically free in 1947. This is eloquently described by Ornit Shani when she argued that

> this was no legacy of colonial rule: Indians imagined the universal franchise for themselves, acted on this imaginary, and made it their political reality. By late 1949, India pushed through the frontiers of the world's democratic imagination, and gave birth to its largest democracy.[19]

The structure of colonial administration was transformed into a design for democratic governance by both 'bold' imaginations and complementary concerted effort by a collectivity towards fulfilling its aspired goals. It was a radical metamorphosis for colonialism was exploitative and sustained itself by refining the policy of *divide-et-impera*, which resulted in India's dismemberment in 1947. The 1950 Constitution laid out an elaborate structure of governance to translate into reality the concern of the founding fathers for democracy. One of the significant steps in this regard was the acceptance of universal adult suffrage, which was immediately agreed upon as soon as the processes for drafting the Constitution for independent India had begun. This was a significant break with the colonial past when franchise was severely restricted and was a device to pursue sectarian politics. The official declaration of 1948 for adult suffrage was thus naturally hailed as a concrete step towards making India truly democratic. It was made clear in the declaration which stated that

> the introduction of adult franchise is intended to confer on every adult, male or female, a right to participate in the establishment of fully democratic system of Government in the country and the provincial Government is therefore anxious that the Electoral Rolls are correctively prepared and no adult, male or female, is as far as possible left unrecorded in the Electoral Rolls.[20]

The purpose here is not to dwell on the processes leading to the acceptance of universal adult suffrage in independent India, but to emphasize the point that this was a key feature of India's constitutional identity. That India is constitutionally democratic, at least politically, is firmly substantiated. Here too, the text-context dialectics visible for the text was translated into practice since the context was favourably disposed towards universal voting rights, which were denied in the earlier dispensation. Inspired by the Enlightenment values and the nationalist struggle, devoted to the collective cause, the 1950 Constitution can be said to have contributed to the creation of a constitutional edifice which was clearly democratic in nature and also texture. The Constituent Assembly laid out and also consolidated the foundation to the extent it was possible, which then grew in strength gradually as the values that informed the processes of constitutionalizing democracy in India became part and parcel of her constitutional identity.

V

Comprising three Parts, the book has six chapters, each of which has a distinct focus and is complementary to the principal theme and argument. With a threadbare analysis of selective aspects of India's constitutional identity, the book puts forward an argument underlining the point that it also evolves because of its obvious contextual character. This is the underlying theme running through six chapters of the book which are divided in three Parts.

The primary focus of Part A is to conceptualize constitutional identity with reference to its intellectual antecedents. As is commonly known, the 1950 Constitution is a creative blending of both derivative and indigenous sources of inspirations. Hence, Chapter 1 focusses on the intellectual impact of the ideas of British liberals on the evolution of India's constitutional identity both during colonialism and its aftermath. Here, it is also emphasized that the British liberal ideas that the founding fathers had imbibed were not readily accepted; instead, they endorsed these ideas which, to them, were a source of empowerment in adverse circumstances. Chapter 2 dealing with the nationalist inputs is an expansion of the argument in the sense that it further develops the intellectual genealogy of India's constitutional identity by drawing on how the colonized accepted the Western liberal ideas while being opposed to the British rule in which an ambience was created in their support. The main theme is also to highlight how British liberalism became 'an ideology of the natives' and an empowering device that brought people of different socio-economic identities together for a common cause. While Part A lays down the foundation, Part B dwells on how India's constitutional identity was fashioned by dealing with a selective set of politico-ideological issues and designs: the former concentrates on those important aspects of the 1950 Constitution that distinctively establishes its unique identity, and the latter delves into those specific constitutional designs that flourishes in independent India to articulate the political-ideological mission that the founding fathers had assiduously pursued. By focussing on the politico-ideological issues, Chapter 3 provides an elaborate account of how they evolve in a context in which liberal democratic ideas seem to have stuck organic roots in India. Given the paucity of space, the chapter has picked up a select set of politico-ideological issues which are considered critical to India's constitutional identity. Similarly, Chapter 4 deals with those specific constitutional designs that remain integral to constitutional democracy in India. It is also shown in this chapter how the classical conceptualization of federalism, for instance, does not appear to be exactly relevant, which defends a wider point emphasizing the critical importance of the context in shaping a constitutional design. Constitutional identity needs to be reinforced in the face of challenges. How is it possible is the theme of Part C which is divided into two chapters? The concern here is to show how judiciary being the custodian of the Constitution discharges its role by reiterating the fundamental politico-ideological priorities on which the Constitution is based. Chapter 5 is a threadbare analysis of the widely quoted Basic Structure Doctrine, which had its roots in a series of judicial pronouncements since the beginning of India's journey as a liberal democratic polity. What is argued here is the point that under no circumstances, the fundamental features of the Constitution can be bypassed. In a similar vein, Chapter 6 is just an expansion of the point, made in the earlier chapter. By drawing on the recent judgements ascertaining that liberty, equality and fraternity are too fundamental to the 1950 Constitution to be fiddled with, the chapter reconfirms the main theme of the book. With an analytical account of some of the recently delivered significant judicial pronouncements, the chapter thus upholds the contention that the core liberal values of liberty, equality and freedom can never be belittled, since it adversely affects the basic constitutional identity that India as a polity unambiguously represents. What is emphasized here is the idea that constitutional identity needs to be safeguarded, and in this respect, the role the political institutions play, especially the judiciary, is of immense significance. A careful perusal of judiciary's contribution shows, in other words, how, being the custodian of the Constitution, it has upheld the fundamental sociocultural and political values from which the 1950 Constitution derives its sustenance. There are occasions, however, when India's judiciary succumbed to the executive diktat, especially during the 1975–77 Emergency; otherwise, there are not many examples showing that the judiciary failed to discharge its role in accordance with its constitutional obligations. As shown in Chapter 6, India's judiciary invokes the cardinal constitutional principles, espoused by the founding fathers, to reconfirm that practices denying justice and freedom to the citizens are ultra vires to the Constitution. Besides its empirical values, this chapter also stands out because it makes an argument which is complementary to one of the main themes of the book, namely India's constitutional identity is not static, but is regularly reinvented by judicial interventions as well.

VI

Constitutional identity is always in a state of flux, since it is being constantly refashioned within those broad philosophical principles which remain critical in its articulation. What is suggested here is the idea that it is neither fixed nor can be changed at will because the ideological values from which it derives its sustenance remain sacrosanct. The book is a restatement of the point by offering two major and one minor arguments drawn on a thorough study of the evolution and consolidation of India's constitutional democracy following decolonization in 1947. The first major argument highlights the fact that constitutional identity is both derivative and indigenous, and a fair understanding of the phenomenon involves a careful analysis of these two sources. The 1950 Constitution of India is undoubtedly a product of Western constitutional liberalism which the Indian nationalists imbibed during the long colonial rule. It also epitomizes processes whereby British liberalism, which also justified colonialism, became an empowering ideology for the colonized, as the history of Indian freedom struggle demonstrates. In other words, by being nurtured in an environment in which constitutional liberalism was privileged, the Indian nationalists gradually imbibed the liberal spirit which they articulated while challenging the colonizers. A text-context dialectical interconnection, the relationship sustained even decolonization. The second argument that the book makes is about how constitutional liberalism survives India's political independence in 1947; that the 1950

Constitution retains a format of governance which was not exactly radically different from that of the past presumably because there was hardly a serious ideological break with what purportedly supported the British rule in India. In other words, since constitutional liberalism remained the principal source of India's governance even after political independence from colonialism, the claims does not seem to be overstretched. The point is simple: by drawing on the core principles of the philosophy of Enlightenment, the 1950 Constitution expressed itself in a language which is unmistakably liberal and structured accordingly in that format. In terms of its identity, it is clearly liberal in both its conceptual roots and also existential manifestation. This does not appear to be strange as the foundational principles that inform the processes leading to the making of the Constitution were derived from the Enlightenment ideas. The minor argument is made by drawing attention to the creative blending of the derivative ideas with those of the founding fathers that the 1950 Constitution represents. This is an obvious contention that independent India's Constitution was also accommodative of the concern of the Gandhians who did not seem to have been taken seriously by the majority of their colleagues in the Constituent Assembly supportive of a liberal Constitution in the Western mould. Nonetheless, by incorporating some of their demands in Part IV of the Constitution (Directive Principles of State Policy), the dominant section in the Assembly paid adequate attention to their concerns. In conceptualizing India's constitutional identity, this was a significant aspect since the Gandhians, despite being marginalized in the Assembly, had also left their imprint in the Constitution, which, however, loomed large as history progressed.

The text is not a biography of the 1950 Constitution, but an elaboration of the processes that finally culminated in making the Constitution what it later became. Implicit here are two concerns: on the one hand, the book seeks to explain why Western liberalism gained precedence over other competing ideological preferences, which also had supporters among the nationalists. The explanation is couched in the text-context dialectical format, which means that liberalism was privileged primarily because it was considered to be a potentially empowering ideology for the colonized. A trajectory of India's constitutional identity also demonstrates that not only was liberalism a preferred ideological dispensation during the nationalist phase, it also remained so even after independence. The transformation of constitutional liberalism from an ideology justifying colonialism to an empowering devise for the nationalists is an interesting narrative that the book seeks to capture by dwelling on the complex texture of India's constitutional identity. What is striking is also the fact that it was a linear progress presumably because, in the making of India's constitutional identity, Western liberalism continued to remain predominant. In other words, the substance of constitutional governance that flourished in colonial India hardly corresponded with that of independent India though the foundational ideas remained the same, since they were rooted in constitutional liberalism. Core to the argument is the claim that India's constitutional identity needs to be understood both as a continuity and as a departure from the past: continuity, because its basic kernel is constitutional liberalism, which informed the whole of endeavours that were undertaken during colonialism and its aftermath; departure since independent India's constitutional democracy had a completely contrasting politico-ideological agenda to fulfil for a liberated nation. Constitutional identity is thus an ideological substance, less a legal marker, demarcating a specific ideational boundary in which the 1950 Constitution of India sets out its policy preferences.

Notes

1 Lawrence Tribe, 'A constitution we are amending: in defence of a restrained judicial role', *Harvard Law Review*, Vol. 97, 1983, pp. 433, 440 – cited in Gary Jeffrey Jacobsohn, 'Constitutional identity', *The Review of Politics*, Vol. 68, 2006, p. 361.

2 I have developed this argument in my *Constitutionalizing India: An Ideational Project*, Oxford University Press, New Delhi, 2018.

3 Gary Jeffrey Jacobsohn, 'Constitutional identity', in Sujit Chowdhury, Madhav Khosla and Pratap Bhanu Mehta (eds.), *The Oxford Handbook of the Indian Constitution*, Oxford University Press, New Delhi, 2016, p. 115.

4 www.ushistory.org/declaration/document/, The 1776 Declaration of Independence, accessed on 16 April 2018.

5 ibid.

6 www.loc.gov/rr/program/bib/ourdocs/13thamendment.html, the Thirteenth Amendment Act of 1865, accessed on 16 April 2018.

7 In his well-researched exposition, entitled 'Thirteenth Amendment to the Constitution of the United States: consummation to abolition and key to the Fourteenth Amendment', *California Law Review*, Vol. 39, No. 2, 1 June 1951, pp. 171–203. Jacobus tenBroek persuasively argued how a particular amendment radically altered the ideological thrust of the US Constitution.

8 http://avalon.law.yale.edu/19th_century/lincoln1.asp, First Inaugural Address of Abraham Lincoln, 1861.

9 Michael Rosenfeld, 'Modern constitutionalism as interplay between identity and diversity', in Michael Rosenfeld (ed.), *Constitutionalism, Identity, Difference and Legitimacy*, Duke University Press, Durham, 1994, p. 8 – cited in Gary Jeffrey Jacobsohn, 'Constitutional identity', *The Review of Politics*, Vol. 68, 2006, p. 365.

10 I have dealt with this aspect of the civil rights campaign in the US in which non-violence was privileged in my *Confluence of Thought: Mahatma Gandhi and Martin Luther King Jr.*, Oxford University Press, New York, 2013.

11 Thomas R Metcalf, *Ideologies of the Raj*, Cambridge University Press, Cambridge, 1998, pp. 215–234.

12 Mithi Mukherjee, 'Justice, war and the imperium: Indian and Britain in Edmund Burke's prosecutorial speeches in the impeachment trial of Warren Hastings', *Law and History Review*, Vol. 23, No. 3, Fall 2005, p. 602.

13 https://archive.org/details/speechesofrighth02burk, the Works of the Right Honourable Edmund Burke, Vol. VIII, Speeches on the Impeachment of Warren Hastings and Letter, George Bell & Sons, London, 1877, p. 217, accessed on 18 June 2017.

14 Mithi Mukherjee, 'Justice, war and the imperium: Indian and Britain in Edmund Burke's prosecutorial speeches in the impeachment trial of Warren Hastings', *Law and History Review*, Vol. 23, No. 3, Fall 2005, p. 627.

15 This section is drawn on my *Constitutional Democracy in India*, Routledge, Oxford and London, 2018, pp. 3–5.

16 Aandras Sajo, 'Constitution without constitutional moment: a view from the new member states', *International Journal of Constitutional Law*, Vol. 2, 2005, p. 243 – cited by Gary Jeffrey Jacobsohn, in his 'Constitutional identity', in Sujit Chowdhury, Madhav Khosla and Pratap Bhanu Mehta (eds.), *The Oxford Handbook of the Indian Constitution*, Oxford University Press, New Delhi, 2016, p. 111.

17 Gary Jeffrey Jacobsohn, 'Constitutional identity', in Sujit Chowdhury, Madhav Khosla and Pratap Bhanu Mehta (eds.), *The Oxford Handbook of the Indian Constitution*, Oxford University Press, New Delhi, 2016, p. 111.

18 David Shulman, *More Than Real: A History of the Imagination in South India*, Harvard University Press, Cambridge, 2012, p. ix.

19 Ornit Shani, *How India Became Democratic: Citizenship and the Making of the Universal Franchise*, Penguin, New Delhi, 2018, p. 1.

20 Election Commission of India, Record Room, Press Communique, Government of United Provinces, 19 November 1948, cited in Ornit Shani, *How India Became Democratic: Citizenship and the Making of the Universal Franchise*, Penguin, New Delhi, 2018, p. 47.

Part A

Conceptualizing constitutional identity in India

Intellectual antecedents

Constitutional identity is articulated in a historical perspective. Hence, this Part divides the discussion into two complementary chapters: on the one hand, this Part focusses on those specific aspects of India's constitutional democracy, which lay out and contributed to the articulation of constitutional identity in specific ways: for instance, by according priority to religion and religious freedom, secularism, reservation and gender, the 1950 Constitution seeks to build and also consolidate a solid constitutional foundation for liberal democracy (primarily of the Western mould) in India. That specific provisions striving to guarantee religious freedom, secularism, reservation and gender-parity were incorporated in the Constitution also confirms that the founding fathers were unanimous in appreciating those values of liberal constitutionalism, which, they felt, were inseparable to India's governance. In a similar vein, the structure of governance that is integral to liberal constitutionalism needs to be built and nurtured, on the other. Hence, federalism was espoused by the framers of the Constitution that has always been upheld in independent India to sustain her multifaceted social, economic and political texture. Article 370 of the 1950 Constitution ensuring special constitutional status to the state of Jammu and Kashmir may, however, appear to be an aberration if one interprets Constitution's federal provisions mechanically without reference to the historical context in which it was incorporated as perhaps the only option to unite a clearly alienated part of the country with the mainland. The most significant endeavour in articulating India's constitutional identity is evident with the formulation of the doctrine of the basic structure by the Supreme Court of India. Reiterating that those politico-ideological values from which the Constitution draws its sustenance cannot, under any circumstances, be bypassed, India's apex court appears to have discharged its role as a custodian of the Constitution in a creative fashion. This is a revolutionary intervention in two ways: first, the basic structure confirms that there are certain constitutional values which are sacrosanct so long as liberal democracy continues in India; second, by being proactively involved in the maintenance of constitutional democracy in India, the Supreme Court of India has truly become an important actor in institutional politics.

As a phenomenon, constitutional identity evolves by following certain core politico-ideological values shaping its articulation in specific fashions.

In fact, these are the foundational pillars that can be ignored at the peril of its existence. In other words, if they are changed, the Constitution will lose its basic character. This is too fundamental for a Constitution to ignore. The idea is clear: for a Constitution is not merely a statement of provisions, it is equally reflective of the conceptual foundation in which it unfolds as a mechanism of governance. In case of India, the story is multifaceted since India is perhaps one of those decolonized polities in which the past influence did not seem to have been less significant even after the attainment of political freedom in 1947 from the British rule. Reasons are plenty: prominent among them was definitely the consensus that the nationalists developed over the acceptance of the ideological-cum-institutional fabric that the colonizers had created and also consolidated in the wake of colonial rule. How was it possible? Explanations need to be couched in terms of the ideational compatibility that the nationalists had shared with their *bete noire*, the rulers. It happened presumably because the former was nurtured in an environment in which liberal constitutionalism was privileged in a sociopolitical milieu in which ideas supportive of the prevalent system were generally encouraged. Primarily, it was an ideational appreciation by the nationalists which, *inter alia*, created an environment where the Westminster form of constitutional democracy seems to have gained precedence. The outcome was inevitable: despite attempts by some of those nationalists who were opposed to imitating what they experienced during colonialism, constitutional liberalism became an acceptable option for independent India. Implicit here is the argument that the design that emerged in India during the British rule did not seem to have been imposed, but had evolved spontaneously since a majority of those who opposed colonialism upheld the system in view of its utility even after decolonization. The argument is a reinforcement of the point that largely due to an ideational endorsement, it was possible for the Westminster mode of governance to strike roots in India; this appears to have been organic in character since endeavours towards its replacement were brutally scuttled, as the revival of constitutional democracy in 1977 after two years of non-democratic rule following the imposition of Emergency in 1975. Constitutional democracy is not just a façade, but an organically evolved system with the tentacles spread around all strata of society. Two important conceptualizations seem critical here: on the one hand, India's constitutional identity is an offshoot of complex processes in which the ideational battle, both during colonialism and its aftermath, over choosing an appropriate option for governance needs to be taken into account for a persuasive explanation. There is also the point, on the other, that constitutional identity is not static, but is being constantly reinvented without, of course, jeopardizing the fundamental character of the governance drawing on constitutional liberalism.

In two complementary chapters, the Part identifies the possible intellectual sources of liberal political ideas supportive of constitutional democracy that gradually became critical in governance in India even after the colonizers were forced to leave.

1 Constitutional identity

The British liberal inputs

Major initiatives by the colonial government[1]

Colonialism expanded its control in India in two distinct ways: first, by tactfully following the divisive *divide-et-impera* strategy that created and sustained the schism between the two major communities of Hindus and Muslims. The British strategy worked favourably because of the socio-economic differences that separated these two communities. In course of time, the divide-and-rule formula not only consolidated the British rule in India, but also created conditions for the politically underprivileged sections to rise as meaningful partners in governance. So, it cut both ways: on the one hand, the chasm between communities, based on genuine socio-economic differences as well, made the task of governance easier for the ruler; this also, on the other hand, led to a process whereby the peripheral communities became a powerful political voice in the nationalist struggle for independence. Second, drawn on the classical liberal democratic tradition, the British ruler introduced several legal steps to consolidate the empire by gradually opening up administration to the Indians. Along with the application of force, the British government also adopted various reform schemes to inject constitutional values that shaped the nationalist campaign to a significant extent. It will therefore not be incorrect to suggest that the British rule survived in India with the least coercion because of the role of the Indian collaborators in defending the empire. Except in the context of the 1942 open rebellion, the collaborative network of support had never shown signs of collapse. The adoption of various reforms by the British government created conditions in which Indians felt attached with the imperial rule that finally disintegrated due to its internal contradictions and also the growing nationalist consolidation opposed to foreign rule. Focussing on the landmark constitutional designs during the British rule, this chapter is an analytical statement on the British politico-legal strategies to consolidate the Raj. These designs, undoubtedly concessions to the ruled, were also devices to weaken the nationalist agitation as and when it became a serious threat to the government. In other words, while the British liberal tradition may have contributed to the constitutional reforms, one cannot deny the growing strength of the nationalist campaign, Gandhian or otherwise, that forced the British to introduce measures to defuse crisis.

The basic argument that this chapter defends relates to the contention that liberalism evolved in India at the patronage of the colonial authority. The analysis draws on the ideas of select British thinkers to argue that the civilizing zeal of the rulers appears to have governed their priorities in India as soon as India became a British colony. The serious differences notwithstanding among those who shaped the cognitive understanding of colonialism, there was hardly a formidable opposition to the continuity of colonial rule till when the British paramountcy was severely challenged by the nationalists. Besides the obvious economic gain, India as a colony was also a laboratory for testing some of the interesting ideas, which were considered to be integrally connected with the fundamental civilizing mission of the colonizers. This was never seriously questioned and the leading thinkers, despite their concern for liberty, fraternity and compassion, appeared to have endorsed the colonial practices as being needed to elevate the colonies to an improved state of being civilized. As will be shown, it was James Mill who endorsed colonialism as it was a panacea for the natives to avoid despotic rule justifying priestcraft. Despite being hailed as an important treatise on British India, Mill's views in the *History of British India* are so simplistic and 'so unremittingly dark, often so pathetically foolish in their lack of nuance' that they are criticized, rightly so, for being rooted in self-obsessed racial prejudices. Nonetheless, Mill's ideas did play a critical role in shaping the attitude of the colonizers at the dawn of colonialism in India, as evidence demonstrates. For the colonizers, the British colonialism was a panacea for the 'barbarian' Indians because it would help them to be civilized and enlightened by being introduced to the philosophy of Enlightenment espousing liberty, equality and fraternity. It is therefore not surprising that even for Edmund Burke who initiated the impeachment motion in parliament against Warren Hastings, the first Governor General of Bengal in 1788 for his misconduct, never questioned the British endeavours towards colonizing India. They were keen to warp governance in India in the format of liberal constitutionalism, of course, at the behest of the British 'patriarchs'. Such a concern led to the unfolding of two important processes: on the one hand, efforts were undertaken to gradually install the institutional fabric of constitutional democracy in India, which gained strength, as history has shown, in the wake of colonial rule; the structure of constitutional governance upholding colonialism derived its sustenance by drawing, on the other, the ideological resources that the colonizers shared with the colonized while administering India. Conceptually, it was an innovative design which had its root perhaps in the ignominious defeat of the British colonizers in the American War of Independence (1775–83). By being vanquished, the rulers had evolved a strategy to accommodate the dissenting voices in India by creating a structure of governance in which Indians were also allowed to participate. Justifying the design as an extension of the philosophy of Enlightenment, the British rulers seem to have put in place, rather perfunctory, a system which the colonized appear to have accepted as days passed by. This segment is thus of critical importance to the principal argument, since it helps us understand how the Enlightenment ideas which led to the consolidation of colonialism in India became a source of empowerment to the colonized in course of time.

An uncritical look at the selective, but major, landmark constitutional initiatives during the colonial rule may lead one to conclude that these were initiated by the British for the Indians. Hence, the spirit of nationalism is underrated. If one goes beyond the surface, what is evident is that the inclusion of Indians in administration was but an outcome of the British effort to defuse popular discontent. Hence, the argument that every constitutional drive was initiated by the Raj does not seem to be persuasive. History reveals that there were situations which forced the British authority to adopt measures to control agitation. For instance, the Congress campaign in the 1880s contributed a lot to the introduction of the 1893 reforms. Behind the 1909 Morley-Minto Reforms lay the *Swadeshi* Movement and revolutionary terrorism. Similarly, the 1919 Montague-Chelmsford Reforms were attempts at resolving crises that began with the Home Rule League and climaxed with the 1919 Rowlatt Satyagraha and the Non-Cooperation Movement of 1910–21. To a large extent, the Gandhian Civil Disobedience Movement (1930–32) accounted for the introduction of constitutional measures seeking to involve Indian politicians in public administration.

Furthermore, the interpretation of these constitutional designs remains partial unless linked with the broader socio-economic and political processes in which they were conceptualized. An attempt to analyse the structure and dynamics of constitutional politics without reference to the broader social matrix and economic nexus is futile because the politico-constitutional structure reflects economic and social networks, religio-cultural beliefs and even the nationalist ideology which impinged on the organized world of administrative and constitutional structure. So, an urgent and unavoidable task for an analyst is not to completely ignore the broader socio-economic context, but to ascertain its relative importance in shaping a particular constitutional initiative. For instance, the 1932 Communal Award was believed to have been initiated by the British to expand political activity among the Muslims in Bengal and Punjab. But, as studies have shown, it was also a concession that the British was forced to grant in order to make the maintenance of the Empire easier.[2] The sharing of power with the native elites was thus prompted by considerations other than merely British initiatives.

The landmark constitutional designs before the 1858 Queen's Proclamation

With the victory of the East India Company in 1757, a new era in India's political history had begun; it was an era of British colonialism that lasted for almost two hundred years. What is fascinating is the unfolding of the British rule in India which also laid out a solid foundation of what later became as constitutional democracy for India. Behind these imperial designs remained two objectives: first, by gradually expanding the base of colonial administration, the British rulers pursued a politico-ideological design of being accommodative of the dominant (and also pliable) sections of the nationalists, which paid them off till the complete independence resolution was adopted in 1929. Even during the heyday of the Gandhi-led anti-British nationalist campaign, there were many leading Indians who appreciated the British rule for being 'truly' liberal. Of them, it was BR Ambedkar who always preferred colonial paramountcy to the rule by the Congress, which actually meant the rule by the upper-caste Hindus. The second objective, which is critical for our purpose, relates to the British concern for building constitutional governance which, the rulers felt, was linked with their so-called civilizing mission in India. Although the design unfolded in phases, there is doubt that it was a goal-driven initiative which culminated in the formation of responsible governments by the democratically elected representatives. So, the idea that germinated with the acceptance of the 1861 Council Act remained dominant not only during the British rule in India, but even in its aftermath.

The unfolding of the colonial design of governance

The nature of the British administration also varied: under the East India Company, the Crown was not directly involved in administration; it was peripherally linked as the supreme authority controlling the Company that functioned under the overall administrative jurisdiction of the British queen. Empowered by the Crown, two institutions were entrusted with the operation of the Company in India: the Court of Proprietors and the Court of Directors. These two Courts were largely independent and decided the course of action for the Company in India. The Queen's charter authorized the Courts to fulfil its goal in India without almost any restriction. The Company functioned in a ruthless manner, guided solely by its commercial interests. Although there were attempts by the Company rulers to bring about reforms in administration, they remained largely academic in nature. Complaints against the 'misrule' of the Company poured in and, as a result, the House of Commons appointed a Committee of Secrecy to look into the authenticity of the complaints. The findings of the Committee went seriously against the Company. The result was the adoption of the Regulating Act of 1773, the first formal articulation of the British supremacy over a part of India that abolished the Dual Government of the Company.

The Regulating Act, 1773

This Act was the first measure of the British Parliament that directly intervened in the affairs of the Company. Although the power of the Company's Directors remained unaltered, the regulation that the Company was required to keep the Treasury Bench informed reduced its independence drastically. The Governor of Bengal, Warren Hastings, was now designated as the Governor General who would be assisted by a Council of four members, recommended by the Crown. According to the Act, the supreme authority rested not with the Governor General, but with the Council, guided by the principle of majority while taking a decision vis-à-vis India. While in India, the Council remained supreme, but it had to function under the supervision, direction and control of the Court of Directors in London.

The Act was a major milestone in India's public administration for four specific reasons: *first*, by restraining the Company, the Act simply endorsed the importance of values in administration. As the Company was involved in public administration in India, it hardly could avoid its obligations to the ruled. The intervention by the Crown clearly suggests that the British government was not at ease with the way the Company was managing its affairs in India. There were many Indians who also expressed their resentment since the administration became a vehicle for fulfilling partisan interests. As GK Gokhale stated,

> the true well-being of the people is systematically subordinated to militarism and the service interests of the European mercantile classes. … Even the efficiency of administration, as has been attained in the past by the existing system, is bound to suffer more and more, owing to the antagonism of the governed to that system.[3]

In such a tense situation, the promulgation of the Regulating Act of 1773 was a concessional design upholding an ideological concern of the rulers in England for the governed in India. There is no denying the fact that colonial interests remained paramount though the Act contributed to a social and political ambience that led to the adoption of ameliorating legal enactments in course of time. *Second*, rejecting the individual-based administration, as epitomized by the Governor, the Act also made the Council accountable to the Crown. This was a significant break with the past because public administration was not merely governance, but governance with a purpose. So, apart from laying the structure of administration, the 1773 Act sought to change the ideological basis of Company rule that was now guided by the well-established principles of administration, evolved in the long tradition of Westminster democracy under the Crown. *Third*, the Act marked the beginning of centralization. The Governor-General-in-Council became the supreme ruler in India, and the Governors of three presidencies of Bengal, Madras and Bombay were reduced to subordinate governments. Within the overall control of the Governor General, the Act, however, demarcated administrative domains of the Governors of the presidencies that were critical to the evolution of public administration in India. By involving the Council in administration, the Act also inaugurated a new trend in the Company's rule that no longer remained, at least theoretically, as arbitrary as before. The Governor General was required to consult the Council and was also made accountable to the British Parliament. *Finally*, the most outstanding feature of the Act was the establishment of a Supreme Court in Calcutta. This Court was founded under the Letters of Patent with Elijah Impey as the Chief Justice and three other judges. Primarily a Court of record, it also had civil, criminal, ecclesiastical, admiralty, equity and supervisory jurisdiction over the whole Presidency and any person in the employment of the Company even outside the Presidency.

As evident, the Act was most critical to public administration in India because (a) it laid down the skeleton of the governmental system of modern India, and (b) all subsequent enactments can be said to have either enlarged or amplified the basic text of the 1773 Act. Despite its limited appeal in today's context, the Act was certainly radical in its approach and content. By holding the Company responsible for the Parliament, the Act sought to shape Company's administration in accordance with the principles of 'formal' democracy. Although the Act recommended unitary command by suggesting the supremacy of the Governor-General-in-Council, it was also a device for 'limited' decentralization because the Governors of the presidencies remained independent, at least administratively, within their respective domains.

The Regulating Act of 1773 was not sufficiently equipped to address the administrative distortions in India under the Company rule. The parliamentary committee under Edmund Burke exposed the arbitrary functioning of the Governor General and Chief Justice and recommended for their recall. But it was not possible because the Board of proprietors refused to respect the recommendation. This led to a constitutional crisis because it also demonstrated the lack, if not absence, of parliamentary control on the Company rule in India. In response, the Pitt's India Act of 1784 was enacted. According to this Act, the Court of Directors was allowed 'free hands' to manage the commercial affairs of the Company in India, while, in political sphere, the authority was vested in a new body, known as the Board of Control comprising six Commissioners. Appointed by the King, the Board had in it the Chancellor of the Exchequer, a Secretary of State and four Privy Councillors. The Board retained full powers of 'superintendence, direction and control' of all operations of the civil and military governments of the British territorial possessions in the East Indies. The Court of proprietors lost its hegemony in Company's affairs except in the election of Directors who were given the authority to make appointments of all posts in India though the Crown was authorized to recall any person in the employment of the Company.

In the evolution of public administration in India, the Pitt's Act was an important benchmark for two reasons: *first*, the Act established the supremacy of the British Crown in territories, controlled by the Company. Administration was now an elaborate arrangement involving those, appointed by the King and accountable to the Parliament. Through various structural mechanisms, the British government sought to create a system of governance in India which was qualitatively different from any of the preceding administrations. *Second*, this Act introduced a new policy in relation to the Indian princes by laying down that the Company should follow a policy of 'non-interference' in their affairs. In other words, the Company was restricted to those areas which were already under its control. The non-intervention policy was short-lived and by the end of the eighteenth century, especially with the arrival of Wellesley as Governor General, the British Empire in India was transformed into the British Empire of India. Wellesley accomplished his task both by military stringency and by strategic 'subsidiary alliances' with the Indian princes. What was remarkable about Wellesley, apart from his role as an empire builder, was his concern for an efficient administration because he believed that without skilled administrators, the Empire could not survive. With this intent, he founded a college at Fort William for the training of the Company's civil servants. From here, one can trace the genesis of Indian Civil Service that was to be founded soon.

The Regulating Act of 1773 and the Pitt's India Act of 1784 were two pieces of legislations to evolve institutions to impose restrains on the East India Company's authority in India and make it accountable to the Crown. While the former created the institution of Supreme Court for administering justice, the latter led to the Constitution of a Board of Control in London to supervise the Company's activities in India. As designs of governance, they were fine though there were severe constraints which crippled their authority to a significant extent. For instance, the Supreme Court was unable to apply the British common law since it was asked to be equally sensitive to the native law just to protect the sentiments of the local collaborators who extended, in exchange, their unconditional support to the rulers. It created a piquant situation which forced the Parliament to appoint a select committee with Edmund Burke as its chairman to devise a mechanism to avoid conflicts between the Company and Parliament. The Pitt's Act of 1784 was the outcome and the Board of Control for the Company which was to be accountable to the Parliament was established. In practice, however, both these Acts had achieved nothing substantial: the issue was addressed, but the result was almost zero because the alleged tacit support of the government allowed the Company to continue in India with its diktat which was not surprising in view of the circumstances.[4]

The Charter Act, 1833

Of all the acts, enacted by the British Parliament to govern the East India Company in India, the Charter Act of 1833 is perhaps the most watershed legislative intervention in India's public administration. Why was such an Act necessary? The administration, in both India and Britain, confronted new circumstances following the rapid expansion of the British Empire in India. The administrative machinery was not adequate in holding the empire together. In Britain, parliamentary reforms led to a new form of governance largely due to the influence of Enlightenment philosophy with its emphasis on enlightened liberalism. There was a clamour for free trade with India, unrestricted immigration of Europeans into India, reform of laws and improvement of education in India. Two ardent liberals who set forth the changes in the British attitude during this period were Macaulay and James Mill; while the former, also a parliamentarian, was the Secretary to the Board of Control, the latter was the Examiner of India correspondence at India House.

As the Company lost its commercial monopoly in India following the acceptance of the Charter Act, all restrictions to European immigration into India were removed. Besides, the Act introduced new devices of administrative control in India, which are as follows: *first*, the Governor General, now designated as Governor General of India, was vested with supreme authority in so far as civil, military and revenue administration were concerned. In the centralized administration, the Governors of other provinces were subordinates to the Governor General who became the pivot of the British administration in India. *Second*, all decisions of the Governor General and Governors overriding the decisions of their respective Executive Councils were to be supported by recorded statement of reasons. This was a rider in the stipulation to restrain those holding supreme authority. *Third*, all legislative powers were vested in the Governor-General-in-Council and the provincial governments lost their legislative powers. Laws approved by the Governor-General-in-Council came to be designated as acts and the endorsement of the Supreme Court for their validity was withdrawn. These acts were applicable to all Courts. *Fourth*, a Law Member who was to be an English Barrister was to be appointed to the Governor-General-in-Council in an advisory capacity. This appointment was certainly a significant step in the Constitution of the Imperial Legislative Council. Macaulay, the first Law Member, was also entrusted with the task of codifying laws for India in his capacity as the President of the Indian Law Commission that came into being at the behest of the Governor General. *Finally*, the Charter Act was also a powerful statement against discrimination in employment under the Company due to religion, place of birth, descent, colour or any of these. Although this principle was theoretically endorsed, the practice was otherwise for reasons connected with colonialism.

Public administration in India gradually became complex with the expansion of the British Empire. While the 1773 Regulation Act ushered in an era of centralized administration of the Company, the 1833 Charter Act marked the culmination of that process by establishing the authority of the Crown over the administration in India. The Governor General became supreme along with the Council. As evident, the Indian administration was largely Weberian in spirit and content: it was hierarchical and centralized involving various layers of administration within the overall structure of British rule. Its purpose was defined by colonialism that remained a determining influence, for obvious reasons, until India's independence in 1947.

The Act for the Good Government of India, 1858

Perhaps the most distinctive Act that radically altered the nature of public administration in India was the Act of 1858, which brought the East India Company's century-old rule to an end. In order to strengthen the colonial rule in the aftermath of the 1857 abortive revolt of the Indian army, which is characterized as the first war of independence, this Act stipulated devices to improve the administrative machinery by which the Indian government was to be superintended and controlled by the Crown in England. The Proclamation was not just a royal deed justifying the Crown's authority, but also articulated the concern which was also derivative of the so-called civilizing mission of the British rulers; it was also a confirmation of what the British liberals strove to achieve by governing India in a particular fashion. By taking over India's administration, the Queen thus proclaimed that

> We shall respect the rights, dignity and honour of native princes as our own; and we desire that they, as well as our subjects, should enjoy that prosperity and that social advancement which can only be secured by internal peace and good government.
>
> We desire no extension of our present territorial possessions; and while we permit no aggression upon our dominations or our rights to be attempted with impunity, we shall sanction no encroachment of those of others.
>
> We hold ourselves bound to the native of our Indian territories by the same obligation of duty which binds us to all our other subjects, and those obligations, by the blessing of Almighty God, we shall faithfully and conscientiously fill.
>
> We disclaim alike the right and the desire to impose our conviction (religious) on any of our subjects. We declare it to be our royal will and pleasure that none be in anywhere favoured, none molested or disquieted by reason of their religious faith or observances, but that all shall alike enjoy the equal and impartial protection of the law; and we do strictly charge and enjoin all those who may be in authority under us that they abstain from all interference with the religious belief or worship of any of our subjects on pain of our highest displeasure.
>
> And it is our further will that, so far as may be, our subjects, of whatever race or creed, be freely and impartially admitted to office in our service, the duties of which they may be qualified by their education, ability and integrity duly to discharge.
>
> We know and respect the feelings of attachment with which the native of India regard their lands inherited by them from their ancestors and we desire to protect them in all rights connected therewith, subject to equitable demands of the State; and we will that generally, generally, in framing and administering the law, due regard be paid to the ancient rights and customs of India.
>
> When, by the blessing of Providence, internal tranquillity shall be restored, it is our earnest desire to stimulate the peaceful industry of India, to promote works of public utility and improvement, and to administer the Government for the benefit of all ours subjects resident therein. In their prosperity will be our strength, in their contentment our security, and in their gratitude our best reward.[5]

The Proclamation provides significant inputs to the Act of 1858. By abolishing the Court of Directors and the Board of Control, the Act transferred the government, territories and revenues from the Company to the Crown with the appointment of Lord Canning as the first Viceroy and Governor General of India. India was to be governed by the English Sovereign that, by implication, suggests the importance of the British Parliament in governance in India. As the pivot of colonial administration, the Secretary of State for India discharged all powers vested earlier in the Board of Control and Court of Directors. As a member of the cabinet, the Secretary of State drew his salary from the revenues generated from India. He was authorized to place the annual statement of accounts of all government revenue and expenditure in India and to submit a report of all moral and material progress in India. To assist him in the discharge of his constitutional and administrative responsibilities, he was provided with a Parliamentary and a Permanent Under-Secretary. A council, designated as the Indian Council, was constituted to help him perform his duties most efficiently. The Council was mainly an advisory aid, and its role was thus limited though on various occasions it acted in a decisive manner to influence the decisions of the Governor General through other constitutional bodies.

The Act of 1858 was not qualitatively different from the earlier acts in the sense that it made no spectacular changes in the colonial administration except that it vested the entire revenue of the country in the Governor-General-in-Council. The provincial governments became totally subsidiary to the Council. Another paramount act which introduced non-official members in the administration was the 1861 Indian Councils Act. The function of the Council was limited to legislation and had no authority to control the executive though it empowered the provincial governments to legislate on provincial matters. The Executive Council was expanded to include the Advocate General of the provinces, in addition to four non-official members who were invariably Indians.

The Indian Councils Act is a remarkable piece of legislation for two important reasons: *first*, it was certainly an important step towards decentralization of power, and in that sense, it was a break with the past. For the first time, steps were taken to provide an alternative to centralized British administration. *Second*, it also introduced Indians in the administration by recommending the inclusion of non-official members. It was a deliberate political design to accommodate the elite Indians in public administration that had an enormous impact especially in the aftermath of the 1857 uprising. Although those who were nominated were either Indian princes or big land owners, it was undoubtedly a significant beginning towards involving Indians in public administration.

In the early part of the Crown administration, two processes seem to have worked. On the one hand, attempts were made to strengthen the

Governor-General-in-Council, and there were steps, on the other hand, towards devolution, especially of, financial power. In this connection, the 1870 Mayo resolution is most remarkable which stated,

> Local interest, supervision and care are necessary to success in the management of funds devoted to education, sanitation, medical charity and local public works. The operation of the resolution in its full meaning and integrity will afford opportunities for the development of local self-government, for strengthening municipal institutions and for association of the natives and Europeans to a greater extent than before in the administration of affairs.[6]

Several acts were enacted to constitute municipalities in Bombay, Calcutta and Madras. The most eventful development in this regard was undoubtedly the 1882 Ripon Resolution that defended the introduction of the local self-government by underlining that it was introduced 'not primarily with a view to improvement in administration. It is chiefly desirable as an element of political and popular education'. In pursuance of this goal, the 1885 Bengal Local Self Government Act was adopted that led to the formation of district local boards in Bengal.

The trajectory of the British rule in its initial phase suggests the phased decentralization of administration and also the growing involvement of the Indians in administration. Two substantial events changed the course of colonialism: (a) the founding of the universities of Calcutta, Madras and Bombay helped develop an articulate opinion of the educated Indians on the British rule. It captured the growing discontent among the Indians who always remained, for obvious reasons, peripheral in administration. (b) The inauguration of the Indian National Congress in 1885 created a new platform to ventilate the grievances of the ruled. This also became a forum for the Indians to articulate demands for better rule. This was the context in which the 1892 Indian Councils Act was promulgated. As the Act underlines, its aim was

> to widen and expand the functions of the Government of India, and to give further opportunities to the non-official and native elements in Indian society to take part in the work of the Government, and in that way, to lend official recognition to that remarkable development both of political interest and political capacity that had been visible among the higher classes of Indian society since the Government of India was taken over by the Crown in 1858.[7]

The Act provided for the enhanced membership of the Councils. It was mandatory for the government to consult the representative bodies and institutions, approved by the government, before selecting nominees for the Councils. Besides legislative powers, the Councils were also empowered to pull the Executive on financial matters though it had no power to either revise or reject decisions on this matter. However, the growing weightage of the Councils is indicative of a sea change in colonial rule. As Morley, the Secretary of State, articulated,

> there are two rival schools of thought, one of which believes that better government of India depends on efficiency, and that efficiency is, in fact, the end of British rule in India. The other school, while not neglecting efficiency, looks also to what is called political concessions.[8]

This declaration laid the foundational principles of the British administration in India. As a first step, a Royal Commission was appointed in 1907 to look into the administration that seemed to have lost its viability in the context of growing discontent among the ruled. The aim of the Commission was to provide an administration which was adapted to the changed social, economic and political realities of India. While recommending the corrective measures, the Commission was guided by the following factors: (i) the difficulties of ruling the vast subcontinent from a single headquarter and the inevitable failure of in the statesmanship and efficiency in administration, (ii) the difficulties of applying uniform schemes of development for the provinces which are socio-culturally diverse, (iii) to instil a sense of responsibility among those engaged in provincial and local administration and (iv) to strengthen the colonial rule by educating people in the values of strong administration. On the basis of the recommendation of the Commission, a bill was introduced in 1908 which became the 1909 Morley-Minto Reforms. As a political scheme seeking to strengthen colonial rule in India, the 1909 Act introduced a profound change with long-term effects in representation of communities in Councils. Once the Muslim league was founded in 1906, there were demands for 'separate electorate' for the Muslims. In his plea to the Governor General, the Muslim League chief, Aga Khan, defended separate electorate for the Muslims on the basis of their 'numerical strength', 'political importance' and 'contribution', which they made 'to the defence of the Empire'. Endorsing the argument, Minto assured Aga Khan that the Muslims 'may rest assured that their political rights will be safeguarded'. So, the 1909 Act is remarkable in the history of representation in India. Muslims were recognized as a separate community, and their electoral rights were also guaranteed accordingly. The British policy of 'divide and rule' was thus formally articulated. Public administration continued to remain partisan, for obvious reasons. Meanwhile, the nationalist movement gained momentum and the political atmosphere in India changed. The 1909 Morley-Minto Reforms failed to address the genuine grievances of the ruled.

Notwithstanding its demerits, the 1909 reform scheme was a break with the past in the sense that it ushered in an era of constitutional governance in India by making representative institutions integral to the British administration. By creating a forum for dialogues between the Indians and the administration, it also consolidated the foundation of democratic politics (though in a very restricted manner) in India; it also gave recognition to the elective principle as the basis of the composition of the legislative council for the first time, which was an advancement of the idea of collaborative governance in which the Indians remained as critical as their British counterparts. An analytical scan of the features of the Morley-Minto Reforms reveals that they were

> an attempt to graft the principle of constitutionalism upon the existing autocracy of British rule; they were also the outcome of the old conception which made the Government of India a benevolent despotism which might, as it saw fit for purposes of enlightenment, consult the wishes of the subjects.[9]

The trend that had begun with the acceptance of the 1909 Reforms continued. Various other acts were enacted to sustain the system of governance that was articulated in the 1909 Reform scheme. With the outbreak of the First World War, a change in the attitude of the British government was visible, which was largely 'strategic' to solicit the support of the Indians in its war effort. The result was the adoption of the 1919 Montague-Chelmsford Reform scheme, which was guided by the committed goal of the government 'to increase association of the Indians in every branch of the administration and the gradual development of self-governing institutions in India'. On the surface, the Reform scheme appeared to be novel and drew on the commitment to make public administration India-friendly, as the four major principles that formed the core of the scheme suggest:

a There should be, as far as possible, complete popular control in local bodies and the largest possible independence for them of outside control.
b The provinces are the domain in which the earlier steps towards the progressive realization of responsible government should be taken. Some measures of responsibility should be given at once, and the aim of the British government is to provide complete responsibility to the Indians in their governance to the extent possible under the present circumstances.
c The Government of India must remain wholly responsible to the Parliament and saving such responsibility, and its authority in essential matters must remain indisputable pending experience of the effect of changes now to be introduced in the provinces. Meanwhile, the Indian legislative council should be enlarged and made more representative, and its influence in the processes of policymaking needs to be enhanced.

There is no denying that the 1919 Act was a politically appropriate strategy in a context when the nationalist movement was growing in importance especially after the arrival of Gandhi on the scene. Although the administration was guided by the colonial spirit, by involving the loyalist Indians in governance, the British rulers provided a new design of public administration in India. In the new dispensation, structural changes were made in administration. The most remarkable step was the adoption of dyarchy. The dyarchy was an administrative device that demarcated functions between those which were to be given to popular control and those which must continue to remain with the British rulers: the former were called 'transferred subjects' and the latter 'reserved subjects'. The Governor-General-in-Council was in charge of the reserved subjects while Governors, acting with the ministers in the provinces, remained supreme in so far as the transferred subjects were concerned.

On the surface, the nature of governance appeared to have undergone radical changes since the enlargement of the electorate created Indian majorities in various councils. But the appearance was misleading since critical roles were retained by the British. The distribution of power under the Government of India Act, 1919, which led to the creation of dyarchy, is illustrative here.

As Table 1.1 shows, the dyarchy was a format of governance which by constitutionally bestowing the authority on the British rulers (and not the

Table 1.1 The division of administrative subjects under the Government of India Act, 1919

Ia: Devolution of subjects of government	
Central	*Provincial*
Military, foreign affairs, tariffs and customs, railway, post and telegraphs, income tax, currency, coinage and public debt, commerce and shipping, civil and criminal law, audit of provincial expenditure	Local Self Government, medical administration and public health, education, public works and irrigation, land revenue administration, famine relief, agriculture, forests, exercise, administration of justice, industrial matters, police and jails, minor ports
1b: Provincial division of subjects of government	
Reserved	*Transferred*
Water supplies, land revenue administration, famine relief, land acquisition, justice, law reports, stamps, mineral resources, posts, water ways, police, newspaper control, European vagrancy, coroners, prisons, money borrowing	Local Self Government, medical administration, public health, sanitation, vital statistics, pilgrimages, education, public works, agriculture, veterinary services, fisheries, cooperative societies, forests, exercise, registration, industry, stores, weights, libraries, elections

Source: Indian Statutory Commission, Volume 4, Memoranda 9, cited in Stephen Legg, 'Dyarchy: democracy, autocracy and the scaler sovereignly of interwar India', *Comparative Studies of South Asia, Africa and Middle East*, Vol. 36, No. 1, 2016, p. 45.

elected representatives) in regard to the reserved subjects made them holders of de facto authority. Since the Viceroy had the veto power, the transfer of authority to the elected representatives was futile. Devolution was thus 'intended to tie in a large element of society to the status quo'.[10] The design was seen to have been politically contrived because 'giving power to the local communities meant that energies that could have applied against the imperial power were dissipated into communal harmony'.[11] An outcome of the grand imperial strategy of *divide-et-impera*, it worked for ruler's benefit though, as the available literature shows, constitutional articulation of British imperial preferences in India always presented a problem for legislators and British colonial officials in India. For drafting and making 'a democratic constitutional design', what was imperative, for obvious reasons, was to ensure that 'Britain's imperial position would not be undermined or worse, eliminated'.[12] Nonetheless, the British authority agreed to go ahead with the reforms presumably because of their self-proclaimed civilizing mission in India that also entailed an endeavour towards evolving a sociopolitical environment for constitutional democracy to strike roots. The constitutional reforms were thus an outcome of concerns for defending Britain as a champion of liberalism and also its tutelary role in developing a conducive milieu.

Despite being unique, the dyarchy was thus doomed to fail simply because of its ideological roots in colonialism. Even the Alexander Muddieman-led committee, which was constituted to examine the functioning of dyarchy, concluded that it crumbled because of its inherent weaknesses and dissensions due to the following factors: (i) the demarcation of authorities between reserved and transferred was meaningless since the *de facto* power always rested with the former; (ii) as a result, there was hardly effective dialogue between the provincial ministers and the Governors or the Governor General; (iii) the Indian ministers were further handicapped since Indian civil service officers hardly cooperated with them; and (iv) the excessive control by the finance department of the Government of India over the transferred subjects.

As evident, the administration was constantly being restructured seemingly to placate the Indians' interests in governance. Although the actual power rested with the British authority, dyarchy was a critical step towards administrative devolution that radically altered the complexion of the British power in India that largely revolved around Governor-General-in-Council. Dyarchy empowered the Governors who exercised independence in regard to transferred subjects in the provinces. Furthermore, the involvement of the Indian ministers had introduced changes, though cosmetic in character, in public administration. Apart from gaining experience in administration, the Indian ministers acquired a first-hand knowledge of how the administration functioned in most partisan manner. This helped them articulate a nationalist agenda which was now readily acceptable to the people at large since it was experience-based. So, dyarchy was very critical to conceptualizing the changing nature of public administration in British India at least in the first two decades of the twentieth century.

The 1935 Government of India Act

Colonialism and centralization of power seem to go hand in hand though public administration in British India underwent changes at least in its content. A change is visible if one follows the evolution of public administration since the adoption of the 1772 Regulating Act. Perhaps the most (and last) significant constitutional measure in India during the British rule is the 1935 Government of India Act that drew on the inputs from the Indian Statutory Commission, the All Parties Conference, the Round Table Conferences and the Joint parliamentary Committee of the British Parliament. Seeking to establish a federal form of government in which the constituent provinces had autonomous legislative and executive powers, the Act paved the way for a parliamentary form of government in which the executive was made accountable within certain bounds to the legislature. This had radically altered public administration in India, including the civil services in the country. Although the well-espoused federation never came into being, the Act was nonetheless a powerful comment against the integrated administrative system of the colonial variety. A perusal of the Act draws our attention to the following features:

a provincial autonomy was recognized by giving the provinces a separate legal identity and liberating them from central control except for certain specific purposes;
b a federation of India was established demarcating domains between the provincial governments and the federal central government;
c dyarchy, discontinued in the provinces, was introduced at the centre. Subjects of foreign affairs and defence were 'reserved' to the control of the Governor General; the other central subjects were transferred to ministers in the provinces;
d the federal principle was recognized in the formation of the lower house of the central legislature though the de facto ruler remained the Governor General.
e separate electorate was retained following the distribution of seats among the minority communities, as devised by the 1932 Communal or MacDonald Award.

The Act redefined 'public' in public administration. Introduction of provincial autonomy enabled the Indian ministers to directly involve in administration though they had to function under the overall restriction of colonialism. Hence, it was characterized as 'a gigantic constitutional façade without anything substantial within it'. The Act was also a sign of the determination of the British government to wrap the Indian question towards electoral politics. By involving Indians in administration, the Act had brought more players in the arena of public administration. There is no doubt that the Act (a) introduced the Indian politicians to the world of parliamentary politics and

(b) as a result of the new arrangement, stipulated by the Act, politics now percolated down to the localities which largely remained peripheral so far. The available evidence also suggests that the Act was the price the British paid for the continuity of the Empire. What thus appears to be a calculated generous gesture was very much a politically expedient step. In fact, the surrender of power, though at the regional levels, caused consternation among the votaries of the British power in India who saw an eclipse of British authority in this endeavour.

The 1935 Government of India Act was certainly a powerful constitutional intervention that the colonial rulers seriously made to accommodate the nationalist zeal within, of course, the colonial administrative format. This is also illustrative of efforts at legitimizing the growing democratic aspirations of the ruled in India through a constitutional device. Interestingly, the 1935 Act remained the strongest influence during the making of the 1950 Constitution for free India. Some 250 clauses of the present Constitution were, in fact, lifted from the Government of India Act. Although the political system of independent India draws its sustenance from universal adult franchise and political sovereignty, rules are undoubtedly derived from its colonial past. The most striking provisions that the Constitution of India derived from its 1935 counterpart are 'the Emergency provisions' that enable the President to suspend the democratically elected governments and fundamental rights of the citizens.

Reviewing the argument

An uncritical look at these selective, but major, landmark constitutional initiatives during the colonial rule may lead one to conclude that these were initiated by the British for the Indians. Hence, the spirit of nationalism is underrated. If one goes beyond the surface, what is evident is that public administration underwent changes largely because of the British effort to defuse popular discontent. Hence, the argument that every constitutional drive was initiated by the Raj is totally unfounded.

The 3 June Plan and Indian Independence Act, 1947

At the end of the Second World War (1939–45), the British politicians realized that the colonial rule in India could no longer be sustained. The Indian nationalists were deadly against its continuation. International opinion was also in favour of decolonization. The perspective in which the Indian question was so far articulated had thus radically changed. True to its pledge, the newly elected Labour government also responded to the situation in a very different way. Illustrative of their commitment is the announcement on 20 February 1947, where Atlee, the British premier, declared that 'His Majesty's Government wish to make it clear that it is their definite intention to take necessary steps to effect the transference of power to responsible Indian hands by a date not later than June, 1948'.[13] Accordingly, Mountbatten, the last viceroy, was vested with all powers to devise an appropriate scheme to settle the Indian question. It was a difficult task. Nonetheless, the viceroy convinced both the Muslim League and the Congress leadership to agree to the partition of Bengal and Punjab and also assured to complete the process by August 1947 instead of June 1948 as decided earlier. It was against this background that the 3 June Plan was prepared, which involved 'at every stage a process of open diplomacy with leaders'.[14] The Atlee government was determined to transfer power as the 3 June Plan was unambiguous in stating that 'it has been the desire of His Majesty's Government that power should be transferred in accordance with the wishes of the Indian people themselves'.[15] It was also made clear that the responsibility of framing the Constitution for independent India and Pakistan should rest with the people of the respective countries. The government declaration further stated that

> His Majesty's Government wish to make it clear that they have no intention of attempting to frame any ultimate constitution for India [or Pakistan]; this is a matter to be decided by the people themselves. Nor is there anything in this plan to preclude negotiations between communities for a united India.[16]

The plan made provision for the Constitution of two Boundary Commissions – one for Punjab and the other for Bengal and if necessary for Assam. In case, the award not being implemented before the transfer of power to the Government of Pakistan in August 1947, the plan provided for 'the notional partition' of the provinces of Bengal and Punjab purely on the basis of demographic composition of the provinces. It further stressed that the Commission 'shall under no circumstances be conditioned by the provisional boundaries and instead look into the matter afresh'.[17]

The 3 June plan appeared to have guided the entire process of what finally culminated in the division of Bengal and Punjab. According to this plan, the provincial Legislative Assemblies of Bengal and Punjab would 'meet in two parts, one representing the Muslim-majority districts and the other the rest of the Province' to decide 'whether or not the Province should be partitioned'.[18] Unlike Punjab where the Legislative Assembly met amidst demonstrations and communal disorders, the voting in Bengal passed off in a comparatively peaceful atmosphere. First, there was a joint meeting of the members from both the Muslim and Hindu-majority districts, presided over by the Speaker of the House, Nurul Amin, in which a majority of 126 members endorsed the demand for a new and separate Pakistan constituent assembly, while ninety members voted for participating in the existing constituent assembly that was elected in 1946. At the second stage, members representing the Hindu and Muslim majority districts met separately. In a meeting chaired by the Maharaja of Burdwan, members from the Hindu-majority districts decided in favour of partition by 58 to 21 votes, while members from the Muslim-majority districts, sitting separately, opposed partition by 106 to 35 votes. However, when the results of the members from the Hindu-majority districts were made known to them, they decided by 107 to 34 votes that a district with a clear Muslim majority should join the proposed Pakistan constituent assembly.

The Indian Independence Act, 1947, that formally transferred power to the people of India was introduced in the House of Commons on 4 July and received the Royal assent on 18 July. Drawn on the spirit of the 3 June Plan, the Act also recognized the independent existence of Pakistan along with India. Since partition was accepted by both the Congress and the Muslim League, it was rather easier for the British government to set out the terms and conditions for the transfer of power. Pakistan was created by bifurcating three Muslim-dominated British Indian provinces – two in the east, Bengal and Assam, and one in the west, Punjab. Sind, Balochistan and North West Frontier Province were also to be included in the new state of Pakistan. As soon as the Independence Act was approved, the British government transferred its responsibility of governing the country to the new dominions. Similarly, the suzerainty of the British Parliament over the princely Indian states lapsed along with all the treaties and agreements between the British government and Indian rulers. This provision provoked criticism from the Congress, and Nehru in his note of 3 July 1947 argued that 'the complete wiping out of all treaties and agreements in force at the date of passing of the Act will create administrative chaos of the gravest kind'.[19] Hence, he was in favour of endorsing the Cabinet Mission's suggestion that 'pending the new agreements, existing arrangements in all matters of common concern should continue'.[20] The Muslim League hailed the Act just like the Hindu Mahasabha: while the League was happy because Pakistan was carved out, the Hindu Mahasabha welcomed partition of Bengal, in particular, as it would give the Hindus an opportunity to govern themselves, which was not possible given the demographic preponderance of the Muslims in the erstwhile undivided province.

The Act set in motion processes that finally led to the transfer of power on 15 August 1947. The Constituent Assembly had already begun its deliberations. The two Boundary Commissions were appointed under the chairmanship of Cyril Radcliffe who submitted his recommendations within less than a month after his first meeting on the subject on 16 July 1947. Drawing on probably the best available legal minds, the Radcliffe Award turned out to be an excellent technical document which, due to the utter negligence of the reality in Bengal and Punjab, remained a bone of contention to those adversely affected by 'this whimsical design' even in the aftermath of freedom. Nonetheless, the 1947 Act remained an important statement on India's freedom from colonialism for two interrelated reasons: *first*, India's struggle for freedom led to a paradox of history because freedom was won with a heavy price in the form of partition of the country; *second*, this was an Act that despite being a formal declaration of the British withdrawal from India seemed to have translated into reality the British apprehension that imperial control of India was no longer tenable.

For the nationalists in India and Pakistan, the 1947 Indian Independence Act was not merely recognition of what they fought for, but also one of the foundational, perhaps most significant, pillars of freedom. The constitutional arrangement that the Act stipulated was respected by all despite being critical of some of the provisions. This itself is indicative of the extent to which the British colonialism succeeded in warping the Indian minds in typical liberal tradition of the Westminster type. There were hardly scathing criticisms of the provisions of the Act; neither the Congress nor the Muslim League challenged the Act except seeking clarifications or offering technical suggestions for implementing some of schemes that the Act found appropriate for smooth transfer of power.

The outcome of the Act was the inauguration of two new nations. India became free on 15 August 1947. A new era dawned, and Jawaharlal Nehru captured that moment in his famous 'tryst with destiny' speech by saying that

> At the stroke of the midnight hour, when the world sleeps, India will awake to life and freedom. A moment comes, which comes but rarely in history, when we step out from the old to the new, when an age ends, and when the soul of a nation, long suspended, finds utterance. It is fitting that at this solemn moment we take the pledge of dedication to the service of India and her people and to the still larger cause of humanity.[21]

While Nehru was optimistic, his colleagues were not so given the multiple sources of discontent that the newly emerged nation was likely to confront. Apprehending that political freedom, by itself, made no sense unless it was articulated to bring about radical changes in governance, which was possible once the sources of social, economic and political discontent were completely eradicated. Hence, Rajendra Prasad, the President of the Constituent Assembly, exhorted that

> India needs today nothing more than a set of honest men who will have the interest of the country before them. There is a fissiparous tendency arising out of various elements in our life. We have communal differences, caste differences, language differences, provincial differences and so forth. It requires men of vision, men who will not sacrifice the interests of the country at large for the sake of smaller groups and areas and who will rise over the prejudices which are born of these differences.[22]

The scene does not appear to be as gloomy as it was made out to be, as he immediately pointed out that 'successful working of democratic constitution requires in those who have to work them willingness to respect the view point of others, capacity for compromise and accommodation'.[23] He was also persuaded to believe that it was not difficult to achieve since 'we have been able to draw this Constitution without taking recourse to voting and division in Lobbies'.[24] Nonetheless, social diversity of India was 'a real, if awkward, fact [which] simultaneously provoked pride in India's civilizational fecundity and plurality, and a fear in its centrifugal potential'.[25] India's partition in 1947 was a testimony to a situation when communal schism was resolved only with the vivisection of the country. One cannot therefore ignore the context in which specific efforts towards constitutionalizing India were made. In other words, what was initiated by the colonial rule in the name of constitutional governance and also those parallel attempts that the nationalists made towards that goal need to be understood with reference to the contemporary democratic politics. Constitutionalism is conceptualized as organically linked with the prevalent socio-economic context. There is a point of view, however, suggesting that it was a design for 'political exclusion of the masses',[26] which both the colonial rulers and their opponents endorsed while articulating their responses for constitutionalizing India. Despite having contrasting political objectives, the colonizers and the colonized were hardly different in their approach to the masses given their 'shared political language of exclusion [which] was intrinsic to constitutional reforms'[27] that were undertaken so zealously during colonialism and its immediate aftermath. As their ideological goal was identical, the nationalists were persuaded to accept that 'in order to achieve any measure of self-government, they had to adopt a language of representation, one that fundamentally agreed with the colonial government that large masses had yet to be tutored in the art of self-government'.[28] It is true, and the argument draws heavily on this, that there existed two worlds: organized and unorganized; in the former, the appeal of constitutionalism was significant, while the latter remained peripheral due to complex socio-economic reasons explaining their exclusion. However, the situation had undergone a sea change with the arrival of Gandhi who tried to bridge the gulf between the organized and the unorganized words for a nationalist goal. There were other ideological forces representing the interests of the peasants, workers and other marginalized sections of society, which also became prominent in struggles which were also directed against socially entrenched vested interests. The point here relates to the argument emphasizing the dialectical interconnection between democratic politics and constitutionalism. Hence, India's constitutional history is not one of absolute consensus, but one that represented a series of conflicts around myriad social, economic and political issues. An analytical scan of what led India to become a constitutional democracy in the aftermath of decolonization reveals that the nationalists favoured the Westminster form of liberal democracy, which they justified as an appropriate mode of governance because (a) it was meant to realize what they had imbibed by virtue of being part of the Empire that drew on the philosophy of Enlightenment and (b) it also had a natural appeal to them since they were nurtured in that tradition. Furthermore, it also demonstrates at another level that the nationalists hardly spoke in one language, and their ideological priorities were chosen accordingly though the Gandhian mode of anti-British protest campaign remained the dominant one. As far as the structure of governance was concerned, the nationalists and their *bete noire* undertook to seek to conceptualize in liberal theoretical mould. For instance, with the increasing importance of Muslims as an independent political entity, it was unavoidable for both the British government and Congress nationalists not to take into account their special politico-ideological needs while devising the 1935 constitutional design for India; in a similar vein, the 1945 Sapru Committee paid significant attention to the communal question though within the nationalist framework to allay the fear of the minorities of being marginalized in what they characterized as Hindu-dominated India.

Concluding observations

The evolution of colonialism in India will continue to remain an interesting area of research for a variety of reasons. Prominent among them is certainly the process in which colonialism sustained its grip in India by creating a strong collaborative network and also by successfully pursuing a divide-and-rule strategy to scuttle efforts at unifying socio-economically separated communities. The strength of British colonialism lies in the fact that unlike their European counterparts, the British rulers expanded and also maintained their presence not merely by coercion, but also by creating circumstances in which they emerged as the best possible option by the Indians who remained highly divisive due to various socio-economic and political reasons. The constitutional landmarks were a clear testimony to those imperial efforts that defused opposition rather easily on most occasions. What was distinct about British colonialism was its success in welding a significant section of population to the system of governance that the British introduced. It was possible perhaps due to its triumph in ideologically moulding people towards liberal political values and ethos. Barring the militant nationalists, most of the nationalists were content with the method of three Ps (petition, prayer and protest) until the rise of Gandhi who radically transformed the complexion of anti-British confrontation. The scene was not the same with the ascendancy of the Extremist nationalists who pledged to fight for India's independence even by deploying coercive means. They were gradually exterminated by following a due process of law, which was, however, managed by the British authority so efficiently that an image of the Empire being true to its commitment to the subjects was built and consolidated. It was therefore not surprising that the nationalists took legal means to save their colleagues from gaol, which also confirms that these constitutionally recognized institutions of governance gained credibility among them despite being staunch opponents of the British rule. Here too, the argument that the nationalists upheld liberal values which, they felt, were protected by these complementary political institutions is reinforced. Fundamental here is the point that the legal stipulations and the institutions that they brought about led to the consolidation of British imperialism by most effectively managing (and also defusing) the nationalist counter-attacks before they became threatening to the Empire. In the process, these institutions also evolved as integrally connected with the evolution of India as a constitutional democracy which was rooted in the British endeavour towards constitutional India, an effort which also received adequate support from the nationalists notwithstanding being opposed to the alien rule.

In view of the uncanny similarities between the colonial institutions and those in independent India, one can safely argue that decolonization was hardly a break with the past. As a result, at least structurally, the institutions that helped the British to expand and consolidate its hegemony were allowed to survive. And, as a corollary to this argument, one can further advance the point that the *weltanschauung* (world view) that flourished in postcolonial India was based on 'the mixed legacies of colonial rule' that upheld the rule of law, bureaucracy, citizenship, parasitic landlords, modern political institutions and 'two-track tradition of protest and participation'.[29] What accounts for relative stability for colonialism in India was certainly its ability to adapt to the changed sociopolitical circumstances and also gradual but steady 'internalization' of domination by the subjects of colonial rule, which provoked an analyst to characterize colonialism as 'an intimate enemy'[30] because the dominated saw the virtues of being dominated for their own betterment. Colonialism was thus not seen as an absolute evil but complementary to India's rise as an independent nation in future. The statement may not be politically correct. Nonetheless, it can safely be argued that colonialism provided critical impetus to various processes that finally resulted in serious political mobilization against imperialism in India. Whether nationalism or democratization – they had their roots in the long history of colonialism and in this sense colonialism remained a significant force behind the rise of India as an independent nation in 1947.

As argued above, it will not be unfair to suggest that these landmark constitutional experiments contributed to the evolution of constitutional democracy in India which does not seem to be overstretched, at one level; being primarily instruments of the Empire, these constitutional designs were, at another level, also meant to expand and consolidate its authority. By championing the distinctive rights of the minorities, especially the Muslims, the British authority utilized a powerful constitutional argument to cause a fissure between the two major communities, Hindus and Muslims, in India. The implication was disastrous as the recognition of Muslims as a separate socio-economic and political entity which required special constitutional protection culminated in the 1947 partition of the country. Hence, it is argued that these constitutional designs had a role in permanently dividing major communities in India on the basis of religion and other socio-economic denominations. Both the Hindus and Muslims redefined their identities through a process of contestation of vision, contestation of beliefs and contestation of history. The period between 1909 and 1947, when major constitutional experiments were undertaken, sharply shows the mutation in the formation of Hindus and Muslims as communities opposed to each other in the political arena. What was distinctive about this period was the growth of the communities as political units always in a permanent adversarial relationship with the members of the 'other' community. This was further consolidated following the introduction of the communal electorate in the 1937 provincial elections. With the acceptance of the principle of majority, Muslims automatically became the most powerful community in Bengal and Punjab by their sheer demographic strength. In other words, religious identity as a demographic category became probably the single most crucial criterion in determining the distribution of governmental power in these Muslim-majority provinces. The 1935 Government of India Act reiterated the divide-and-rule strategy by formally recognizing that Muslims needed to be treated separately as a distinct, but neglected minority in India. This was a decisive constitutional intervention because not only did it establish the principle of majority as sacrosanct in democracy, but it also made the Muslims self-conscious of their critical importance in governance in India. It is now possible to argue that the 1935 Act definitely shifted the centre of political activity in Bengal to the east of the province. Not by virtue of any inherent superiority of the Muslims, but simply because in a democratically elected legislature, as a contemporary report underlines, 'the weight of numbers tells and the teeming millions of East Bengal – sixty percent of their being Muslims outweighed in point of numbers the more educated Hindus of the South, West and extreme north of the province'.[31] The migration of power to the countryside took place in the context of a major realignment in the social bases of political power, which was manifested in the decline of the urban-based Indian National Congress in East Bengal and the consequent consolidation of the Krishak Praja Party that caught the imagination of the majority community, the Muslims, in no time.[32] Adequate attention to this aspect of India's political history thus substantiates the claim that despite being supportive of constitutional democracy in India, these constitutional designs, true to their historical role of being imperial instruments, had also a share in consolidating divisive politics in India which finally resulted in India's partition.

Notes

1 The chapter is drawn on chapter 1 of my *Constitutional Democracy in India*, Routledge, Oxford, 2018.

2 I have shown this in my 'The communal award of 1932 and its implications in Bengal', *Modern Asian Studies*, Vol. 23, No. 2, 1989, 493–523.

3 DG Karve and DV Ambedkar, *Speeches and Writings of Gopal Krishna Gokhale*, Vol. 2, Asia Publishing House, London, 1966, p. 129.

4 This argument is well-elaborated in the available literature which includes, among others, (a) CH Philips, *The East India Company, 1784–1834*, Manchester University Press, Manchester, 1961; (b) Lucy S Sutherland, *The East India Company in Eighteenth Century Politics*, Clarendon Press, Oxford, 1962; (c) Ramkrishna Mukherjee, *The Rise and Fall of the East India Company*, Monthly Review Press, New York, 1974; and (d) Jeremy Bernstein, *Dawning of the Raj: The Life and Trials of Warren Hastings*, Ivan R Dee, Chicago, 2000.
5 www.csas.ed.ac.uk/mutiny/confpapers/Queen%27sProclamation.pdf, *The Proclamation of the Queen in the Council to the Princes, Chiefs and People of India*, 1 November 1858, accessed on 17 June 2017.
6 India Office Records, London, *Report on the Administration of Bengal, 1871–72*, Government Press, Calcutta, 1872, p. 11.
7 The text of the Act is available in www.sdstate.edu/projectsouthasia/loader.cfm?csModule=security/getfile&PageID=861833, accessed on 25 May 2016.
8 The statement of John Morley is quoted from DA Hamer, *John Morley: Liberal Intellectual in Politics*, Oxford University Press, Oxford, 1968, p. 111.
9 MV Pylee, *Constitutional Government in India*, Asia Publishing House, London, 1960, p. 73.
10 Walter Reid, *Keeping the Jewel in the Crown: The British Betrayal of India*, Penguin, New Delhi, 2016, p. 31.
11 ibid.
12 Arvind Elangovan, 'Constitutionalism, political exclusion and implications for Indian constitutional history: the case of Montgue Chelmsford reforms (1919)', *South Asian History and Culture*, 2016, p. 6.
13 Prime Minister Atlee's statement in the House of Commons – reproduced in VP Menon, *The Transfer of Power in India*, Orient Longman, Madras, 1993, Appendix IX, p. 507.
14 Mountbatten's statement – quoted in HV Hodson, *The Great Divide: Britain-India-Pakistan*, Hutchinson, London, 1969, p. 204.
15 Statement made by the His Majesty's Government on 3 June 1947 – reproduced in VP Menon, *The Transfer of Power in India*, Orient Longman, Madras, 1993, Appendix X, p. 510.
16 ibid.
17 *The Statesman*, Calcutta, 8 June 1947.
18 Statement made by His Majesty's Government on 3 June 1947 – reproduced in VP Menon, *The Transfer of Power in India*, Orient Longman, Madras, 1993, Appendix X, p. 511.
19 A note on 3 July 1947 by Jawaharlal Nehru – reproduced in VP Menon, *The Transfer of Power in India*, Orient Longman, Madras, 1963 (reprint), Appendix XII, p. 4.
20 ibid.
21 Jawaharlal Nehru's 'Tryst with destiny' speech delivered at the dawn of independence in India on 15 August 1947 – quoted from B Shiva Rao (ed.), *The Framing of India's Constitution: Select Documents*, Vol. I, Universal Law Publishing Co., New Delhi, 2004 (reprint), pp. 558–559.
22 Rajendra Prasad's address in the Constituent Assembly on 26 November 1949, *Constituent Assembly Debates*, Vol. XI, Lok Sabha Secretariat, New Delhi, 2003, p. 993.
23 ibid.
24 ibid.
25 Uday S Mehta, 'Indian constitutionalism: crisis, unity and history', in Sujit Choudhury, Madhav Khosla and Pratap Bhanu Mehta (eds.), *The Oxford Handbook of the Indian Constitution*, Oxford University Press, New Delhi, 2016, p. 53.

26 Arvind Elangovan, 'Constitutionalism, political exclusion and implications for Indian constitutional history: the case of Montague-Chelmsford reforms (1919)', *South Asian History and Culture*, Vol. 7, 2016, p. 14.
27 ibid.
28 ibid.
29 Subrata Mitra, 'Constitutional design, democratic vote counting and India's fortuitous multiculturalism', Working Paper, November 2004, South Asia Institute, Heidelberg University, pp. 29–34.
30 Ashis Nandy, *The Intimate Enemy: Loss and Recovery of Self under Colonialism*, Oxford University Press, New Delhi, 1989 (reprint).
31 *India Office Records*, London, Tyson Papers, Eur E 341/41, John Tyson's note, 5 July 1947.
32 I have dealt with this aspect of political mobilization in Bengal in my *Partition of Bengal and Assam: The Contour of Freedom*, Routledge, London & New York, 2004.

2 Constitutional identity

The nationalist inputs*

The 1950 Constitution of India is drawn on the fundamental liberal values which flourished during the long colonial rule. Liberal ideas were articulated both by the British liberals and their Indian counterparts. While the former was paternalistic in their attitude, the latter held liberalism as perhaps the only empowering ideological design of governance which was appropriate for India. In contemporary scholarship, three important types of liberalism have been identified: colonial liberalism, nationalist liberalism and radical liberalism. Drawn on their paternalistic concern for the colonized, the colonial liberals contributed to the consolidation of a system of governance which would prepare Indians to appreciate rule-driven administration. Although they differed in their assessment of the situation in India, they agreed that colonialism was beneficial to the rise of India as a well-governed polity in due course. While they strongly felt that representative democracy was certain to flourish in Australia and America given identical civilizational identity, India was simply incapable of self-government, argued one of most influential liberal thinkers, JS Mill, because of the lack of social homogeneity. Nonetheless, liberal ideas of limited government and the rule of law, equality before law and education as a means of social empowerment were gradually introduced in India by the wake of the colonial rule. A careful study of the British rule in its initial phase suggests that liberalism created a space for the growing involvement of the Indians in administration. Two substantial events changed the course of colonialism: (a) the founding of the universities of Calcutta, Madras and Bombay helped develop an articulate opinion of the educated Indians on the British rule. It captured the growing discontent among the Indians who always remained, for obvious reasons, peripheral in administration. (b) The inauguration of the Indian National Congress in 1885 created a new platform to ventilate the grievances of the ruled. This also became a forum for the Indians to articulate demands for better rule. The outcome of which was the 1892 Indian Councils Act. As the Act underlines, its aim was

> to widen and expand the functions of the Government of India, and to give further opportunities to the non-official and native elements in Indian society to take part in the work of the Government, and in that

* Part of the chapter appeared in my earlier works.

> way, to lend official recognition to that remarkable development both of political interest and political capacity that had been visible among the higher classes of Indian society since the Government of India was taken over by the Crown in 1858.[1]

The Act provided for the enhanced membership of the Councils. It was mandatory for the government to consult the representative bodies and institutions, approved by the government, before selecting nominees for the Councils. Besides legislative powers, the Councils were also empowered to pull the Executive on financial matters though it had no power to either revise or reject decisions on this matter. However, the growing weightage of the Councils is indicative of a sea change in colonial rule. As Morley, the Secretary of State, articulated,

> there are two rival schools of thought, one of which believes that better government of Indian depends on efficiency, and that efficiency is, in fact, the end of British rule in India. The other school, while not neglecting efficiency, looks also to what is called political concessions.[2]

This declaration laid one of the foundational principles of the British administration in India. As a first step, a Royal Commission was appointed in 1907 to look into the administration that seemed to have lost its viability in the context of growing discontent among the ruled. The aim of the Commission was to provide an administration which was adapted to the changed social, economic and political realities of India. While recommending the corrective measures, the Commission was guided by the following factors: (i) the difficulties of ruling the vast subcontinent from a single headquarter and the inevitable failure in the statesmanship and efficiency in administration, (ii) the difficulties of applying uniform schemes of development for the provinces which are socioculturally diverse, (iii) to instil a sense of responsibility among those engaged in provincial and local administration and (iv) to strengthen the colonial rule by educating people in the values of strong administration. On the basis of the recommendation of the Commission, a bill was introduced in 1908 which became the 1909 Morley-Minto Reforms. As a political scheme seeking to strengthen colonial rule in India, the 1909 Act introduced a profound change with long-term effects in representation of communities in Councils. This is the beginning of a trend that gradually unfolded, as will be shown below by dwelling on the legislative steps that gave impetus to the steady growth and consolidation of representative institutions in India. By drawing on the ideational inputs that inform the processes of constitutionalizing India, the chapter substantiates the argument that the Constitution of India is an outcome of long-drawn battle of ideas in which both the colonialists and their opponents had participated. The chapter is thus both an endorsement of the argument and an endeavour to pursue further research in constitutionalizing India.

Nationalist and radical liberals

Liberalism reached the Indian shore through the colonial liberals who, however, had strong reservation about its application in India. Nonetheless, they inspired the early nationalists who were politically baptized through those texts which articulated the liberal approach to politics and governance. Liberalism gained a hegemony in part because of 'the Anglicization of public life'.[3] The political ideas of JS Mill, Herbert Spencer and August Comte, among others, were spread to the English-educated classes through English and later vernacular newspapers, books and pamphlets. The influence was so well-entrenched that even the Indian National Congress had no qualms to openly appreciate the British rule because it purportedly drew on the fundamental ethos of liberalism. In its eleventh annual session, Indian National Congress thus declared that

> to England, we look for inspiration and guidance [because] English history has taught us those principles of freedom which we cherish. ... We have benefitted by the education that we receive and by the material civilization which annihilates time and distance, and brings us together to feel a common interest in our own elevation under a vivifying influence of a literature and a history, the like of which the world has not known in the past for its triumphs in the emancipation of mankind.[4]

However, the delegates were highly disappointed since colonialism in India had already manifested in its most brutal form. Hence, they made an appeal to the rulers

> to gradually change the character of her rule in India, to liberalize it, ... so that in the fullness of time, India may find itself in the great confederacy of free states, English in their origin, English in their character [and] English in their institutions.[5]

So, the main concern was to imbibe the spirit of liberalism in governance. Their main ideal was their representation in the legislature. The demand was continuously made by the Congress since it would allow the Indians to voice their concerns in legislative forums. While justifying the demand, Dadabhai Naoroji, a prominent Moderate liberal, strongly argued for expansion of representation to include Indians in the legislature. As he stated,

> what makes us proud to be British subjects, what attaches us to this foreign rule with deeper loyalty than even our own past Native rule, is the fact that Britain is the parent of free and representative government, and, that we, as her subjects and children, are entitled to inherit the great blessing of freedom and representation'. ... Britain would never be a slave and could not, in her very nature and instinct, make a slave.

> Her greatest glory is freedom and representation, and as her subjects, we shall have these blessed gifts.[6]

What Naoroji had initiated was reinforced by his successors, like Pherozeshah Mehta (1845–1915), Surendranath Banerjea (1848–1925) and GK Gokhale (1866–1915), who also insisted that institutions of representation were seen as the *sine-qua-non* of human freedom. They were also persuaded to believe that it was possible for them to express their views freely in public forums since colonial rulers drew on liberalism. 'It is under the civilizing rule of the Queen and the people of England', thus argued Naoroji, 'that we regularly meet, unhindered by none and are freely allowed to speak our minds without the least fear and least hesitation'.[7] In a similar vein, he further admired British rule by saying that

> we understand the benefits [that] the English rule has conferred upon us; that we thoroughly appreciate the education that has been given to us, the new light which has been poured upon us, turning us from darkness into light and teaching us the new lesson that kings are made for the people and not people for their kings; and this new lesson we have learned amidst the darkness of Asiatic despotism only by the light of free English civilization.[8]

A careful reading of the early nationalists' intervention reveals that they upheld liberalism to the hilt since they were convinced of its utility as an empowering ideology for the colonized. Hence, they insisted on constitutionalism, gradual reforms and an appeal to the English traditions, which helped build the liberal ethos as integral to governance in Britain. The arguments that the early nationalists made in favour of liberalism had two complementary components: on the one hand, what it entails was their concern for political transformation following the fundamental principles of liberalism; their critique of the British rule in India was, on the other hand, drawn on the fact that it had failed, to a significant extent, 'to live up to its own mission as the bearer of liberal and modern institutions and values in India'.[9] They were appalled, in other words, because 'Britain was failing to complete the appointed role, as evidenced by its selfish economic and political policies in India, and by its distrust of the very class that it had brought forth'.[10] What was basic to their arguments was the effort to articulate liberalism in spirit and content and they felt discontented since the British rule in India was not adequately liberal.

Notwithstanding the debilitating effect of colonialism in India, the early liberals seem to have found the British rule most conducive for the growth of a liberal society in India. In their perception, representative institutions and free press were always identified as critical to the material and moral progress of a country which was plagued by archaic customs and primordial social values. As Surendranath Banerjea noted,

> the three great boons which we have received from the British Government are High Education, the gift of a free press and local Self-Government. ... But High Education is the most prized, the most deeply cherished of them all. It is High Education which has made local Self-Government the success that it is admitted to be. It is again High Education which has elevated the tone of the Indian press.[11]

In the creation of a liberal India, the institutional changes were as much critical as the change in the prevalent mindset that had undergone a massive transformation with the introduction of English education, the early nationalists claimed. By recognizing the immense utility of English education, the Deccan Sabha thus exhorted that

> the greatest gift [of the British rule] has been to bring within our reach the blessing and benefit of English education which has helped us to avail of and assimilate the civilizing elements which accompany and distinguish [the rule by the British parliament].[12]

This was an unqualified appreciation of how the English education contributed to the consolidation of liberal ideas in society. It was strongly felt that efforts towards building a liberal society were likely to fail unless it was complemented by a conducive mindset which was possible only by accepting English education. Being critical of political liberals and social Tories, MG Ranade, another vocal liberal, thus stated that

> you cannot be liberal by halves. You cannot be liberal in politics and conservative in religion. The heart and head must go together. You cannot cultivate your intellect, enrich your mind, enlarge the sphere of your political rights and privileges, and, at the same time, keep your hearts closed and cramped. It is an idle dream to expect men to remain enchained and enshackled (sic) in their own superstition and social evils, while they are struggling hard to win rights and privileges from their rulers. Before long these vain dreamers will find their dreams lost.[13]

On another occasion, Ranade emphasized the importance of a strong state, guided by the rule of law in combatting the well-entrenched social evils. In other words, he was in favour of a strong state which was necessary to establish a liberal social format as well. The argument was forcefully made when he stated that

> the history of the suppression of infanticide and Sati shows that these institutions which had grown as excrescences upon the healthy system of ancient Hindu society, were checked and can only be checked by the strong arm of Laws, and once they are denounced as crimes they disappeared from the face of the country.[14]

Justifying state intervention as legitimate, he further argued that

> the diseased corruptions of the body cannot and should not be dealt with in the same way as its normal and healthy developments. The sharp surgical operation and not the homoeopathic infinitesimally small pill is the proper remedy of the first class of disorder and the analogy holds good in the diseases of the body politic as well as the material body in dealing with the parasitical growth of social degeneration.[15]

Two important ideas stand out: first, the early liberals were persuaded to believe that unless there were adequate institutional backups, the Westminster form of liberal democracy would remain elusive. Their insistence on having those institutions was thus a natural choice. Second, they were also aware of the fact that without supportive value systems, not only would the liberal institutions fail to strike organic roots in India, but they would also become merely cosmetic.

While the Moderate liberals pursued a policy reconciliation within the British rule, their Extremist counterparts championed violence, if necessary, to harm the ruler. Their idea of swaraj approximated to self-government of the liberal variety though the Extremists felt that 'as long as the source of power is situated in Whitehall there cannot be even a beginning of the democratic processes'.[16] What was basic in their politico-ideological campaign was the demand for freedom which would facilitate the formation of a political system of their choice. Hence, it was suggested that the new system involved

> the abdication of the right of England to determine the policy of the Indian government, the relinquishment of the right of the present foreign despotism to enact whatever law they please, the abandonment of their right to tax the people according to their own will and to spend the revenues of the country in any way they like.[17]

Their aim was to form a government according to what the people of India thought, which was evident in what Lala Lajpat Rai mentioned by saying that 'in order to be free we must form, guide and control the national will in such a way as to make it irresistible'.[18] What was unique in the Extremist perception was their belief that sovereignty rested with the people. Unlike the Moderates, Aurobindo, one of the most vocal Extremists, made his preference very clear by stating that 'only by becoming responsible to the people and drawn from the people can the government be turned into a protector instead of an oppressor'.[19] Appreciative of liberal democracy since it drew its sustenance from the people, he reinforced his argument by saying that

> the only effective way of putting an end to executive tyranny is to make the people and not irresponsible Government the controller and

> paymaster of both executive and judiciary. The only possible method of stopping the drain is to establish a popular government which may be relied on to foster and protect Indian commerce and industry conducted by Indian capital and employing Indian labour. This is the object which the new politics, the politics of the twentieth century, places before the people of India in their resistance to the present system of Government, not tinkerings and palliatives, but the substitution for the autocratic bureaucracy, which at present misgoverns us, of a free constitutional and democratic system of government and the entire removal of foreign control in order to make way for perfect national liberty.[20]

Despite their strong criticism of the colonial rule which led to devastations in India, the Extremist thinkers expressed their keenness in adopting a liberal democratic system of governance for two reasons: first, liberal democracy was perhaps one of those forms of government which derived its strength from people; the fact that it nurtured popular sovereignty attracted the Extremists regardless of the fact that it had evolved in Britain. Second, the idea appears to have swayed the Extremist thinkers presumably because of their personal experience of the system of governance that existed in England during their stay as students or otherwise; they thus believed that liberal democracy was not only a libertarian ideology, but also appropriate for meaningfully translating popular sovereignty in spirit and content.

There are therefore reasons to believe that the early liberals helped create some of the conditions for the rise and consolidation of India's political democracy. Supportive of the democratic institutions that articulated liberalism in practice, they also contributed to develop a space for debates over the feasibility of a system of governance that owed its sustenance from liberalism. What is, however, paradoxical was the fact that their concern for class interests, including property rights, clouded their vision for social democracy. As a result, they, despite being critical of inequality during colonial rule, failed to provide a conceptually persuasive analytical framework for combatting well-entrenched poverty which also had social roots. This confirms the argument that liberalism in India was contextually constructed, which means that the classical British liberal ideas were 'deconstructed and reassembled to reflect Indian conditions and structures of thought'.[21]

While the early liberals were keen to build the institutional fabric of the nation since it was, in their perception, unavoidable to realize the fundamental liberal ethos, the radical liberals, especially Jyotirao Phule (1827–90) and BR Ambedkar (1891–1956), strongly argued for rearranging of the prevalent social systems to avoid birth-driven discrimination. Influenced by Thomas Paine's *Rights of Man*, Phule was persuaded to believe that since 'the creator has bestowed upon all men and women equal religious and political liberties, … [they] should therefore have equality before law and equality of opportunity for entry into the civil service or municipal administration'.[22] Anticipating some of the ideas that BR Ambedkar was to articulate in future, he attributed social discrimination to Brahmin domination in Hindu society. Being critical of MG Ranade for his appreciation of 'Hindu tradition', he maintained that this was a ploy to retain a discriminatory social arrangement in which *sudras* (untouchables) would always remain subservient to the upper caste, particularly Brahmins. His appreciation of the British rule was governed by his firm belief that it was meant by 'the Creator to rescue the sudras from slavery [and hence he urged upon them] to exploit the golden opportunity given by the British rule to get themselves emancipated from Brahman domination'.[23] What Phule suggested was further developed by BR Ambedkar who, while challenging the existent heritage-dependent hierarchical social order in India, also welcomed the British rule for being liberal in its approach to governance. He was a vocal supporter of positive constitutional and political discrimination in favour of the untouchables. BR Ambedkar created and also expanded normative spaces involving not just equality, liberty and rights, but also self-respect and dignity for the historically disadvantaged segments of the population. There is a caveat here because Ambedkar's notion of constitutional liberalism can be said to have redefined its basic thrust by insisting on the group autonomy and dignity (and not merely individual autonomy and dignity) against coercion, whatever the source – the state, society or any other institution. It was an effort that was translated into reality in the 1950 Constitution of independent India, which created a template for liberty, equality and fraternity regardless of class, clan and ethnicity. By interrogating the foundational values of Hinduism that tended to justify social inequality, Babasaheb gave a voice to the critique that subjected the sociologically justified caste divisions to a thorough scrutiny. In his conceptual framework, the human agency remained central which also reflected a Deweyan emphasis on the role of human beings in the making and unmaking of the world that we lived in. It was thus perfectly compatible with his overall ideological position when he declared that

> do not depend … for the abolition of caste slavery upon God or Superman. Your salvation lies in political power and not in making pilgrimages and the observance of fasts. Devotion to scriptures would not free you from bondage, want and poverty.[24]

Central to his argument was a belief in human efforts in re-conceptualizing social mores and values which were contrary to liberal interpretations of human civilization. While defending liberalism, Ambedkar also introduced a unique moral and political framework in public reasoning which owed much to the European variety of Enlightenment paradigm combining social virtues (such as benevolence, compassion and tolerance) with scepticism and reason and the American variety of republican values. The idea of every person having the right to life, liberty, free speech and pursuit happiness, and the duty of the state to ensure that they were not violated remained critical in Ambedkar's understanding of liberalism, which had clear contextual roots. Being 'an eclectic thinker'[25] who was also sensitive to the social brutalities that he suffered due to his birth as a Mahad, he supported 'vigorous state action to empower the untouchables and lower castes',[26] which, however, ran counter to the fundamental ethos of classical liberalism. Nonetheless, there are imprints of English liberal idealists, like TH Green (1836–82) and LT Hobhouse (1864–1929), who insisted on community, individual welfare rights and as an activist he devised his own model of state-driven social transformation in which his own experiences of humiliation because of the accident of birth remained critical. Hence, it is fair to argue that Indian liberals, including the radical liberals, reinvented what derived from their understanding of British liberalism in the Indian context. The shift from constitutional liberalism of the early nationalist era to 'the quasi-socialistic communitarianism of 1900 and after'[27] is illustrative here. It is therefore not odd to find that by championing the idea of secular freedom and equality, Gandhi set in motion an ideological search that was not exactly derivative of classical British liberalism. It was an idea that was creatively interpreted in the context of the struggle that he led in South Africa and later in India against the denial of the basic rights of freedom and equality because of the deviant nature of a so-called liberal state. The Mahatma posed a clear challenge to the typical Western articulation of the basic values of liberalism that justified racial stereotypes by drawing on the Christian ideas of the value of individual, early bourgeois idea about the transition from a state of nature to civil society, and the ideas of progress that informed industrial capitalism, among others. By evolving his critique of liberalism on the obvious logical fallacy of the way the exponents of exploitation viewed liberalism, Gandhi powerfully challenged the regimes (in South Africa and India) that simply failed to be liberal because they clearly deviated from the classical liberal creed.

A thorough analytical scan of the multiple traditions of liberalism that figured prominently in the writings and also deeds of the nationalists in India reveals that liberalism remained a critical ideological force. Beginning with the Moderate liberals in the early part of India's nationalist movement to Gandhi, Ambedkar and their partners, liberalism did not seem to have lost its appeal despite being conceptualized differently in different phases of India's struggle for freedom. There is no denying the fact that liberalism appealed to the Indian nationalists in the context of the Anglicization of the public life which was reinforced possibly because it became an empowering ideology in their battle against colonialism. It was further strengthened by the constitutional designs that evolved in the wake of the British rule in India, as will be shown below, which, by creating a template of governance, seem to have governed, to a significant extent, the nationalists' preference. The end result was that despite having drawn on contrary ideological perspectives, the nationalists and their *bete noire* upheld liberal constitutional values while seeking to pursue their respective political aims.

Major designs towards constitutionalizing India

The Constitution of India had both colonial and nationalist imprints. By devising mechanisms of sharing power with their Indian counterparts, the colonial rulers set in motion processes of constitutionalizing India, which drew its inspiration from the fundamental ethos of British Enlightenment. There were concerted efforts by the alien state, in other words, to conceptualize constitutional governance within the theoretical framework of liberalism. The inevitable outcome was the growing support for the Westminster model of democracy as perhaps a panacea for all troubles that the colonized had to face. Despite occasional challenges to liberal democracy by those who did not seem persuaded, parliamentary democracy had prevailed over other ideological options since Indian National Congress and its allies were convinced of its effectiveness as a form of governance for India. How was it possible? At one level, the increasing acceptance of liberal democracy was an offshoot of the British initiatives to involve the Indians in administration, which was primarily a colonial strategy to weaken the efforts against colonialism. This was further strengthened by those nationalist leaders, from the Moderates to Gandhi and Jawaharlal Nehru who, unlike the former, demanded complete independence, who, by being ideologically baptised in liberalism during their growing-up years, appeared to have found its merit which was strong enough to sway them for what they stood for. The book thus makes two arguments: first, the structure of governance that evolved during colonialism and its aftermath was drawn on the fundamental principles of liberal democracy that was rooted in the efforts that the colonial government undertook as a strategy by dispersing power; in other words, the idea had gradually percolated down to the grass roots presumably because it generated a hope among a sizeable section of the colonized who now became part and parcel of colonial governance. Second, the fact that the leading nationalists accepted liberalism as an empowering ideology strengthened its base in India; it was therefore not surprising that the Moderates who never pressed for complete independence and their opponents converged by being appreciative of liberal constitutional values, which also confirms that the British-initiated processes of constitutionalism continued to remain critical whenever the nationalists articulated their preferences for a specific kind of Constitution.

Keeping these two arguments in view, the book thus proposes to pursue the discussion in two complementary parts: on the one hand, there will be an analytical account of all the legislative endeavours that the colonial government adopted to efficiently manage administration in the context of the growing disenchantment of the colonized with colonialism; the discussion shall also be devoted to explore, on the other hand, the nationalist alternative which, despite having been drawn on contrasting political perspectives, was not radically different in tenor presumably because of the nationalist faith in liberalism as a libertarian ideological design.

Major initiatives by the colonial government

Colonialism expanded its control in India in two distinct ways: first, by tactfully following the divisive *divide-et-impera* strategy that created and sustained the schism between the two major communities of Hindus and Muslims. The British strategy worked favourably because of the socio-economic differences that separated these two communities. In course of time, the divide and rule formula not only consolidated the British rule in India, but also created conditions for the politically underprivileged sections to rise as meaningful partners in governance. So, it cut both ways: on the one hand, the chasm between communities, based on genuine socio-economic differences as well, made the task of governance easier for the ruler; this also, on the other hand, led to a process whereby the peripheral communities became a powerful political voice in the nationalist struggle for independence. Second, drawn on the classical liberal democratic tradition, the British ruler introduced several legal steps to consolidate the empire by gradually opening up administration to the Indians. Along with the application of force, the British government also adopted various reform schemes to inject constitutional values that shaped the nationalist campaign to a significant extent. It will therefore not be incorrect to suggest that the British rule survived in India with least coercion because of the role of the Indian collaborators in defending the empire. Except in the context of the 1942 open rebellion, the collaborative network of support had never shown signs of collapse. The adoption of various reforms by the British government created conditions in which Indians felt attached with the imperial rule that finally disintegrated due to its internal contradictions and also the growing nationalist consolidation opposed to foreign rule. Focussing on the landmark constitutional designs during the British rule, this chapter is an analytical statement on the British politico-legal strategies to consolidate the Raj. These designs, undoubtedly concessions to the ruled, were also devices to weaken the nationalist agitation as and when it became a serious threat to the government. In other words, while the British liberal tradition may have contributed to the constitutional reforms, one cannot deny the growing strength of the nationalist campaign, Gandhian or otherwise, that forced the British to introduce measures to defuse crisis.

An uncritical look at the selective, but major, landmark constitutional initiatives during the colonial rule may lead one to conclude that these were initiated by the British for the Indians. Hence, the spirit of nationalism is underrated. If one goes beyond the surface, what is evident is that the inclusion of Indians in administration was but an outcome of the British effort to defuse popular discontent. Hence, the argument that every constitutional drive was initiated by the Raj is totally unfounded. History reveals that there were situations which forced the British authority to adopt measures to control agitation. For instance, the Congress campaign in the 1880s contributed a lot to the introduction of the 1893 reforms. Behind the 1909

Morley-Minto Reforms lay the *Swadeshi* Movement and revolutionary terrorism. Similarly, the 1919 Montague-Chelmsford Reforms were attempts at resolving crises that began with the Home Rule League and climaxed with the 1919 Rowlatt Satyagraha and the Non Cooperation Movement of 1910–21. To a large extent, the Gandhian Civil Disobedience Movement (1930–32) accounted for the introduction of constitutional measures seeking to involve Indian politicians in public administration.

Furthermore, the interpretation of these constitutional designs remains partial unless linked with the broader socio-economic and political processes in which they were conceptualized. An attempt to analyse the structure and dynamics of constitutional politics without reference to the broader social matrix and economic nexus is futile because the politico-constitutional structure reflects economic and social networks, religio-cultural beliefs and even the nationalist ideology which impinged on the organized world of administrative and constitutional structure. So, an urgent and unavoidable task for an analyst is not to completely ignore the broader socio-economic context, but to ascertain its relative importance in shaping a particular constitutional initiative. For instance, the 1932 Communal Award was believed to have been initiated by the British to expand political activity among the Muslims in Bengal and Punjab. But, as studies have shown, it was also a concession the British was forced to grant in order make the maintenance of the Empire easier.[28] The sharing of power with the native elites was thus prompted by considerations other than merely British initiatives.

The evolution of colonialism in India will continue to remain an interesting area for research for a variety of reasons. Prominent among them is certainly the process in which colonialism sustained its grip in India by creating a strong collaborative network and also by successfully pursuing a divide-and-rule strategy to scuttle efforts at unifying socio-economically separated communities. The strength of British colonialism lies in the fact that unlike their European counterparts, the British rulers expanded and also maintained their presence not merely by coercion, but also by creating circumstances in which they emerged as the best possible option by the Indians who remained highly divisive due to various socio-economic and political reasons. The constitutional landmarks that we have discussed above are a clear testimony to those imperial efforts that defused opposition rather easily on most occasions. What was distinct about British colonialism was its success in welding a significant section of population to the system of governance that the British introduced. It was possible perhaps due to its triumph in ideologically moulding people towards liberal political values and ethos. Barring the militant nationalists, most of the nationalists were content with the method of three Ps (petition, prayer and protest) until the rise of Gandhi who radically transformed the complexion of anti-British confrontation.

These landmark constitutional experiments had a role in permanently dividing major communities in India on the basis of religion and other socio-economic denominations. Both the Hindus and Muslims redefined their identities through a process of contestation of vision, contestation of beliefs and contestation of history. The period between 1909 and 1947, when major constitutional experiments were undertaken, sharply shows the mutation in the formation of Hindus and Muslims as communities opposed to each other in the political arena. What was distinctive about this period was the growth of the communities as political units always in a permanent adversarial relationship with the members of the 'other' community. This was further consolidated following the introduction of the communal electorate in the 1937 provincial elections. With the acceptance of the principle of majority, Muslims automatically became most powerful community in Bengal and Punjab by their sheer demographic strength. In other words, religious identity as a demographic category became probably the single most crucial criterion in determining the distribution of governmental power in these Muslim-majority provinces. The 1935 Government of India Act reiterated the divide-and-rule strategy by formally recognizing that Muslims needed to be treated separately as a distinct, but neglected minority in India. This was a decisive constitutional intervention because not only did it establish the principle of majority as sacrosanct in democracy, but it also made the Muslims self-conscious about their critical importance in governance in India. It is now possible to argue that the 1935 Act definitely shifted the centre of political activity in Bengal to the east of the province. Not by virtue of any inherent superiority of the Muslims, but simply because in a democratically elected legislature, as a contemporary report underlines, 'the weight of numbers tells and the teeming millions of East Bengal – sixty percent of their being Muslims outweighed in point of numbers the more educated Hindus of the South, West and extreme north of the province'.[29] The migration of power to the countryside took place in the context of a major realignment in the social bases of political power.

The 1935 Government of India Act was certainly a powerful constitutional intervention that the colonial rulers seriously made to accommodate the nationalist zeal within, of course, the colonial administrative format. This is also illustrative of efforts at legitimizing the growing democratic aspirations of the ruled in India through a constitutional device. Interestingly, the 1935 Act remained the strongest influence during the making of the 1950 Constitution for free India. Some 250 clauses of the present Constitution were, in fact, lifted from the Government of India Act. Although the political system of independent India draws its sustenance from universal adult franchise and political sovereignty, rules are undoubtedly derived from its colonial past. The most striking provisions that the Constitution of India derived from its 1935 counterpart are 'the Emergency provisions' that enable the President to suspend the democratically elected governments and fundamental rights of the citizens.

There is no doubt that the postcolonial state in India inherited its habits of governance from colonial practices. And, its *weltanschauung* (world view) is based on 'the mixed legacies of colonial rule' that upheld rule of law, bureaucracy, citizenship, parasitic landlords, modern political institutions and 'two-track tradition of protest and participation'.[30] What accounts for relative stability for colonialism in India was certainly its ability to adapt to the changed sociopolitical circumstances also gradual but steady 'internalization' of domination by the subjects of colonial rule, which provoked an analyst to characterize colonialism as 'an intimate enemy'[31] because the dominated saw the virtues of being dominated for their own betterment. Colonialism was thus not seen as an absolute evil but complementary to India's rise as an independent nation in future. The statement may not be politically correct. Nonetheless, it can safely be argued that colonialism provided critical impetus to various processes that finally resulted in serious political mobilization against imperialism in India. Whether nationalism or democratization, they had their roots in the long history of colonialism, and in this sense, colonialism remained a significant force behind the rise of India as an independent nation in 1947.

Major nationalist initiatives

One of the first serious endeavours in this direction was made in the 1927 Madras Congress that sought to evolve constitutional governance in India. Known as the Swaraj Constitution, it was also an outcome of a series of discussion involving several political parties, including the Muslim League. Realizing that without consensus among the major communities, no effort towards making a Constitution was likely to succeed, and an attempt was made to frame a resolution in such a way as to create confidence among them, especially the Muslims. The resolution that the Congress had adopted was thus explicit in stating that

> having regard to the general desire of all political parties in the country to unite together in settling a Swaraj Constitution, and having considered the various drafts submitted to it and the various suggestions received in reply to the Working Committee's circular, [the Madras Congress] authorizes the Working Committee … to draft a Swaraj Constitution for India on the basis of a Declaration of Rights, and to place the same for consideration and approval before a special convention … consisting of the All India Congress Committee and the leaders and representatives of the other organization … and elected members of the central and provincial legislatures.[32]

On paper, it was a grand design though it did not succeed because of the failure of the Congress to counter the apprehension of the Muslims that they were likely to be marginalized in the proposed constitutional arrangement although the Committee assured that no community would be allowed to dominate over other. Asserting that the aim was not to 'give domination to one over another but to prevent the harassment and exploitation of any individual or group by another [the Committee insisted] on the fullest guarantee of religious liberty ... [and] cultural autonomy'.[33] In order to establish group rights in its most substantial form and content, the Committee argued for 'joint or mixed electorates' and discarded Separate Electorates completely 'as a condition precedent to any rational system of representation'.[34] Characterizing Separate Electorates as 'bad and harmful for the growth of a national spirit',[35] the Committee also marshalled arguments to suggest that Separate Electorates ended up creating a permanent fissure between the minority and majority community. Hence, it was argued that 'under Separate Electorates, the chances are that the minority will always, have to face a hostile majority, which can always, by sheer force of numbers, override the wishes of the minority'.[36] The aim of the Nehru Committee was to counter the League's insistence on special constitutional protection to the Muslims by guaranteeing Separate Electorates, which was never appreciated given its obvious divisive character. Nonetheless, special care was taken to protect cultural autonomy of the minorities which, felt the Committee, was needed to sustain India's socio-economic diversity. So, the conceding of group rights was not a concessional measure, but a politically contrived design for the sake of sustaining the national spirit.

The 1928 constitutional draft, prepared by the Motilal Nehru Committee, was finally rejected due to lack of consensus. Nonetheless, it was one of the first serious endeavours that the Indian nationalists had undertaken to constitutionalize India following the fundamental principles of liberalism, which unfolded in the wake of the British rule. In order to realize these principles in public life, the Committee admitted having imitated the British system of governance, which was evident in its submission that recommendations were not 'original'. The Committee was said to have been content 'to follow models which have been tried and tested in other parts of the world and which even the framers of the Montague-Chelmsford constitution professed to follow'.[37] The Committee however maintained that the proposed Constitution was not exactly derivative of the available constitutions since drawing up the Constitution, it 'deliberately declined to be overcome by one type or the other'. Aware of India's peculiar socio-economic circumstances, the members strove to provide 'for the development of fullest possible provincial life compatibly with national interests'.[38] Another bone of contention was the minority rights which figured prominently in the Report which introduced group rights in the shape of cultural and religious rights of minorities partly to allay the fears of the religious minorities that they would be swamped in a Hindu-dominated India, partly to stave off the demand for separate electorates, and partly to devise a principle that helped the Congress to regulate inter-group relations.[39] Similarly, the Committee recommended for adult suffrage despite strong criticism even by the Congress. Two points of criticism were made: first, it was argued that without being adequately educated, the voters would fail to exercise franchise 'intelligently'; second, in view of the vastness of the country and the lack of transport, it would be difficult, if not impossible, for the voters to go to the booth to exercise their rights, which would make the system redundant. As a counter to these arguments, the Committee retorted that 'the repeated exercise of the right to vote is in itself a powerful educative factor'.[40] And, it was further argued that 'the average Indian voter understands his business and [that he] can form an opinion that affects him directly'.[41] What was unique about the Nehru Report was an attempt to conceptualize group rights in a liberal way, since it also endorsed individual rights by insisting on adult suffrage. This was a revolutionary step which also confirms the nationalists' concern for creating a constitutional arrangement on the basis of their understanding of liberal constitutionalism.

Dissensions surfaced as soon as the Nehru recommendations were made public. Even Jinnah who appreciated Motilal's effort in drafting a Constitution for united India rejected the recommendations demanding that the residual powers should rest with the provinces rather than the centre to scuttle the rise of a unitary and authoritarian Hindu-dominated state. Other Muslim groups joined hands and in January, 1929, an All Parties Muslim conference was held in Delhi, and they agreed to abandon the Report that hardly addressed the Muslim concern. While Muslims dissociated from the Report as it was far from their expectations, there were dissidents even within the Congress. Led by Jawaharlal Nehru and Subhas Chandra Bose, a powerful faction within the Congress formed 'Independence India League' that demanded complete independence rather than dominion status as suggested by the Nehru Committee. While elucidating the difference between dominion status and independence, Nehru stated that dominion status 'envisages the same old structure, with many bonds visible and invisible tying us to the British economic system: [complete freedom] gives, or ought to give us, freedom to erect a new structure to suit our circumstances'.[42] Critical of those defending dominion status, Nehru further argued

> for them the problem is one of changing colour of administration, or at most having a new administration … [and] not a new state'. … They can only conceive of a future in which, they or people like them will play the principal role and take the place of the English high officials.[43]

The 1928 Calcutta Congress thus saw an open split between those who defended dominion status and those who advocated complete independence. It was more or less a foregone conclusion that in view of the growing importance of the radical section within the Congress, it had no alternative, but to insist on complete independence. With the acceptance of the complete independence resolution in the 1929 Lahore Congress, it was decided to boycott the legislature and the Congress members were asked to resign. Furthermore, the All India Congress Committee was authorized to launch civil disobedience, including non-payment of taxes wherever it deemed appropriate. Gandhi rose as the undisputed leader and was made the sole authority to decide the time and manner of the launching of the civil disobedience movement.

Like the 1928 Motilal Nehru constitutional draft, the 1945 Sapru Committee also prepared a constitutional design following the fundamental ethos of liberalism. Here too, the institutional arrangements that Indians had inherited as colonial subjects were accepted as integral to the making of a liberal Constitution for India. Admitting that it was the British initiatives that led to the consolidation of liberal democracy in India, the Committee had begun its recommendations by quoting Montague's famous declaration in the House of Commons on 20 August 1917, which corroborated the idea by declaring that

> the policy of His Majesty's Government, with which the Government of India are in complete accord, is that of the increasing association of Indians in every branch of the administration and the gradual development of self-governing institutions with a view to a progressive realization of responsible government in India as an integral part of the British Empire.[44]

This was not a favour that the British government extended, but was the outcome of the challenges that the ruling authority was apprehending in view of the growing discontent. It was a powerful strategy to seek to quell the circumstances that were quite volatile as the nationalists were being regrouped under charismatic Gandhi. The idea was also appreciated by a hardcore colonialist, like Curzon who found the suggestion most appropriate since, as he argued,

> with the modern ideal of nationalism and self-determination making in the circumstances of the times so strong an appeal, the peoples of countries such as India attached much more importance to being governed, even though not so well-governed, by themselves, than they did to being even superbly governed by another race.[45]

By referring to the early British initiatives, the Sapru Committee justified that the idea of self-government was nothing new; instead, it was perhaps a natural outcome of the British endeavour towards constitutionalizing India in a liberal democratic format. On the basis of this understanding, the Committee built its argument for a constitutional structure that drew on the fundamental ethos of liberalism. Here too, the members appeared to have been persuaded by his erstwhile colleagues who prepared the 1928 Nehru Report which, despite having accepted dominion status within the Empire, also defended self-government. Being favourably disposed towards the Westminster form of liberal democracy, they thus insisted that 'the future of India lies in adopting a democratic constitution and taking all the risks which a change from the present system of government to a state of real democracy must involve'.[46] Similar to its 1928 counterpart, the Committee strongly argued for adult franchise with a proviso that under the existing circumstances, 'it may be excusable to give communities divided on religious lines the right to a fair and adequate share of opportunities for service in the legislature and of executive power'.[47]

The Constituent Assembly (1946–49) and its role

Seeking to lay out the background for the Constituent Assembly that drafted free India's Constitution, it is conceptually pertinent to focus on two specific constitutional steps that the British government undertook just on the eve of the 1947 transfer of power. While the 3 June Plan set out the agenda for the transfer of power, the 1947 Indian Independence Act translated that into reality. Framing a Constitution for independent India was not an easy task. Beginning with the 1942 Cripps Mission, the idea of involving Indians for drafting their Constitution was being debated. Although the 1946 Cabinet Mission enthusiastically supported the formation of a constituent assembly to prepare the Constitution for free India, its members were convinced that 'a solution involving the partition of the Punjab and Bengal would be contrary to the wishes and interests of a very large proportion of the inhabitants of these Provinces'.[48] Nonetheless, the subcontinent was partitioned and two independent nations – India and Pakistan – were born in 1947. The Constituent Assembly for India met, for the first time, on 9 December 1946 and, in less than three years, the Constitution of India was produced and was adopted by the nation on 26 November 1949. Besides elaborating the processes that led to the making of the Constitution, the chapter draws on the socio-economic and political circumstances of the era and also the philosophical predilections of the founding fathers to delve into the riddle as to why India's Constitution incorporated some of the draconian provisions of the 1935 Government of India Act despite being opposed to it when it was introduced.

With the adoption of the 1947 India Independence Act, Indian became politically free. This may suggest that freedom was a colonizers' gift which does not seem justified simply because India's political independence came after a protracted struggle by the freedom-fighters for independence. It was an outcome, in other words, of an all-round effort, both organized and spontaneous, which finally led to the withdrawal of the British from India. Implicit here is the idea that India's struggle for freedom was fought at many levels: there are occasions, especially in the context of the 1942 open rebellion, when the masses rose in revolt spontaneously against the foreign rule involving the subalterns who came forward in response to a call given by the Mahatma before his arrest. On the whole, the battle for independence was the culmination of a sustained anti-British campaign. Freedom was a clear break with the past which Jawaharlal Nehru captured by saying that it was a moment

> 'which comes but rarely in history, when we step out from the old to the new, when an age ends, and when the soul of a nation, long suspended, finds utterance. It is fitting that at this solemn moment we take the pledge of dedication to the service of India and her people and to the still larger cause of humanity'.[49]

That independence brought political freedom was beyond question; however, what bothered the nationalists who presided over India's destiny following decolonization was whether this was adequate to purge the country of the social and economic ills which caused mass discontent, for obvious reasons. This was a genuine concern shared by the nationalists when they embarked on making the constitution for independent India. The issue was most clearly articulated by the President of the Constituent Assembly, Rajendra Prasad who exhorted that India required those men and women who would selflessly work for her well-being. While pursuing this point, Prasad further stated that

> 'we need ... a set of men [and women] who will have the interest of the country before them. There is a fissiparous tendency arising out of various elements in our life. We have communal differences, caste differences, language differences, provincial differences and so forth. It requires men of vision, men who will not sacrifice the interests of the country at large for the sake of smaller groups and areas and who will rise over the prejudices which are born of these differences'.[50]

Being aware of the schism among the Indians on account of well-entrenched socio-economic chasms, he also emphasized that "successful working of democratic constitution requires in those, who have to work, the willingness to respect the view point of others, capacity for compromise and accommodation'.[51] It was not a difficult task, Prasad believe, given the fact that Indians despite ingrained socio-economic differences among themselves fought together against an alien rule. This was a source of confidence for him which he underlined by saying 'we have been able to draw this Constitution without taking recourse to voting and division in Lobbies'.[52] The argument has substance since the 1950 Constitution was drafted largely by consensus and accommodation of contrary views.[53] The exercise was successfully conducted in a situation when India was passing through perhaps the worse crisis in her journey as an independent polity following the British withdrawal in 1947. The joy of freedom was, in other words, marred by partition.[54] Nonetheless, the nationalists, especially those who toiled hard to draft a constitution for free India, succeeded in preparing a unique constitution which put in place India's liberal democratic fabric. A herculean task indeed, the making of India's Constitution represented tireless endeavours of the members of the Constituent Assembly who joined hands for constitutionalizing India despite odds. In view of the composition of the Constituent Assembly, the point that it was not democratic may appear plausible though a perusal of the history of constitution making elsewhere reveals that the exercise has historically been undertaken by a handful of men and women presumably because of its technical nature. The point does not seem to be persuasive since the ideas that inform the makers of the constitution are too important to be wished away. In case of India, the values of the Enlightenment philosophy remained the fundamental guiding principle. Not only did the nationalists organize the campaign for freedom around these cardinal principles of Enlightenment, they also accepted liberal constitutionalism as a mode of governance for independent India. Discarding the Gandhian village swaraj, the Constituent Assembly endorsed liberal democracy of the Western variety with the belief that it was most appropriate for the nascent nation. Was it just a blind imitation? Perhaps not. If one goes through the processes of constitutionalization of India, one is persuaded to believe that 'in order to achieve any measure of self-government, [the makers of the constitution] had to adopt a language of representation and [they were convinced that] large masses had yet to be tutored in the art of self-government'.[55] It is true that involvement in self-government in its undiluted form is not possible so long as fraternity, one of the cardinal principles of liberal democracy, is absent which BR Ambedkar captured when he forcefully mentioned that

> 'isolation and exclusiveness make them anti-social and inimical towards one another. Isolation makes for rigidity of class consciousness, for institutionalizing social life and for the dominance of selfish ideas within the classes. Isolation makes life static, continues the separation into a privileged and underprivileged, masters and servants'.[56]

Basic here is the idea of social communion that Babasaheb sought to develop while laying out India's constitutional fabric. Being one of the architects of the 1950 Constitution, he can be said to have put in place the ideological priorities that govern the deliberations in the Constituent Assembly. Gandhi's idea of village swaraj was thoroughly discussed, but did not seem to have swayed the majority; as a result, liberal constitutionalism supportive of individual being the centre of governance was preferred. Interestingly, a careful scan of the 1928 Constitution (also known as the Motilal Constitution) and 1945 Constitution (which the Sapru Committee prepared) demonstrates that even before the issue was discussed in the Constituent Assembly the Congress nationalists, in general, always favoured liberal constitutionalism.

The Constituent Assembly and the making of the Constitution

The making of free India's Constitution by the Constituent Assembly over a period of little more than three years is reflective of the efforts that the founding fathers undertook to translate into reality the nationalist and democratic aspirations of an independent polity following decolonization. Furthermore, while the Constitution is a continuity at least in structural and procedural terms, it was also a clear break with the past since the 1950

Constitution drew on an ideology that sought to establish a liberal democratic polity following the withdrawal of colonialism. There can be no greater evidence of the commitment to constitutionalism and rule of law on the part of the founding fathers than the Constitution that they framed despite serious difficulties due to partition. The commitment to liberal democratic values, as the Constituent Assembly proceedings suggest, remained paramount in the making of the Constitution.

Set up as a result of negotiations between the nationalist leaders and the members of the Cabinet Mission over the possible constitutional arrangement in post-war India, the Constituent Assembly was not, it is argued, convened 'by any national provisional government but by the British government [to bring together] the delegates of the major political parties'.[57] The task of the Constituent Assembly was to draft a Constitution for India. The objective resolution that Jawaharlal Nehru moved was, according to BR Ambedkar, 'an expression of the pent-up emotions of the millions of this country'.[58] While defending the objective resolution, Nehru argued strongly for democracy and socialism: he strongly defended 'democracy' as the most appropriate system of government that 'fit in with the temper of our people and be accountable to them'.[59] Similarly, socialism, he firmly believed, would bring about economic democracy to India. For him, political independence was futile unless it was supported by democratic governance and socialistic vision. Hence, he was critical of the princely states that were reluctant to relinquish monarchy for democracy. As a true democrat who had no doubt that socialism was the ultimate solution for India's stark poverty, Nehru set the tenor of the discussion in the Assembly by providing a philosophical layout for free India's Constitution. Nonetheless, the political context in which the Constitution was being deliberated was full of uncertainty because of (a) Hindu-Muslim rivalry and (b) reluctance of most of the princely states to join independent India. While the former led to the dismemberment of India following the British withdrawal in 1947, the latter necessitated threat or application of coercion, on occasions, to geographically unify India by bypassing the claim of the existing rulers of the princely states. By staying away from the Assembly, the Muslim members clearly stated their preference for Pakistan that gained momentum especially after the adoption of the 1940 Lahore resolution. The 1946 Calcutta and later Noakhali riots confirmed the Congress apprehension that it was possibly strategically correct to accept partition to avoid further bloodbath. What was clear when the Constituent Assembly met for drafting the Constitution was that Pakistan was inevitable and a strong state was required to fulfil its socio-economic goals.

The outcome

Despite being appreciative of India's pluralistic social texture, there was a near unanimity among the Assembly members for a strong state.[60] Even those who were critical of the Emergency provisions also defended a centralized state to contain tendencies threatening the integrity of the country.

Emergency provisions in the Constitution were justified because 'disorder' or 'misgovernance' endangers India's existence as 'a territorial state'. Such concerns could only have reflected, argues Paul Brass, 'another kind of continuity' between the new governing elite and the former British rulers, namely 'an attitude of distrust' of the ordinary politicians of the country and 'a lack of faith' in the ability of the newly franchised population to check 'the misdeeds' of their elected rulers.[61] Nonetheless, the fear of 'disorder' was probably the most critical factor in favour of the arguments for a centralized state despite its clear incompatibility with the cherished ideal of the nationalist leaders for a federal state. BR Ambedkar's contradictory stances on federalism, for instance, thus may appear whimsical independent of the circumstances. In 1939, Ambedkar was clearly in favour of a federal form of government for its political viability in socioculturally diverse India.[62] By 1946, he provided a radically different view by saying that 'I like a strong united Centre, much stronger than the Centre we had created under the Government of India Act of 1935'.[63] While presenting the final report of the Union Powers Committee, Jawaharlal Nehru also argued in favour of a strong state by stating that

> [w]e are unanimously of the view that it would be injurious to the interest of the country to provide for a weak central authority which would be incapable of ensuring peace, of coordinating vital matters of common concern and of speaking effectively for the whole country in the international sphere.[64]

As evident, federalism did not appear to be an appropriate structural form of governance in the light of the perceived threats to the existence of the young Indian nation. Hence, the Constitution-makers recommended for a strong centre because the constitutional design of a country is meant to serve 'the normative-functional requirements of governance'. The Constitution was to reflect 'an ideology of governance' regardless of whether they articulate the highly cherished ideals of the freedom struggle that a majority of the Assembly members nurtured while participating in the freedom struggle. As GL Mehta believed that 'we have to build up the system on the conditions of our country [and] not on any abstract theories'.[65] In the same tune, Alladi Krishnaswamy Ayyar argued that 'our constitutional design is relative to the peculiar conditions obtaining here, according to the peculiar exigencies of our country [and] not according to a prior or theoretical considerations'.[66] In the making of the Constitution for governance, they were guided more by their views on state craft which would surely have been different without the traumatic experience of partition and communal bloodbath preceding the inauguration of the Constitution in 1950. Hence, one can safely suggest that 'hard-headed pragmatism and not abstract governmental theories' was what guided 'the architects of our Constitution'.[67]

Yet, it was not the entire Assembly that wrote the document. It was clearly the hard work 'of the government wing of the Congress, and not the mass party' and the brunt of the task fell upon 'the Canning Lane Group [because] they lived while attending Assembly sessions on Canning Lane'.[68] There is another dimension of the functioning of the Assembly, which is also instructive. According to Granville Austin, Indian's constitutional structure is perhaps 'a good example' of decision-making by consensus and accommodation, which he defends by examining the debates on various provisions of the Constitution.[69] Scholars, however, differ because, given the Congress hegemony in the Assembly, views held by the non-Congress members were usually bulldozed. As SK Chaube argued that at least on two major issues – political minorities and language – both these principles were conveniently sacrificed. As regards political minority, there was no consensus and the solution to the language was, as Austin himself admits, 'a half-hearted compromise'.[70] By dubbing the Assembly as 'a packed house', the shrunk Muslim League expressed the feeling of being alienated from the house. Even Ambedkar underlined the reduced importance of the Assembly since on a number of occasions, as he admitted, 'they had to go to another place to obtain a decision and come to the Assembly'.[71]

Decision by consensus may not be an apt description of the processes of deliberation. But, as the proceedings show, there was near unanimity on most occasions, and divisions of opinion among the Congress Party members who constituted a majority were sorted out politically. As Ambedkar admits, '[t]he possibility of chaos was reduced to nil by the existence of the Congress Party inside the Assembly which brought into its proceedings a sense of order and discipline. ... The Party is therefore entitled to all the credit for the smooth sailing of the Draft Constitution in the Assembly'.[72] As Shiva Rao informs, on a number of controversial issues, efforts were made to eliminate or at least to minimize differences through informal meetings of the Congress Party's representatives in the Constituent Assembly.[73] If the informal discussion failed to resolve the differences, 'the Assembly leadership ... exercised its authority formally by the Party Whip'.[74] As evident, in the Constituent Assembly, no attempt was made to force decision, the accent being on unanimity presumably because 'the leaders were alive to the fact that the constitution adopted on the principle of majority vote would not last long'.[75] It was not therefore surprising that Rajendra Prasad, the president of the Constituent Assembly, preferred to postpone the debate and allowed them to work out agreed solutions rather than take a vote that might, as he apprehended, result 'in something not wanted by anybody'.[76]

Two important points emerge out of the preceding discussions: *first*, the making of the Indian Constitution was a difficult exercise not only because of the historical context, but also due to the peculiar social texture of the Indian reality that had to be translated in the Constitution. The collective mind in the Assembly was defensive as a consequence of rising tide of violence taking innocent lives immediately after partition. *Second*, the founding fathers seem to have been obsessed with their 'own notion of integrated national life'. The aim of the Constitution was to provide 'an appropriate ordering framework' for India. As Rajendra Prasad equivocally declared on the floor of the Assembly, '[p]ersonally I do not attach any importance to the label which may be attached to it – whether you call it a Federal Constitution or a Unitary Constitution or by any other name. It makes no difference so long as the Constitution serves our purpose'.[77] On the whole, a unitary mind produced 'an essentially unitary constitution doused with a sprinkling of permissive power for a highly supervised level of constituent units'.[78] This was not the goal of the nationalists and, of course, their leader, Mahatma Gandhi, who always stood for decentralized village republic. Besides confirming that constitutionalism in India was not entirely derivative, this assumption directs our attention to the argument that the Indian Constitution was 'cosmopolitan' in character not only 'in its fidelity to the universal principles of liberty, equality and fraternity', but also due to fact that its text and principles, its values and its jurisprudence were drawn from 'the major cross-currents of global constitutional law'.[79]

Concluding observations

Constitution-making is an arduous task, more so, in a socioculturally diverse society like India. As is argued above, the Constitution was the culmination of a process in which contrasting ideas converged to evolve an acceptable set of principles for a socioculturally and economically diverse population. The account is historical too because the ideas that became pre-eminent in the Constituent Assembly had their roots in the tumultuous days of India's freedom struggle in which various waves of thought were also discernible. By arguing that the Constitution of India was the outcome of a complex ideational battle in different phases of India's struggle for freedom, the book challenges the conventional notion that it is merely a mindless, if not haphazard, borrowing of constitutional provisions and practices prevalent elsewhere. The argument supporting the contention that the Indian Constitution is a borrowed doctrine seems vacuous, given the fact that it is also a break with the past. One of the most significant breaks was to constitutionally recognize the principle of representative government in its unalloyed form through universal adult suffrage, an ambition that the nationalist had been nurturing since the adoption of the 1928 Motilal Nehru Report. Besides the emergent need of tackling contingent circumstances following the partition which created a strong demand for the continuity of the available colonial administrative machinery, the founding fathers also felt the need of a strong administration to translate into reality their ambitious plan of transformation. It has thus been persuasively argued that '[w]hile continuity was sought in the service of the break in this way, the claim of break itself was called upon to justify certain continuities'.[80] A careful study of the arguments that were marshalled in favour of incorporating mechanisms and institutions from the colonial era confirms the point.

A cursory look at the processes that influenced constitutionalism in India reveals that there are three critical areas – social justice, liberal constitutionalism and group representation – in which an ideational battle took place involving those who were responsible for charting out a specific course for India's constitutionalism to follow. The aim here is primarily to understand how these ideas were articulated in a series of efforts which culminated in the Constituent Assembly when the founding fathers sat together to make a Constitution for independent India in a historical perspective which is both derivative and context-driven: derivative because it was drawn on liberalism that had no parallel in India, and context-driven since Indian socio-economic and ideational reality did not seem to favour liberal socio-economic and political practices. A daunting task indeed, the book will thus not only be intellectually refreshing, but also allow us to conceptualize the making of India's Constitution in a completely new perspective.

Notes

1 The text of the Act is available in www.sdstate.edu/projectsouthasia/loader.cfm?csModule=security/getfile&PageID=861833, accessed on 25 May 2016.
2 The statement of John Morley is quoted from DA Hamer, *John Morley: Liberal Intellectual in Politics*, Oxford University Press, Oxford, 1968, p. 111.
3 CA Bayly, *Recovering Liberties: Indian Thought in the Age of Liberalism and Empire*, Cambridge University Press, Cambridge, 2012, p. 346.
4 file:///C:/Users/Sony/Downloads/GIPE-014672.pdf, accessed on 19 August 2016: Report of the Eleventh Indian National Congress, held in Poona in 1895, p. 3.
5 ibid., p. 13.
6 https://ia802608.us.archive.org/30/items/essaysspeechesa00paregoog/essaysspeechesa00paregoog.pdf, accessed on 19 August 2016: Chunilal Lallubhai Parekh (ed.), *Essays, Speeches, Addresses and Writings of the Honourable Dadabhai Naoroji*, Caxton Printing Works, Bombay, 1887, p. 321.
7 ibid., p. 332.
8 ibid., p. 333.
9 Sanjay Seth, 'Rewriting histories of nationalism: the politics of "Moderate Nationalism" in India, 1870–1905', *American Historical Review*, Vol. 104, No. 1, February 1999, p. 104.
10 ibid.
11 Surendranath Banerjea's presidential address, 1902, Indian National Congress in AM Zaidi (ed.), *Congress Presidential Addresses*, Indian Institute of Applied Political Research, New Delhi, Vol. 2, p. 118.
12 *Address of the Deccan Sabha*, p. 9 – cited in Sanjay Seth, 'Rewriting histories of nationalism: the politics of "Moderate Nationalism" in India, 1870–1905', *American Historical Review*, Vol. 104, No. 1, February 1999, p. 113.
13 file:///C:/Users/Sony/Downloads/Miscellaneous-Writings-Of-M-G-Ranade.pdf, accessed on 20 August 2016: Address by MG Ranade in The Second Social Conference, Allahabad, 1888 in The Miscellaneous Writings of late Hon'ble Mr Justice MG Ranade, Sahitya Academy, New Delhi, 1992, p. 88.
14 ibid., p. 81.
15 ibid., pp. 81–82.
16 Lala Lajpat Rai, *Ideals of Non-Cooperation*, Ganesh and Company, Madras, 1921, p. 50.

17 Bipin Chandra Pal, *Swadeshi and Samaj: The Rise of New Patriotism*, Yugayatri Prakashak Limited, Calcutta, 1954, p. 55b.
18 Lala Lajpat Rai, *Ideals of Non-Cooperation*, Ganesh and Company, Madras, 1921, p. 98.
19 https://books.google.co.in/books?id=LL9JAAAAMAAJ&printsec=frontcover#v=onepage&q&f=false, accessed on 20 August 2016, Aurobindo Ghose, *The Doctrine of Passive resistance*, Arya Publishing House, Calcutta, 1948, p. 11.
20 Ibid., pp. 15–16.
21 CA Bayly, *Recovering Liberties: Indian Thought in the Age of Liberalism and Empire*, Cambridge University Press, Cambridge, 2012, p. 346.
22 Rajendra Vora, 'Two strands of Indian liberalism: the ideas of Ranade and Phule', in Thomas Pantham and Kenneth Deutsch (eds.), *Political Thought in Modern India*, Sage, New Delhi, 1986, p. 107.
23 ibid., p. 108.
24 Address of BR Ambedkar to a felicitation function, Bombay, 4 March, 1933 – reproduced in Narendra Jadhav (ed.), *Ambedkar Speaks*, Vol. 1, Konark Publisher Pvt. Limited, New Delhi, p. 422.
25 CA Bayly, *Recovering Liberties: Indian Thought in the Age of Liberalism and Empire*, Cambridge University Press, Cambridge, 2012, p. 305.
26 ibid., p. 310.
27 I borrow this expression from CA Bayly who developed the idea in his *Recovering Liberties: Indian Thought in the Age of Liberalism and Empire*, Cambridge University Press, Cambridge, 2012, p. 346.
28 I have shown this in my 'The communal award of 1932 and its implications in Bengal', *Modern Asian Studies*, Cambridge, Vol. 23, No. 3, 1989, 493–523.
29 India Office Records, London, Tyson Papers, Eur E 341/41, John Tyson's note, 5 July 1947.
30 Subrata Mitra, 'Constitutional design, democratic vote counting and India's fortuitous multiculturalism', Working Paper, November, 2004, South Asia Institute, Heidelberg University, pp. 29–34.
31 Ashis Nandy, *The Intimate Enemy: Loss and Recovery of Self under Colonialism*, Oxford University Press, New Delhi, 1989 (reprint).
32 The resolution is quoted in quoted in *The Nehru Report: The Anti-Separatist Manifesto, 1928*, Vol. I, Machiko & Panjathan, New Delhi, 1928, p. 25.
33 *The Nehru Report: The Anti-Separatist Manifesto, 1928*, Vol. I, Machiko & Panjathan, New Delhi, 1928, p. 35.
34 ibid., p. 36.
35 ibid., p. 36.
36 ibid., p. 36.
37 *The Nehru Report: The Anti-Separatist Manifesto, 1928*, Vol. II, Machiko & Panjathan, New Delhi, 1928, p. 62.
38 Ibid., p. 65.
39 Neera Chandhoke pursues this argument in her 'The political consequences of ethic mapping', Crisis State Development Research Centre (discussion paper no. 14), LSE, December 2005 (mimeograph), pp. 12–14.
40 *The Nehru Report: The Anti-Separatist Manifesto, 1928*, Vol. II, Machiko & Panjathan, New Delhi, 1928, p. 67.
41 ibid.
42 Jawaharlal Nehru, *An Autobiography: With Musings on Recent Events in India*, John Lane the Bodley Head, London, 1941, p. 418.
43 ibid., p. 417.
44 *Constitutional Proposal of the Sapru Committee, 1945*, Padma Publications, Bombay, 1945, p. 10.

45 Curzon's statement of 20 August 1917 in the House of Commons in response to Montague's declaration is cited in *Constitutional Proposal of the Sapru Committee, 1945*, Padma Publications, Bombay, 1945, p. 11.
46 *Constitutional Proposal of the Sapru Committee, 1945*, Padma Publications, Bombay, 1945, p. 325.
47 ibid., p. 326.
48 MV Pylee, *Constitutional Government in India*, Asia Publishing House, London, 1963 (reprint), p. 127.
49 Jawaharlal Nehru's 'Tryst with destiny' speech, delivered at the dawn of independence in India on 15 August 1947 – quoted from B. Shiva Rao (ed.), *The Framing of India's Constitution: Select Documents*, Vol. I, Universal Law Publishing Co, New Delhi, 2004 (reprint), pp. 558–559.
50 Rajendra Prasad's address in the Constituent Assembly on 26 November 1949, *Constituent Assembly Debates*, Vol. XI, Lok Sabha Secretariat, New Delhi, 2003, p. 993.
51 ibid.
52 ibid.
53 Uday S Mehta, 'Indian constitutionalism: crisis, unity and history', in Sujit Choudhury, Madhav Khosla and Pratap Bhanu Mehta (eds.), *The Oxford Handbook of the Indian Constitution*, Oxford University Press, New Delhi, 2016, p. 53.
54 Arvind Elangovan, 'Constitutionalism, political exclusion and implications or Indian constitutional history: the case of Montague-Chelmsford reforms (1919)', *South Asian History and Culture*, 2016, p. 14.
55 ibid.
56 ibid.
57 Shibanikinkar Chaube, *Constituent Assembly of India: Springboard of Revolution*, Manohar, New Delhi, 2000, p. 49.
58 *Constitutional Assembly Debates* (CAD hereafter), Vol. I, p. 104.
59 *CAD*, Vol. I, p. 62.
60 Mohit Bhattacharya, 'The mind of the founding fathers', in Nirmal Mukarji and Balveer Arora (eds.), *Federalism in India : Origins and Development*, Vikas Publishing House, New Delhi, 1992.
61 Paul Brass, 'India, Myron Weiner and the political science of development', *Economic and Political Weekly*, 20 July 2002, pp. 21–32.
62 BR Ambedkar, *Federation versus Freedom*, Gokhale Institute of Politics and Economics, Poona, 1939.
63 *CAD*, Vol. 1, 1946, p. 102.
64 *CAD*, Report of the Union Powers Committee, Vol. V, 20 August 1947, p. 58.
65 *CAD*, Vol. V, p. 79.
66 *CAD*, Vol. XI, p. 839.
67 Mohit Bhattacharya, 'The mind of the founding fathers', in Nirmal Mukarji and Balveer Arora (eds.), *Federalism in India: Origins and Development*, Vikas Publishing House, New Delhi, 1992, p. 89.
68 Granville Austin, *The Indian Constitution: Cornerstone of a Nation*, Oxford University Press, New Delhi, 1999, p. 17, 317.
69 ibid., pp. 311–321.
70 ibid., chapter 12 (language and the constitution: the half-hearted compromise). pp. 264–307.
71 *Hindustan Times*, 27 November 1949.
72 *CAD*, Vol. VII, p. 974.
73 Shiva Rao, *The Framing of India's Constitution*, Vol. V, Universal Law Publishing, New Delhi, 2004, p. 835.

74 Granville Austin, *The Indian Constitution: Cornerstone of a Nation*, Oxford University Press, New Delhi, 1999, chapter 12 (language and the constitution: the half-hearted compromise), p. 315.
75 Rajni Kothari, *Politics in India*, Orient Longman, New Delhi, 2005 (reprint), p. 107.
76 Rajendra Prasad's press statement, *Hindustan Times*, 29 December 1949.
77 Rajendra Prasad's statement made after the Constitution was inaugurated on 26 of January 1950, *The Times of India*, 29 January 1950.
78 Mohit Bhattacharya, 'The mind of the founding fathers', in Nirmal Mukarji and Balveer Arora (eds.), *Federalism in India: Origins and Development*, Vikas Publishing House, New Delhi, 1992, p. 103.
79 Sujit Choudhury, Madhav Khosla and Pratap Bhanu Mehta, 'Locating Indian Constitutionalism', in Sujit Choudhury, Madhav Khosla and Pratap Bhanu Mehta (eds.), *The Oxford Handbook of the Indian Constitution*, Oxford University Press, New Delhi, 2016, pp. 4–5.
80 Sandipta Dasgupta, '"A language which is foreign to us": continuities and anxieties in the making of the Indian constitution', *Comparative Studies of South Asia, Africa and Middle East*, Vol. 34, No. 2, 2014, p. 240.

Part B

Comprehending constitutional identity

A constantly shifting and restructured phenomenon

In order to grasp and conceptualize constitutional identity, this Part delves into certain specific constitutional designs that the 1950 Constitution of India put in place. The theme is too vast to be captured in one monograph. In order to address the concern persuasively, the Part therefore focusses, in a selective way, on those areas of constitutional concerns which are critical in conceptualizing constitutional identity in India. The goal here is to defend an argument that constitutional identity despite being drawn on specific constitutional provisions is also changeable in view of the rapidly transforming socio-economic milieu. There are innumerable instances showing that India's constitutional identity undergoes metamorphosis in circumstances where newer politico-ideological values and norms are privileged. This Part provides an analytical account of the changing/and changed texture of India's constitutional identity also by reference to the historical context in which it is articulated.

Reinforcing the idea that constitutional identity is articulated in specific formats, this Part is immensely significant for two important reasons: first, by arguing that constitutional identity is conceptualized in definite politico-constitutional ideas, the Part delves into those aspects of India's constitutional democracy which hold, as it were, its kernel or substance. Since constitutional identity is being constantly reworked, the Part also draws our attention to the processes in which newer issues and demands are accommodated within the widely acceptable format of democratic governance. While keeping the fundamental character in place, the Constitution is being changed to take care of newer concerns and requirements, which is reflective of Constitution being a living organism. Second, despite being selective, this Part identifies those core values on which India's constitutional identity rests. That constitutional liberalism emerged and gained precedence over other ideological priorities in independent India also confirms how it succeeded in spreading its tentacles across multiple social, economic and political spectra. What is also striking is the fact that many initiatives that were taken in independent India to adapt the Constitution to the changed milieu are also derivative of the desires of consolidating constitutional democracy in India. A careful study of these conceptual-foundational ideas in Chapter 2 will thus help us comprehend India's constitutional identity in a completely new perspective.

In two interrelated chapters, this Part provides a threadbare account of critical areas of India's constitutionalism to demonstrate how constitutional identity is transformed. Drawn on the conceptual claim that the Constitution of a country is a living organism, the chapters in this Part make a couple of arguments to theoretically grasp the principal concern of this exercise: first, notwithstanding the fact that the 1950 Constitution of India upheld a system of governance on the basis of the foundational values of the British liberalism, it, however, underwent significant changes, especially since the mid-1960s following massive democratization with the increasing involvement of the peripheral sections of India's demography in institutional politics. With the consolidation of demands for a legitimate share in power for the Dalits and Other Backward Classes (OBCs), the chapter thus introduces the second argument by suggesting that newer legal-constitutional designs had to be devised to constitutionally recognize their claim. Similarly, the concern for gender-parity which did not seem to have had constitutional recognition that it later received, figures prominently in the constitutional discourses. Example can be multiplied to pursue the argument that constitutional identity is both static because it cannot be altered so easily and also transformational since it changes to be adaptive to the circumstances in which newer socio-economic and political values gain precedence.

As it is difficult to focus on each and every aspect of the phenomenon, this Part selectively analyses India's constitutional designs and practices to conceptually articulate constitutional identity in India. Since this is not merely a study of the phenomenon with reference to India's Constitution, the aim here is also to assess the claim by drawing upon the wider socio-economic and political processes in which constitutional identity gets articulated out of an incessant, but waged at different levels, ideational battle. Core to this Part is the idea that Constitution is not just a compilation of set of rules, but conveys a specific form of governance which is drawn on the fundamental ideological ethos of the philosophy of Enlightenment, being complemented by its indigenization during the nationalist movement and its aftermath.

3 Politico-ideological issues

This chapter provides a threadbare account of critical areas of India's constitutionalism to demonstrate how constitutional identity is transformed. Drawn on the conceptual claim that the Constitution of a country is a living organism, the chapter makes a couple of arguments to theoretically grasp the principal concern of this exercise: first, notwithstanding the fact that the 1950 Constitution of India upheld a system of governance on the basis of the foundation values of the British liberalism, it, however, underwent significant changes, especially since the mid-1960s, following massive democratization with the increasing involvement of the peripheral sections of India's demography in institutional politics. With the consolidation of demands for a legitimate share in power for the Dalits and OBCs, the chapter thus introduces the second argument by suggesting that newer legal-constitutional designs had to be devised to constitutionally recognize their claim. Similarly, the concern for gender-parity which did not seem to have had constitutional recognition that it later received now, figure prominently in the constitutional discourses. Example can be multiplied to pursue the argument that constitutional identity is both static because it cannot be altered so easily and also transformational since it changes to be adaptive to the circumstances in which newer socio-economic and political values gain precedence.

As it is difficult to focus on each and every aspect of the phenomenon, this segment of the chapter delves into six specific areas of India's constitutional designs and practices to conceptually articulate constitutional identity in India. Since this is not merely a study of the phenomenon with reference to India's Constitution, the aim here is also to assess the claim by drawing upon the wider socio-economic and political processes in which constitutional identity gets articulated out of an incessant, but waged at different levels, ideational battle. Core to this section is the idea that the Constitution is not just a compilation of set of rules but conveys a specific form of governance which is drawn on the fundamental ideological ethos of the philosophy of Enlightenment, being complemented by its indigenization during the nationalist movement and its aftermath.

Contextual peculiarities

A constitutional design is built on certain specific politico-ideological ethos which are sought to be articulated in the text. Since the Enlightenment philosophy remains an important source of ideological inspiration for the founding fathers, majority of the 1950 constitutional provisions were drafted to imbibe its spirit. The aim of the Constitution makers was to develop a truly democratic system of governance as they were persuaded to believe that it was the best option for governing an immensely diverse country like India. As the debate in the Constituent Assembly demonstrates, the 1950 Constitution was hardly a borrowed doctrine because it evolved out the intense debate among the members of the Assembly over a period little less than three years between 1946 and 1949. This section delves into those areas of India's Constitution which are clearly derivative of the ideological concerns of the founding fathers who strongly endorsed liberal constitutionalism while underplaying the Gandhian notion of *village swaraj*, which Gandhians supported as perhaps the only option for India's inclusive growth as a nation state. As well as putting these ideological concerns in a historical perspective for a better understanding, this section also draws attention to the changing socio-economic and political contexts in which they are articulated, given the fact that there are many landmark judicial pronouncements which, by reinterpreting, also expanded the sense in which specific constitutional provisions are understood. The purpose of this section is thus two-fold: (a) with a discussion of the intellectual antecedents of specific constitutional provisions, it situates the analysis in a historical context when a specific kind of ideological predilection was preferred; and (b) in view of the argument that the Constitution acquires its identity by being sensitive to the prevalent socio-economic and political concerns, the section also draws on those major court verdicts which are endeavours for strengthening the liberal democratic foundation of Indian polity.

Religion and religious freedom

Religion is both a source of amity and enmity at the same time. History is a witness to many instances, where human beings fought with one another for religious causes which confirms that religion cements a bond among the socio-economically disparate groups of people. This may appear strange though it is true that regardless of socio-economic differences, people tend to flock together in response to a religious call. Given the unfolding of events in India, it can be safely argued that religion is usually one of the primary variables determining the contours of life of the majority, if not all, of the people in India. The influence of religion is so pervasive in the life of people that it becomes very difficult to visualize any activity of life, both public and private as well as in long or short term in shaping of which religion does not play a subtle role. However, 'religion is India is not dogmatic. It is a rational synthesis which goes on gathering into itself new conceptions as philosophy progresses. It is experimental and provisional in its nature. . .'.[1] It is for this reason that India has never remained a uni-religious society. As a way of life, Hinduism has kept on reinventing itself leading to not only consolidation of the element of heterogeneity within itself, but also branching out of a number of other sects or religious denominations even though retaining a number of critical elements of Hinduism in the main. Later, arrival of Semitic religions such as Islam, Christianity and Zoroastrian at different junctures of history further enriched the plural landscape of religion in India. Describing the dynamic nature and importance of religion in the social life of the country, Madan writes so succinctly:

> In India, religion is like an axis that transforms as it turns, propelling society through history. Religion's many expressions – the Sikh, Jain, Hindu, Buddhist, Sant, and Muslim traditions – radiate like spokes, connecting the social in one great wheel of the universe. The ways of *dharma*, *karma* and *bhakti* enact its movement in everyday life; with secularism and pluralism, both evolving from these principles, Nehru and Mahatma Gandhi built the nation. Through its historical landscape, Indian society accompanies the spiritual in the same way that … a person's fortune sets, rises and moves with him through life.[2]

Amidst such a mosaic of religious plurality, even before the process of drafting the Constitution began, it was a foregone conclusion that India would be a secular polity with equal respect for all the religions. In fact, a section of the Congress leadership was well aware of the fact that the landscape of religious plurality in India has been dominated by the Hindu religion, given its numerical preponderance. It was in the subconscious mind of these people that their long-term move for independence and claim of the Indians being united in their urge for swaraj would be seriously dented in case they are not seen agreeable on the nature of future polity and peaceful coexistence of all the religious communities. Such a state of things could be contrived only when the religious groups other than the Hindus are assured of legally incontrovertible protective mechanism for their right to religion in any future constitutional design for the country. A number of leaders of the party, therefore, argued for special attention being paid to this fact and stipulates formidable protective measures for the other religions to ensure equality of all religions in the eyes of the state. For instance, as early as in 1925, in the Commonwealth of India Bill drafted by Annie Besant, freedom of conscience was envisaged as one of the seven fundamental rights for the people of India.[3]

However, as a collective policy decision of the party, such an opinion found its concrete articulation for the first time in the proposals of the Nehru Report submitted in 1928. Drafted to be presented as an anti-separatist manifesto, the tone of the report was out and out pliant to the issues and concerns of the religious minorities in order to retain their confidence in the secular and considerate nature of the post-independent polity of India. It explicitly noticed the probability of 'one community domineering over another'[4] in the post-independent scenario in India and felt the need for evolving redoubtable protective mechanism for religious minorities. Such a mechanism, for the committee, could not have been better than a resolute declaration of fundamental rights that could not have been violated in any circumstance. The committee was categorical in stating that

> another reason why great importance attaches to a Declaration of Rights is the unfortunate existence of communal differences in the country. Certain safeguards are necessary to create and establish a sense of security among those who look upon each other with distrust and suspicion. We could not better secure the full enjoyment of religious and communal rights to all communities than by including them among the basic principles of the Constitution.[5]

Interestingly, in the wake of the general understanding emerging in the constituent assembly to secure for all the people the fundamental right to free practice of religion, a note of caution was presented by a few members of the assembly regarding the perpetuation of obscurantist, discriminatory and inhuman elements of certain religions. The fear was that on the strength of the zealously guarded and absolutist nature of fundamental right to free practice of religion, the self-proclaimed custodians of religions might tend to continue with the deplorably antisocial practices identified with certain religions. That way, such a right would prove to be counterproductive to the project of social transformation to establish a liberal democratic society in India based on the principles of justice, liberty and equality. In this regard, the submissions of Rajkumari Amrit Kaur were quite indicative of her concerns about weeding out the anti-women elements from practices of different religions. She was emphatic that the fundamental right to religion needn't exclude the possibility of effective state intervention towards securing a just and equitable place for all the people in the practices of any religion, and to forbid the perpetuation of discriminatory and inhuman practices especially against women.[6] Thus, the constituent assembly had to tread cautiously, while finalizing the provisions on fundamental right to religion, given the urge to make such rights sacrosanct, on the one hand, and subjecting them to the imperatives of impending social revolution, on the other.

Constitutional intent and judicial interpretation

With the underlying issues and objectives of making the right to religion as a fundamental right getting deciphered in both the discourses during the national movement as well as in the constituent assembly, elaborate provisions on different aspects of religious freedom have accordingly been enshrined in the Constitution. However, two distinct observations can be made on the nature and working of various provisions on religious freedom in India. One, the eclectic nature of the provisions on religious freedom has clearly given a new meaning to the idea of secularism which has hitherto been understood as watertight separation of religion from state. Two, the complex landscape of religious plurality in the country as reflected in different mainstream religions and their sects, along with other denominations, has got further muddied with many of them claiming to be distinct religious order, thereby producing a great deal of litigation and judicial pronouncements on the matter. Further, a broader view of the religious freedom has been taken in the Constitution so as to not only grant the positive freedoms to the people for free profession, practice and propagation of religion, along with the freedom to manage the religious affairs in both institutional and functional realms, but also to insulate from undue interferences by the state such as forcible payment of taxes for promotion of any particular religion or attendance at religious instructions or worships in certain educational institutions.

The foundational premise of the religious freedom in India is set by Article 25 of the Constitution, which guarantees freedom of conscience and free profession, practice and propagation of religion to all the persons equally. The entitlements granted by this article are applicable to all the persons in the country whether citizen or non-citizen. It is, in fact, this sweeping reach of the provision that so many religious preachers from different countries get tempted to come to India not just to practise, but profess and propagate their religion quite often leading to conversions and emergent tensions in the existing social fabric in certain areas. In order, therefore, to delimit the scope of profession and propagation of a religion to just endeavours for benign spread of the basic tenets of a religion, instead of aggressive pursuits aimed at converting the vulnerably benighted and forlorn people, certain state governments enacted legislations to regulate the conversion of naive people in the name of propagating one's religion. Such legislations were soon challenged in courts as not only beyond the legislative competence of the state governments, but also for violating the spirit of Article 25(1).

On this issue, the authoritative judgement was delivered by the Supreme Court in the case of *Rev. Stanislaus vs. State of Madhya Pradesh*. On the question of competence of the state governments to pass such legislations, the court ruled that the states are very much within their right to enact such legislations on the ground of maintenance of public order given the propensity of deceitful conversions leading to tensions in society. In deciding on the issue of anti-conversion laws violating the right to propagate one's religion as guaranteed in the Constitution, the court was more forthcoming. It held that the anti-conversion laws cannot be presumed to violate the right to propagate one's religion because what the Constitution guarantees is benevolent propagation of one's religion, not forcible or deceitful conversion of docile people. The court even went to the extent of calling such conversions as violating the right to freedom of conscience of the converts which cannot be permitted under the garb of converter's right to freedom of profession and propagation of his religion. Explaining the moot points involved in the provision of Article 25(1), the court asserted:

What the Article grants is not the right to convert another person to one's own religion by an exposition of its tenets. It has to be remembered that Article 25(1) guarantees freedom of conscience to every citizen, and not merely to the followers of one particular religion, and that, in turn, postulates that 'there is no fundamental right to convert another person to one's own religion because if a person purposely undertakes the conversion of another person to his religion, as distinguished from his effort to transmit or spread the tenets of his religion, that would impinge on the 'freedom of conscience' guaranteed to all the citizens of the country alike.'[7] Though the line of argument evolved by the five-judge Constitution bench of the Supreme Court on the right to propagate one's religion and its implications for the right to freedom of conscience of others has been criticised on the ground that 'successful propagation of religion would result in conversion,'[8] its verdict in the case stands as law of the land conclusively establishing that right to propagation does not intrinsically contain the right to conversion within itself.

With a proactive judiciary, the ambit of the Right to Freedom of Religion has been, observes the Supreme Court of India, widened by the judicial interpretation that what is guaranteed by Articles 25 and 26 is 'the right of the individual to practise and propagate not only matters of faith and belief but also all those rituals and observances which are regarded as integral parts of a religion by the followers of its doctrines'. Being sensitive to secular values which are ingrained in India and articulated in its unfolding, the Indian judiciary had also played a critical role in defending those constitutional ideas which the founding fathers upheld as concomitant to their desire for making the country a level-playing field for minorities. A perusal of the past affirms the assumption that the Constitution champions the minority rights in two ways: by putting a specific constitutional design in place for protecting the rights of the minorities, the Constitution has, on the one hand, contributed to the development of a mechanism which cannot be so easily stifled because of the presence of an alert judiciary, on the other hand, which, through its multiple pronouncements, also conveys the message that constitutional values in support of the minorities shall always remain prior to any other considerations. As well as defending the minority rights, the apex court also upheld the view that the state was authorized to put an embargo on religious activities which were repugnant to the values that it nurtured for the sake of peace and tranquillity in the society.

While the major contestation on explicating the religious freedom in India has revolved around the provisions under Article 25, a number of other articles also guarantee substantive rights on other aspects of the right to religion. For instance, under Article 26, the freedom to manage religious affairs may be considered as the manifestation of what has been stipulated under the provisions of Article 25. In other words, while Article 25 guarantees the right to religion in terms of an individual's freedom of conscience and freedom to profess, practice and propagate one's religion, Article 26 secures the institutional manifestation of such right by providing for an individual's right to manage religious affairs. It is an undeniable fact that in India religious places including some of the biggest religious complexes are there everywhere. These places have been the centres of faith and devotion of millions of people whose management has been carried on by certain individuals or bodies in an autonomous manner. Such places continue to exist, being managed as per their traditional rituals and religious systems, only by dint of the freedom guaranteed under the provisions of Article 26. Interestingly, this article also provides freedom to every religious denomination to own and acquire movable as well as immovable properties, which has been at the base of creation of the chain of religious places in different parts of the country. When it comes to visualize the public face of religion through different religious denominations and places of worship, the provisions of Article 26 stand as a guarantor to these bodies.

As regards the religious rights of people, an interesting entry in the Constitution happens to be Article 27, which saves the people from payment of taxes for promotion of any particular religion. At the outset, given the secular nature of Indian polity as well as freedom of religion guaranteed to all the people, the need for such a provision appears to be quite intriguing. However, when one looks at the past and future portents of the ruling echelons in the country, the justification for the insertion of such a provision becomes quite clear. For instance, given the long traditions of religious plurality in the country, certain rulers during the medieval times toyed with the idea of imposing religious taxes on the followers of the religions not subscribed to by the ruling class. In spite of being painful and derogatory to the dignified existence of individuals at that time, such taxes were levied and collected by the rulers at the point of swords. Though such a scenario appears quite remote, if not improbable altogether, in the present times, the framers appear to become doubly sure that such an idea should not get even an iota of acceptance in the minds of the people. As part of the secular character of state in India, while there does not exist any space for levying of any religious tax, usage of such proceeds, if any, for the promotion of any particular religion is simply out of place as per the stipulations of Article 27.

The last aspect of religious freedom under the Indian Constitution relates to the freedom as to attendance at religious instructions or religious worship in certain educational institutions under Article 28. The essence of the provisions under this article is in fact to carry forward the ethos of secularism in the country. As such, the article forbids imparting of any religious instructions in any educational institution wholly maintained out of state funds. But again given the deep rooting of religious sentiments and practices in almost all walks of life of the people, the article provides for two exceptions to the general rule outlined in clause of 1 of the article. As per clause 2 of Article 28, the provisions of clause 1 would not be applicable in such institutions which have been established with the avowed purpose of imparting religious instructions. But imparting of such instructions would not be mandatory for anybody who does not want to attend them. Thus, Article 28 weaves a complex web of teaching religion in such a way that the imperatives of secularism as well as religion are met at the same time.

The framework of religious freedom in Indian Constitution treads the difficult path of securing right to religion to the people in a polity whose intrinsic character is completely secular. In such a Constitutional design, the most intractable challenge arises in stipulating the religious rights in such a way that they do not appear to compromise with the secular character of the state. Such difficulties are not faced in the classical secular polities where state has nothing to do with the religious freedom of the people. It neither supports nor prohibits the religious activities of the people. But the ambivalent position of the state vis-à-vis religious rights of the people presents before it the typical challenge of getting involved in the religious activities without being looked as partisan or discriminatory to any particular religion. Moreover, as the state has been given the authority to regulate the enjoyment of religious freedom on the ground of public order, morality and health, its actions on these counts should also be impartial and non-discriminatory. These complexities of the right to freedom of religion in India have given birth to intense litigation on the part of both individuals as well as religious denominations virtually making the courts as the keeper of faith of the people.

The constitutional design of religious freedom in India has worked well insofar as the preservation of secular credential of the state amidst the competing claims of religious pluralism is concerned. The provisions enshrined in the Constitution have practically been followed in letter and spirit thereby retaining the religiosity of the Indian society despite the avowed goal of the Constitution to constitute India into a secular polity. Though the overstretching of certain provisions such as the freedom to propagate one's religion has produced societal tension between followers of two religions, the occasional intervention of courts in such matters has helped in keeping the issues in cold, if not leading to their resolution altogether. Further, the periodic change of government with different attitudes towards particular religions though has offered them some space to reorient the governmental policies towards different religions; the limited leg space provided by the Constitution in this matter has helped in containing the play of politics in the matters of religion. That way, more than seven decades of successful working of the constitutional freedoms regarding religion has indeed proved the wisdom and farsightedness of the framers of the Constitution in constituting India as a secular polity despite guaranteeing most extensive religious freedom to all its people.

Secularism

Indian variety of secularism is a mixed bag in the sense that it hardly corresponds to the conventional wisdom on the phenomenon. It was creatively articulated underlining the complexities of typical non-Western contexts. At the dawn of independence, there had emerged a consensus for the Nehruvian *dharma nirpekshta* (state neutrality to religions) which appeared to have set the tempo when clauses 17 and 18 (that later constituted the Right to Freedom of Religion in the Constitution) were put to discussion in the Constituent Assembly. The principle of religious liberty to all was the operative norm which the Constituent Assembly upheld while preparing the Constitution for the country. So, communities being separated due to religious identity were to be treated as being equal in the public domain since it was constitutionally endorsed. The Right to Freedom of Religion also ensured that communities were not only allowed to profess, practise and propagate a religion of their choice, but also had access to public resources and the freedom to participate in the political arena. The constitutional arrangement that evolved in its wake was undoubtedly secular though there are anomalies, as mentioned above, if one draws attention to, for instance, the prevalence of separate civil codes for different communities. Nonetheless, the Constitution of India stipulates, it can be argued, a policy of fairness in dealing with the communities constituting the nation. This has two major implications: on the one hand, the constitutional provisions do not compartmentalize the public and private domains as strictly separate; instead, by recognizing the distinct cultural rights of the communities, they seem to blur the distinction. In order to protect their distinctiveness, the Constitution guarantees, on the other hand, the right to establish institutions to retain their culture and language. This is reflective of the endeavour on the part of the founding fathers to make the Constitution as an instrument which is fair in dealing with different religious communities equally rather than negating or suppressing their religious identities. There is another point that also merits serious attention. Secularism in India seems to have undergone a sea change in its texture since the 1995 Hindutva judgement which endorses the Gandhian notion of *sarvdharma sadbhava* as being critical to its manifestation in the Indian context. As is shown, the 2016 Supreme Court pronouncement confirms this by forcefully arguing that being religious is not, under any circumstance, an impediment to being secular. This is perfectly possible in a multireligious society like India where religion is dominantly a way of life that shapes individual social choices and preferences. What is most important is the inculcation of values supportive of *sadbhava* or tolerance to all religions with the idea that they are parts of a collectivity. Implicit here is the idea that despite being different in religious terms, there exists a commonality across communities by virtue of sharing the same sociocultural universe. So, they are instinctively tied to one another, an idea which Gandhi imbibed with his sustained engagement with a reality that he confronted while devising his unique design of secularism which is neither derivative of the Western experiences nor exactly indigenous, but a creative blending of the two.

In constituting India as a secular polity, the Constitution makers, in a way, were responding to the complex realities of the social life of its people. Given that religion lays at root of the sociocultural life of people in the country, it was obvious that religion could not be kept away from influencing the working of state in ways more than one. What apparently further queered the pitch of secularism have been the centuries-old traditions of multireligiosity in India. So, one thing was clear that religion had to be situated in such a way in the Indian polity that it remains an important aspect of the social life of people without infringing upon the prospective secular nature of the polity. However, the Western conception of secularism in making state neutral to or away from religious aspect of people's life could not have been materialized in India. So, the choice apparently available for the framers of the Constitution was to evolve a unique concept of secularism which would keep religion in the reckoning of state's interactions with people's life in the spirit of harmonious coexistence of all the religions. That way, secularism, as is practised in the country gets reflected in equal respect and support for all the religions on the part of the state.

Indigenously, two competing phrases – *sarva dharma sambhava* and *dharma nirpekshata* – are generally used to grasp the nature of secularism in India. While the roots of the former lay in the tradition of harmonious coexistence of all religions, the later connotation reflects the Western conception rooted in the separation of religion from state or at least state's indifference to religious aspect of people's life. Literally, *sarva dharma sambhava* stands for goodwill and respect towards all religions. This has, in fact, been the classical framework of Gandhian thought in which secularism is understood in terms of *sarva dharma sambhav* or harmonious coexistence of all the religions. This has also been the essence of the *sanatana* (eternal) pattern of Hindu life which characterized the way of life Gandhi professed and lived throughout. In such a conception of life, a person can be highly religious in accordance with his own faith and belief, but with accommodative outlook towards other religions as well. There is no scope for exclusivity in such a view of secularism and every person is ordained with natural rights to practise his own religion without coming in the way of others to enjoy similar rights. Such a view of secularism 'is in accordance with the ancient religious tradition of India. It tries to build up a fellowship of believers, not by subordinating individual qualities to the group mind but by bringing them into harmony with each other'.[9] Elaborating such a conception of secularism, he further writes,

> when India is said to be a Secular State, it does not mean that we reject the reality of an unseen spirit or the relevance of religion to life or that we exalt irreligion. It does not mean that secularism itself becomes

> a positive religion or that the State assumes divine prerogatives... We hold that not one religion should be given preferential status... This view of religious impartiality, or comprehension and forbearance, has a prophetic role to play within the National or International life.[10]

In contrast to the eternal indigenous spirit of *sarva dharma sambhava,* the notion of *dharma nirpekshata* derives its intellectual roots from the Western conception of secularism. In the west, given the watertight separation of religion from state, there does not exist any scope for the state to have an active role in restriction or promotion of religions. At the best, a state can remain indifferent or neutral towards one and all religions. The same canons of secularism have been sought to be applied to the Indian scenario as well by equating secularism with *dharma nirpekshata* in the post-independent times. Drawing intellectual inspiration from the perspectives of the modernist elements of the national leadership, mild reverberations of such an idea of secularism could be sensed in the statements such as 'a secular state does not mean an irreligious state: it only means that we respect and honour all religions'.[11] However, as Rajeev Bhargava points out, such an understanding of secularism became more pronounced in the post-Nehru period culminating in the insertion of the word 'secular' in the Constitution of India.[12] In this scenario, the state was increasingly portrayed as totally indifferent or neutral to all the religions and religion is purely a matter of private life of the people with no relation to the activities or institutions of the state.

Given the volatility of the issues involved in constituting India as a secular nation along with guaranteeing right to freedom of religion to all its citizens, intense and at times acrimonious debates took place in the constituent assembly while finalizing the provisions relating to these matters. The spectrum of debate in the assembly on the issues of religious freedoms and secularism ranged so wide that it was indeed very difficult for the assembly to actually arrive at any unanimous decision on the subject. In the absence of the desired unanimity, occasionally such matters had to be put to vote to express assembly's disapproval of certain proposals. For instance, two contrasting positions on invocation of God in the beginning of Constitution, and insertion of the word 'secular' in consonance with the spirit of the socialist ideology were vehemently argued for in the assembly. Representing the former point of view, members such as HV Kamath, Shibban Lal Saksena and Pandit Govind Malaviya presented resolutions in the assembly to include the invocation 'In the name of God' in the Preamble to the Constitution, which was found by many as articulating the 'narrow, sectarian spirit'[13] of the members. On Kamath's insistence, his resolution was put to vote to be defeated comprehensively. Similarly, in sharp contrast to Kamath's resolution, Brajeshwar Prasad introduced his resolution to constitute India into 'a secular cooperative commonwealth',[14] with the twin purposes of lifting the subdued morale of the minorities as well as reinforcing the socialist ethos cultivated during the national movement. However, the other members in the assembly reminded Prasad of the liberal democratic traditions of the country and laughed out the futility of his proposal. Thus, the assembly was categorical in rejecting the extreme opinions on religion and secularism as critical aspects of the future polity of India.

Amidst the competing claims of extreme opinions, when the constituent assembly set on to 'creating a secular state in a religious society',[15] a number of plausible options were available before it. Though the two general voices articulating 'no-concern and equal-respect positions on secularism'[16] appeared catchy to sections of the assembly, their uncritical and unqualified acceptance was simply improbable owing to the complexities of the religious landscape of the country. So, what presumably could the assembly do was to take a middle ground in order to bring about some sort of balance between the imperatives of religious freedoms and separation of religion from state. In this context, two significant pointers are quite discernible from the discussions in the constituent assembly and the provisions that eventually became part of the Constitution. First, despite substantial support for the no-concern perspective on secularism in the constituent assembly mainly from the socialist members, that position could not become the guiding principle of secularism in India, given the intricate and all pervasive nature of religion in the minds of the people. Second, in view of the wider and unintended theoretical as well as juridical implications of the insertion of the term 'secular' in the Constitution, the framers decided against placing secularism as one of the key constituent elements of the Indian polity. What the constituent assembly, therefore, did was to leave the idea of secularism as an open-ended subject over which appropriate decisions could be made by the future generations as per their understanding and requirement. Nevertheless, the spirit of secular polity was surely established by the Constitution makers by stipulating a number of such provisions at different places in the Constitution whose tone and tenor have indeed been secular.

Before insertion of the word 'secularism' in the Preamble to the Constitution through the forty-second amendment in 1976, secularism as a letter did not appear anywhere in the Constitution though its spirit has remained omnipresent throughout the law of the land. The basic reason for such a considered decision of the constituent assembly was presumably not to portray the nature of Indian polity in the same frame as of the secular European nations, where religion does not have truck with state activities. Moreover, framers of the Indian Constitution appeared more concerned about making secularism as the pervasive virtue of political life rather than a dogma of state structure. They seemed inclined that the people of India enjoy the greatest of religious freedoms without feeling religion as a ground of any discrimination in their interactions with the state. That way, secularism, instead of getting just confined to the religious variables, turned out to be the guiding principle of state policy to secure an equal and non-discriminatory framework of life for all. On such a premise, any attempt at explicating the constitutional articulation of secularism in India needs to transcend the confines of the provisions relating to the religious freedoms, and touch upon all such articles that seek to materialize the virtues of equality and non-discrimination in the Indian polity.

The constitutional vision of secularism in India has most profoundly been expressed through the provisions enshrined in the chapters on fundamental rights and directive principles of state policy. Insofar as fundamental rights are concerned, two distinct sets of fundamental rights may be taken as indicative of minds of the framers of the Constitution to establish secular polity in the country. At the outset, the basic framework of two fundamental rights, i.e. right to equality and right to freedom under Articles 14 and 19, respectively, lay the secular foundations of polity not only by ruling out any kind of discrimination on the basis of religion and other such sectarian grounds, but also by positively guaranteeing the right to freedom of speech, expression and other related freedoms to all persons without any unreasonable restrictions. Indeed, it is on the basis of these rights that various religious as well as cultural and educational rights guaranteed under different articles are to be enjoyed by the people. In nutshell, the general framework of fundamental rights in India is such that all sorts of primordial affinities have been ruled out to be determinant in the governmental support to the people in living a happy and contended life based on the enjoyment of the rights enshrined in chapter three of the Constitution.

While the scheme of rights provided under the framework of rights to equality and freedom lay the background of secular polity by both prohibiting discrimination on the basis of religion, among others, and guaranteeing various positive rights, the primary onus on giving practical shape to the secular foundations of polity rests on the provisions enumerated under Articles 25–28. Collectively, these four articles address the major, if not all, concerns relating to positive contours of secularism in India through which people could exercise their free will in choosing and practising their religion. The moot point in this regard relates to the extent to which a person can take his freedom of conscience and free profession, practice and propagation of religion. In the rich body of case laws pertaining to these issues, the courts have stood the ground that while the right to practise one's religion is absolute and unfettered, the right to propagation of one's religion cannot be taken to carry out conversions of gullible followers of other religions. Though some jurists have taken such restricted judicial constructions as compromising with the religious freedom of people, there cannot be denying the fact that constitutional provisions on religious freedom in India rival some of the classical liberal democratic societies in the world.

Among the unique characteristics of secularism as articulated in the constitutional design, certain important aspects relate to the issues of social reform as well as acquiescence of state with the religious sentiments of followers of different religions about which relevant provisions have been made in the chapter on directive principles of state policy. In this context, the provision relating to the enactment of uniform civil code for all the people under Article 44 is a case in point. Despite the fact that Muslims take this article as affront to their right to religious freedom and erosion of Muslim personal law, the fundamental spirit behind this provision may be taken as greater secularization of Indian society, at least on the matters that relate to the dignity of persons in society. At the same time, Constitution also addresses the sentiments of the Hindus by stipulating under Article 48 prohibition of slaughter of cows and calves along with other milch animals. These articles, in a way, are indicative of the positive interventions towards reforming and preserving the social and cultural aspects of the life of the followers of different religions.

In sum, the constitutional articulation of secular nature of Indian polity is scattered over different provisions of the Constitution. Such provisions, pertaining to both the individual and collective life of people, have their basic purpose of establishing and cementing the secular fabric in the country within the framework of a liberal democratic polity. The benchmark of religious freedom that is considered as the core component of secularism in the country has been stipulated by the courts as essentially guaranteeing the freedom of conscience and practice of one's own religion to the fullest extent as long as the same does not come in the way of enjoyment of similar freedoms by others. Apart from these, a number of other ancillary articles of the Constitution also fortify the secular nature of Indian polity. As Bakshi writes so succinctly,

> The constitution of India stands for a secular state. The state has no official religion. Secularism pervades its provisions which give full opportunity to all persons to profess, practice and propagate religion of their choice. The constitution not only guarantees a person's freedom of religion and conscience, but also ensures freedom for one who has no religion, and it scrupulously restrains the state from making any discrimination on grounds of religion. A single citizenship is assured to all persons irrespective of their religion.[17]

On account of the implied nature of constitutional intent on secularism in India, the underlying implications and theoretical underpinnings of the concept have been a subject of creative constructions by both statesman and scholars. Soon after the implementation of the Constitution, inquisitive minds started posing questions regarding the true intent and extent of secularism in the country. Interestingly, on such questions, appropriate answers were tried by none other than Jawaharlal Nehru himself. In comparison to the Gandhian notion of secularism rooted in eternal ethos of Indian culture and traditions, Nehru articulated a modernist view of secularism whose contextual framework seems to have been derived from the west, but adapted as per the imperatives of the Indian social life. Explaining his idea of secularism in India, Nehru maintained that

> it does not obviously mean a state where religion as such is discouraged. It means freedom of religion and conscience, including freedom of those who have no religion. It means free play of all religions, subject only to their not interfering with each other or with the basic conceptions of our state.[18]

In conclusion, it may be argued that irrespective of the different shades in which secularism has been understood by different people, it indeed characterizes one of the foundational values of the postcolonial polity in India. In fact, secularism may be argued to be the only model of managing the religious diversity given the adoption of a liberal democratic political system after independence. Secularism, in a way, reflected the normative protest of the nationalist leadership in India against the two-nation theory propagated by the Muslim League in order to brand India as the country of Hindus and Pakistan as the home of Muslims. As such, a sectarian stand was patently against the age-old social, religious and cultural traditions of India, it was natural that the Indian leadership opposed such a conceptualization of India and resisted the creation of Pakistan on the basis of religion. But the real challenge before the Indian leadership emerged in the post-independent times when they set on to draft the Constitution for the country and stipulate the foundational value premises of the Indian polity. It was at this critical juncture of history that framers of the Constitution showed their ingenuity and utmost wisdom in drafting one of the most liberal and democratic constitutions in the world in which the universal values of humanity and brotherhood got fullest manifestation. Despite ensuring the fullest religious freedom to all citizens of the country, the Constitution safely kept the realm of religion outside the vortex of state. Such a fine balance in the religion and state is rare to see in any country as religious as India is. Notwithstanding the religious discords cropping up sometimes among the people, the secular fabric of the country remains as vibrant as ever to present India as a model of harmonious coexistence among believers of different religions.

Reservation

Reservation is a tool to ensure equality of status and opportunity. The socio-economic backwardness of communities due to age-old exploitation for reasons connected with well-entrenched social prejudices is sought to be addressed by putting in place multiple schemes of reservation for public jobs and other facilities. The purpose is to bring these socio-economically excluded groups at par with other communities. The constitutional guarantee for the scheduled castes (SCs) and scheduled tribes (STs) set in motion processes of empowerment, leading to the breakdown of social barriers in a significant way. Hence, it is argued that the supportive provisions are 'social not only it seeks to interrogate the system of hierarchical social relations, but more fundamentally it seeks to alter these social relations along egalitarian lines'. These provisions, adequately backed by constitutional-legal means, create a space where the dominant power structure, supported by the prevalent social relations, is being fiercely challenged by those who so far remain peripheral for historical reasons. In that respect, they are truly revolutionary in character.

In India, reservation refers to the special provisions envisaged in the Constitution for keeping aside a stipulated percentage or number of seats in the government jobs or state-run educational institutions for certain disadvantaged sections of society. It is in the nature of affirmative action to help the hitherto marginalized sections of society climb the ladders of socio-economic development and secure a respectable place for them in society. Though the idea of reservation somewhat stands in contravention to the concept of absolute equality, the same has been accepted as valid and legal course of action in view of securing the larger objective of creating an equitable and egalitarian social structure in India. It is for this reason that reservation is sometimes also referred to as positive discrimination to contextualize the apparent paradox between the principle of equality and the pressing requirements of social justice. Interestingly, reservation as a policy measure for uplifting the status of the disadvantaged section has not been visualized as a permanent feature of the Indian Constitution. On the contrary, it has been considered as some sort of contingent measure to provide early preferential treatment to the members of the specific communities, so that they are able to break free from the shackles of centuries-old social and economic disabilities and regain the status of citizenship with the rest of the people in society.

For a proper understanding of the logic and dynamics of reservation in India, it is important to dwell deep into the social equalities and the resultant disadvantages that it bring for a substantive section of society. At certain junctures of history, the social structure in India got perverted into a graded inequality in which different sections of people got divided into the advantaged and disadvantaged ones. While the former tended to remain upwardly mobile in the socio-economic parameters, the latter got themselves further marginalized due to the vicious play of caste system in the country. The social structure of India eventually became so perverse that the people belonging to certain low castes got socially marginalized to such extent that even their shadows became intolerable for the so-called high-caste people. However, such a state of things could never have been acceptable to the saner elements, given the gross violations of human values in such social practices. So, while a number of social reform movements took off and succeeded in bringing about enormous social awakening among the masses regarding the inhumanity inherent in such derogatory practices, their persuasive value could not have been enough for bringing about radical transformations in the outlook of people. Moreover, such endeavours on the part of enlightened people would not have secured the disadvantaged people substantive and concrete gains of life, which could play formidable role in reshaping their socio-economic position in society.[19] Thus, in order to bring about substantive social transformations, the policy of reservation appeared most plausible as it could not only guarantee the representation of disadvantaged people in the state structures, but also act as a significant persuader in uplifting the social and economic conditions of such people.

Some form of preferential treatment for the disadvantaged sections in order to bridge the equality deficit of the Indian society was part of the public discourse even during the national movement. Though the operational shape and medium for putting in place such measures were bone of contention among leaders, there appeared a large degree of agreement in them for making special provisions for certain disadvantaged sections in order to push their way through the social hierarchy. For instance, on the one side stood Mahatma Gandhi who argued for societal action and voluntary endeavours on the part of the common people to root out the curse of untouchability and secure a dignified and respectful place for the persons of lower castes. But on the other side was Ambedkar who was fully convinced that unless statutory and legal arrangements are in place to secure for the marginalized sections certain preferential treatment and special protective mechanism, they would not be able to make substantive gains amidst the numerous adversities surrounding their life. So, when the constituent assembly started debating the issues relating to reservation and other special measures for the protection and promotion of the interests of low-caste people, the debate did not turn out to be as acrimonious as it could have been, given the clash of interests among the different sections of society.

In the Constituent Assembly, there existed two perspectives on the issue of reservations with particular reference to the intended beneficiaries as well as the nature and extent of reservation. For instance, while, after informed debate, the members agreed for providing reservation for the members of SCs and STs, they could not agree on extending the same benefits to the members of OBCs and women with the same urgency. At the same time, the members could also not agree on extending the benefits of reservation of seats in the legislative bodies to the members of the OBCs and women despite extending the same to the members of the SCs and STs. The basic reason behind such a divergent perspective has presumably been the tendency on the part of the Constitution makers to relate social status of different groups with their relative economic position. On this count, while the people belonging to the SCs and STs were found to be both socially and economically marginalized, the OBCs appeared to suffer only from lack of high social status without suffering from the same level of economic deprivation as the members of the SCs and STs used to suffer. It is probably for this reason that the framers made definitive provisions for the SCs and STs to provide proportionate reservation to them in different aspects of governmental structures such as legislative bodies, educational institutions, and jobs, among others. But when it came for stipulating reservation for the people belonging to the OBCs, the framers thought it fit to leave the matter to be decided by the governments later on.

In accordance with the general consensus emerging in the Constituent Assembly, elaborate provisions have been made in the Constitution to provide for special measures in the form of reservation for the various disadvantaged sections of society. With regard to the definiteness of the provisions, Constitution stipulates two different sets of provisions. In the first place, drawing on the colonial legacies and fulfilling the promises made during the course of the national movement, the Constitution makes specific provisions for SCs and STs. In other words, for the SCs and STs, the provisions are definite, elaborate, all-inclusive and effective right from day one. As regards reservation of seats for OBCs and other disadvantaged sections of society, the Constitution makes just indicative provisions without defining the nature, extent, scope and timeframe of such reservations. The understanding behind such an ambivalent attitude in the Constitution may be located in the differing perceptions on the nature and extent of the backwardness of these communities vis-à-vis the SCs and STs who were found to be suffering from the most perverse and miserable kind of marginalization. For this reason, the question of reservation of seats for these sections was left open-ended with the responsibility now coming upon the incumbent government to walk the extra mile in bestowing the benefits of reservations for them.

The constitutional stipulations on reservation are quite extensive and varied. Primarily, these provisions have been placed in the chapters three, four and sixteen detailing the provisions relating to fundamental rights, directive principles of state policy and special provisions relating to certain classes, respectively. Interestingly, in the chapter on fundamental rights, the references to reservation for different groups of people under Articles 15 and 16 are made more as qualifying signposts to the general formulations on the doctrinal thrust of a given right. Among others, these references are in the nature of explicit exceptions to the normative connotations of the specific fundamental rights in order to provide axiomatic validity to the legislations and other measures in furtherance of the reservation policy. In other words, these provisions are probably to save the main provisions envisaging reservation for the weaker sections of society in jobs, educational institutions as well as legislative bodies. Given the contentious nature of the provisions on reservation, the governmental initiatives on that count would surely have been challenged in the courts. Had these saving clauses been not explicitly made part of the provisions on fundamental rights, the courts in all likelihood would have been tempted to declare the measures for reservation as contravening the provisions on fundamental rights.

Other enabling provisions calling upon the state to take special measures for furthering the interests of the SCs and STs have been made under Articles 46 and 164. Placed in the chapter on directive principles of state policy, Article 46 stands as a general directive to the state to initiate measures for promoting educational and economic interests of the weaker sections including SCs and STs. This directive principle presumably derives its plausibility from the fact that for the long-term improvement in the social and economic conditions of the weaker sections, what would be more effective and fruitful strategy would be their educational empowerment rather than providing jobs and other material gains. In compliance with this directive, a number of states have established special educational institutions at different levels along with hostels for the children belonging to weaker sections in order to provide them holistic education at no cost. To further reinforce the political and administrative arrangements for initiating and implementing policies and programmes for development of SCs and STs, Article 164 envisages for the appointment of a particular minister to act as the nodal person for undertaking the welfare of the STs though he may be entrusted with the responsibility of looking into the issues of the welfare of SCs and OBCs as well in the states such as Chhattisgarh, Jharkhand, Madhya Pradesh and Odisha. Such a provision is obvious given the sizeable number of people belonging to these categories and residing in these states.

The primary constitutional mandate for reservation of seats for the weaker sections has been provided through the provisions enumerated under different articles of chapter sixteen. For instance, under Article 330, the Constitution mandates the reservation of seats for SCs and STs in the Lok Sabha in proportion to the population of these communities in different states and union territories. Similar provisions have been made for the legislative assemblies of the states and union territories, where seats have to be reserved for the members of the SC and ST community in proportion to their population.

In a way, the reservation of seats for the weaker sections of society in India reflects the acceptance of reservation as the mainstay of the constitutional as well as governmental efforts towards improving the social and economic conditions of these people. However, with regard to these provisions, two distinct observations seem pertinent. One, these measures have been considered to be short-term measures to provide quick solace to the weaker sections by providing them quotas in jobs and even promotions. In the long term, what was considered to be the primary concern of the government was to focus on the educational and other material support to the people belonging to these communities, so that they can feel empowered and well-equipped to compete with the people belonging to the general category. However, in the course of time, there has happened a kind of swapping of objectives as a result of which now job reservations have come to be the prime concern of the government with the educational support taking backseat in the governmental initiatives. Two, the provision for reservation has been envisaged to help the weaker sections improve their social and economic conditions in such a way that they no more remain second to the people belonging to the general category in any walk of life. Since the implementation of the policy of reservation, a number of families have indeed been able to corner the benefits of reservation and the trend continues even till date. In other words, the benefits of reservation have been cornered by a select few without showing any tangible evidence that their social and economic conditions have improved substantially enough to jump the fence of the weaker section and join the mainstream of the general category. As a result, the constitutional vision of reservation seems to have become a kind of ritual whose benefits are going straight to the select few of the SCs and STs.

Despite the clear-cut constitutional mandate for reservations for weaker sections of society, the issue has not remained away from the intense litigation over the years. The initial disputes on the subject related to the identification of a particular caste as being SC or a tribe as ST. Later, the identification issues turned murkier with the offspring of inter-caste marriages seeking status of SC or ST. On these issues, the authoritative judgement as of today has come from the Kerala High Court in the *M. C. Valsala v State of Kerala.*[20] The court held that in case of the children being born of inter-caste marriage of which mother or father happens to be SC or ST, the benefits of reservation can be claimed by the children only after proving that he or she is subjected to the same kinds of discriminations, disadvantages and handicaps which a person born as SC or ST suffers ordinarily. On rest of the matters, thanks to the categorical statements contained in different provisions of the Constitution, the reservation for SC and ST has now been taken as settled fact.

Despite having stirred the sensibilities of both the socially advantaged and disadvantaged sections of society, the 1990 Mandal initiative is a powerful input that has brought about radical changes in Indian polity and society. The grammar of entitlement has become an integral part of the language of politics in contemporary India. There can be a debate on how to execute the decision, but all political parties are unanimous in accepting the logic and reality of the Ninety-Third Amendment Act (2005), confirming reservation in all institutions of higher learning. The appointment of the Oversight Committee in 2006 to suggest steps to expand the OBC quota without adversely affecting the equilibrium in admission to institutions of higher learning is a strategy to defuse social tension in the country. Yet, the 2006 controversy had also shown 'how entrenched social prejudices remain and how deep runs the hostility to change in areas where it matters the most'. Despite the obvious social implications, social justice in the discourse supportive of OBC reservation redefined deprivation not in terms of lack of economic entitlement, but primarily in terms of 'social disabilities, which were the consequences of social hierarchies, rather than economic arrangements'. Instead of conceptualizing deprivation as being an inevitable outcome of specific socio-economic circumstances, the Mandal formula explained the phenomenon in terms of caste affiliation. The Mandal debate has thus two important consequences: on the one hand, it linked democracy 'instrumentally to social justice' by arguing for quotas for the OBC in public employment and higher education; this will result in, on the other, democratization of the space, which so far remained beyond OBCs' reach. A group's exclusion or under-representation in institutions of authority is thus seen 'not so much as a consequence of unjust socio-economic inequalities but as its cause'. Conceptually, the argument for OBC reservation may have lapses though it has raised those important social issues which hardly received adequate attention in the past presumably because of the hegemonic grip of the dominant social groups over constitutional governance in India. In that sense, the Mandal debate marks an important shift in the debates and discussions over public justification for reservations. After Mandal, caste as a basis of collective struggle for gaining equality in positions and social status became 'a term of respectable usage' among the marginalized. It is now being seen as 'an empowering device to enhance one's meager entitlements in society'. The shift thus involved a reinterpretation of the nationalist goal of a more equal and just society by empowering the disadvantaged and recognizing the socially denigrated groups in addition to reduction in socio-economic disparities.

Ever since the implementation of the Mandal commission recommendations for reservation of seats in government services as well as educational institutions, a new wave of litigation has set on. In this regard, the pioneering judgement was delivered by the Supreme Court in the *Indra Sawhney v Union of India*.[21] In this particular case, the constitutional validity of the government's decision to grant 27 per cent reservation to the members of the Backward Castes (BCs) in central public services was challenged. In deciding the case, the Supreme Court held the constitutional validity of the government's order, but added a number of qualifications and provisos in the extension of the benefits of reservation to the people belonging to the OBCs. The court made it clear that caste alone could not be the marker of social and educational backwardness in the Indian society. It devised the formula of creamy layer to weed out the affluent and relatively advanced sections from the ambit of the OBC reservation reasoning that their continuation to enjoy the benefits of reservation for OBCs would be violation of the right to equality enshrined in Article 14 of the Constitution. The issue of the OBC reservation again came up for hearing before the Supreme Court when the constitutional validity of the ninety-third amendment to the Constitution was challenged in the case of *Ashok Thakur v Union of India*.[22] In this case also, the Supreme Court upheld the constitutional validity of the OBC reservation.

In upholding the constitutional validity of reservations, the courts in India have in fact shown their progressive character. Given the public contestations on the objective, basis and mode of providing reservations for weaker sections, there would have been a clear possibility that the court would have taken a stand contrary to the measures of the government. However, given the categorical acceptance of reservation as a method of carrying out the project of social justice in the Constitution, the general attitude in the public has increasingly got attuned to accept reservations as a fact of life. But the working of reservations have surely aroused serious doubts regarding the efficacy of reservation as the most appropriate method of bringing about a turnaround in the lives of the weaker sections of society. On a number of occasions, demands have been raised for taking reservations as a dynamic process in which the beneficiaries of the affirmative actions need to be edged out of the reckoning to provide opportunity for others to reap the benefits of such policies. While the courts agreed to this line of argument in the case of the OBCs, they refused to apply the same canons of creamy layer in the case of SC and ST as they have done in case of the OBCs.

Another point of contention with regard to the efficacy of reservations has been the shrinking space of the public employment opportunities where the reservation provisions are applicable. After the inauguration of the neo-liberal economic policies in the country, the public sector is increasingly vacating spaces to be occupied by the private sector. Such a trend is further likely to continue and accelerate in the times to come. In such a scenario, the demand for extension of the constitutional mandate for reservation of seats in jobs and educational institutions in private sector has been raised vehemently from various quarters.[23] But such demands are being resisted on the ground that the constitutional mandate is for guaranteeing reservation of jobs only in the public sector and the government-run educational institutions. Extension of reservation to private sector would be violation of the fundamental right to freedom of profession, vocation, trade and business. Thus, the idea of reservations in reality seems to have run out its utility and is poised for reinvention if it is to remain as the meaningful instrument of social justice in the country.

Gender question

Following the growing democratization the issues such as women empowerment and gender rights have gained massive importance in contemporary political discourses in India. Despite having paid adequate attention, the founding fathers did not seem to pursue the matter to the extent it was expected presumably because they had other pressing priorities. The issue thus remained unresolved though it is being continuously raised especially in the wake campaigns for democratizing governance. That women were sociopolitically tortured and exploited beyond imagination is an age-old phenomenon. Protests were mounted though the roots were hardly touched presumably because of the well-entrenched prejudices against gender-neutral governance. In simple theoretical terms, it can be explained in terms of patriarchy being hegemonic in relation to the issues of gender. The aim here is to comprehend the complex unfolding of the trajectories leading to the articulation of gender equality as a constitutional goal. As the role of judiciary is critical in sustaining the Constitution and the values from which it derives its sustenance, this segment, by dwelling on some of the major judicial pronouncements, traversed a relatively less trodden path in contemporary Political Science scholarship.

Indian Constitution is considered as the document outlining the framework of a social revolution in the country. Such a social revolution was naturally an avowed objective of the Indian Constitution given the enormous issues of social cleavages and inequalities in the Indian society. Over the years, certain sections of society got marginalized schematically in such a way that their individual as well as collective existence as part of Indian society was characterized by inequality and discrimination. So, when the Indian Constitution was in the process of being framed, it was quite obvious in the minds of the framers that any promise of a democratic polity in the country would appear to be hollow without being based on the foundations of an equitable and egalitarian society. It is probably in such a normative framework of the framing of Indian Constitution that the idea of social revolution may be contextualized. However, in any conceptualization of the idea of social revolution, apart from the other major issues and concerns, what also needs to be a primary factor is probably the gender question.

In deciphering the contents of gender question in the countries like India, two issues arguably stand out prominently. At the very outset, the broader contours of the social, economic as well as political frameworks of life need to be designed in such a way that the citizenry of the country is taken as a common denominator without reference to any discriminatory or disproportionately and unduly advantageous positions to traditionally dominant sections of society. In other words, every single citizen of the country needs to have same position and constitutional entitlements in different spheres of life. As such, men and women need to be conferred the same citizenship rights. But another important dimension of gender question pertains to the special provisions that needed to be made in the Constitution to provide for positive discrimination in favour of women. This dimension, indeed, attains added importance in the societies like India where women have traditionally been subjected to all sorts of discriminations and subjugations. Right from the personal laws to the higher echelons of public life such as effective participation in the decision-making processes as well as proportionate representation of women in various public bodies, subordinate and negligible position of women vis-à-vis men seem galore. In such circumstances, what has been felt to be ordained by the Constitution is a comprehensive framework of protective as well as promotional provisions through which not only various kinds of injustices against women can be checked, but also their stakes as equal partner in different aspects of public life could be secured.

Hence, in figuring out the relevant provisions of the Constitution on the gender question, it is quite pertinent to see as to what extent the Constitution addresses these questions.

As a matter of fact, even before the advent of the feminist movement in the world, gender questions have always been prominent part of the public discourse in India.[24] Even during the national movement, it was one of the cherished dreams of the national leaders to encourage and ensure the participation of women in large numbers in the movements launched from time to time against the colonial rule. In fact, in making the movements launched by Gandhi mass movements, the role of women was quite significant. Moreover, many women took active part in the national movement and rose to the position of top leadership of the Congress party. At the same time, many leaders argued for gender equality as the foundational value of the future polity of the country by calling for provisions that there would not be any disqualification of disability of a citizen of the country on the basis only of sex.[25] Subsequent to the independence, when the elections for the Constituent Assembly took place, a number of women got elected to the assembly and played a prominent role in making the deliberations of the assembly enriching and meaningful. It is indeed heartening to note that the central leadership of the Congress was determined to get as many women candidates elected to the Constituent Assembly as possible, and for that purpose certain specific suggestions were made by name to get them elected to the assembly.[26] When the constituent assembly met to debate the basic contours of the Constitution, the women members raised a number of pertinent points relating especially to women and played a pivotal role in engendering the varied provisions of the Constitution.

Interestingly, in the deliberations of the Constituent Assembly, the gender questions appeared in quite unconventional form while discussing the nature and extent of the fundamental rights. At one end, imperatives of protecting rights of women led the assembly to desist from making certain fundamental right unqualified, whose unfettered enjoyment might compromise with the rights of women. Given that in the traditional and custom-ridden societies like India, there existed a host of religious practices, social customs and cultural traditions that are found to be discriminatory and injurious to the dignity and status of women. Societal sanctions to such perverse norms are often claimed on the ground of religious practices or social customs. Hence, when the fundamental rights relating to religion and culture were being debated in the assembly, members, particularly Rajkumari Amrit Kaur, argued for putting reasonable restrictions on these rights, so that they cannot be invoked to perpetuate the inhuman practices patently against the prestige and dignity of women. Further, when the right to equality was being discussed, it was argued that though the right to equality needs to be one of the benchmarks of life of the people, the provisions guaranteeing such rights need not prevent the state from making positive interventions in order to protect the interests of the vulnerable sections of society such as women and children. Thus, the nature of debate in the Constituent Assembly on the issue of gender was quite complex as the general framework of fundamental rights needed to be contextualized in the realm of protection and promotion of the rights of women.

Gender question has been addressed in the Constitution of India in three different formats. In the beginning, general framework of equal rights for both men and women have been stipulated, apart from reaffirming the cherished resolve of the Constitution to constitute a democratic polity in the country in which humanistic values would characterize the different aspects of life of the people. That way, the Preamble sets the tone by outlining the virtues of life that it seeks to secure for all its citizens. For instance, when it declares that justice: social, economic and political; liberty of thought, expression, belief, faith and worship; and, equality of status and of opportunity; would be secured for all the people of India, the Preamble indeed reaffirms the pious intention of the Constitution makers to secure these rights without any discrimination. The significance of such a declaration can be appreciated in traditional societies such as India when one looks at the discrimination and injustices women are subjected to at virtually every step of their life.[27] So, while it may not be easy and quick to achieve the goals set by the Preamble, it surely indicates the democratic and egalitarian ethos of the society in which women may now visualize themselves. Concrete manifestation of such a general right is expressed in certain provisions of the Constitution such as Article 326, which provides that every citizen of India aged eighteen shall be eligible to exercise right to vote without any unreasonable restriction. In a way, the universal adult suffrage guaranteed under the Constitution may be considered as a revolutionary step on the part of the Indian Constitution makers when one looks at the trajectory of securing women's right to vote in many other countries.

The chapter on fundamental rights is the other place where the issues of women's rights have been addressed. In this context, the foundational right seems to be the provisions relating to the different aspects of right to equality. Though the basic formulation with regard to essence of right to equality has been provided under provisions of Article 14, which forbids state from denying to any person equality before law or the equal protection of the law, the operational dynamics of this right has further been elaborated under the provisions of Article 15. Under Article 15, the general direction that the state shall not discriminate against any citizen on certain unreasonable grounds including sex acts as the formidable fiat against the innumerable variety of discriminations that women are subjected to in different walks of life even for the non-state bodies. This article acts as the general reminder to all the stakeholders that women must be treated with equal position and status of men in all aspects of life including access to various services and different opportunities of life. On the positive side, Article 15(3) clarifies the position that the general framework of right to equality would not come in the way of the state from making any special provision for women and children. Taking advantage of this constitutional concession, a number of measures at different levels have been initiated towards bettering the condition of women in society, including their participation in the elected bodies at local levels. Apart from the articles on right to equality, different other fundamental rights also have implicit or explicit references for the protection and promotion of rights of women. The cumulative impact of all these provisions has been that the normative justification for any kind of discrimination against women is summarily rejected, thereby setting the stage for the concerted attempts at bringing about the silent social revolution in the country. Likewise, the egalitarian provisions contained in Article 16 also provide a major benchmark for assuring substantive equality in the Indian Constitution.[28]

A perusal of the Constitution reveals that the futuristic perspective on the rights of women has been ordained in different provisions enshrined in the chapter on directive principles of state policy. There is no denying the fact that discrimination against women has been existing in the Indian society at both social and economic levels with required justifications drawn from the religious or socio-economic practices. Given that undoing such discriminatory practices needed a lot of background preparedness as well as socio-religious persuasions on the part of the different stakeholders, such remedial measures could be placed in the form of fundamental rights of women. Instead, what was found more plausible was to place them as directive principles of state policy, so that they remain directions for the state to implement them with the only grace of sometime afforded to them. On the whole, there are at least three important directive principles whose essence is to do gender justice in a given area of life. For instance, Article 39 contains certain principles of policy to be followed by the state for bettering the life of people. Among many other subtle principles aimed at securing equality of women with men in certain specific areas, the most significant provision has been stipulated under Article 39(c), which states that the state should strive towards securing equal pay for equal work for both men and women. This is a sort of path-breaking directive, given the widespread prevalence of gross inequality between men and women in terms of pay for them despite performing similar types of activities, particularly in the unorganized and non-state sectors.

In view of the fact that as part of their reproductive activity, women have to bear the child and undergo the labour pain, naturally, they need to be entitled for fairly long period of maternity leave. Realizing the seriousness of the matter and securing such a kind of leave for the working women, Article 41 directs the state to ensure that maternity relief including maternity leave becomes a standard practice in working of both public and private organizations. Finally, the most radical measure towards addressing the pressing questions of gender justice, Article 44 calls upon the state to make efforts for securing to all the citizens a uniform civil code throughout the territory of

India. The salience of this provision towards securing gender justice in India can be imagined from the fact that as part of claimed religious or cultural practices, women have been subjected to a number of discriminatory and unjust personal practices leading to innumerable miseries and harassments for them in different parts of the country. In order to mend these discriminatory and unjust social- and religion-based personal laws of different people, this article enjoins upon the state the responsibility of putting in place a uniform civil code. However, given that such a move may not be agreeable on part of all the stakeholders, it does afford the grace of time to the state for achieving the objective. Still, what needs to be appreciated is the intention of the Constitution to secure for all the women similar kind of personal laws, so that their common concerns relating to marriage, divorce, maintenance and adoption, among others, may be taken care of uniformly irrespective of the religious or sociocultural background of a woman. Thus, the constitutional vision on the issues of gender justice in India is both comprehensive and long term, so that the vision for a just society for women becomes a reality in the country.

The constitutional framework for rights of women has been subjected to judicial scrutiny on the hands of the courts in different cases. In this regard, one of the most contested constitutional provisions related to the moves on the part of several state governments to initiate special measures for the protection and promotion of rights of women. For instance, in *Dattatreya Motiram More v State of Bombay*,[29] the petitioner contended that the special provisions made for women under Article 15(3) violated the provisions under Article 15(1). In this case, the Bombay High Court held that though provisions of Article 15(1) lay down the general framework of right to equality in India, the same has been qualified by certain other articles such as Article 15(3) in obvious recognition of the need for special measures for certain disadvantaged sections of society which might not be able to enjoy the right to equality if they are not provided with certain distinct protective and promotional measures. The court therefore reasoned that instead of violating the provisions of Article 15(1), the thrust of Article 15(3) is, in fact, to strengthen the spirit of the former by helping an important section of society come up to the level of the rest.

In another important case *Vishakha v State of Rajasthan*,[30] the petitioner contended that the provisions of Articles 14 and 15 on right to equality are violated in cases where sexual harassment of women takes place at workplace, and therefore, state must initiate substantive measures to check such harassment of women, so that the right to equality may be ensured for them at workplace. In expressing its agreement with the contentions of the petitioner, the Supreme Court even went a step further to hold that sexual harassment at workplace not only violates the rights guaranteed for women under provisions of Articles 14 and 15, but also stands in contravention with the provisions of Article 23 that secure rights against exploitation to the citizens of India. The Court held that unless a woman ensures a free and fair environment at workplace, how could she be expected to stand in a position of equality with other colleagues at the workplace. The Court, therefore, directed the states to adopt a comprehensive framework against the sexual harassment of women at workplace and put in a place an effective administrative mechanism to effectively implement the guidelines of the framework.

Two contemporary issues, namely a uniform civil code and reservation of seats for women in the national parliament and state legislative assemblies seem to have hogged the limelight in contemporary feminist discourse in India. Conceptually, these twin issues are tuned to the wider concern for freedom and equality. Uniform civil code cannot be accepted so easily, since it involves a clear violation of fundamental tenor of the *Shariat* laws. This thus amounts to a threat to India's secular identity though the continuity of separate civil code for the Muslims negates gender equality in general. The issue has thus created a logjam which none of the political stakeholders are willing to address presumably due to obvious sociopolitical repercussions. Similarly, the arguments over the reservation of seats for women in the legislature are justified as essential to fulfil the constitutional goals of freedom and equality. The 1989 Supreme Court Shah Banu judgement, despite not having made adequate progress in this regard, had certainly set in motion the campaign for gender-parity; it was a path-breaking initiative which received tremendous boost in the 2017 Triple Talaq judgement of the Supreme Court, which outlawed the *Shariat* practice of Talaq as being constitutionally contrary.

The introduction of the Eighty-First Amendment Bill in 1996 by the United Front government brought back the gender issue to the centre stage of Indian politics. Women needed to be empowered and reservation through a legal enactment was perhaps the most effective device to bypass the patriarchal prejudices responsible for gender discrimination. The efforts have also received severe opposition because it is alleged that a blanket reservation policy is likely to protect the privileged section of women, given their instant access to political power due to their specific socio-economic roots. The argument opposing reservation thus draws on the fact that women in India are socially fragmented, and it would be conceptually misleading and empirically wrong to conceive of a situation in which women at various social strata articulate a single voice because of their identical biological persona as women. The imbroglio cannot be sorted out so easily. Nonetheless, these debates have established beyond doubt that women are no longer just a voice, but a critical voice challenging the conventional outlook on freedom and equality while providing creative inputs to conceptualize gender equality and women empowerment in the wider social, economic and political context.

In sum, issues related to gender equality found prominent articulation in the constitutional design of India. While it has been running theme of the Constitution to forbid any kind of gender discrimination or inequality based on sex, it also sought to make positive interventions in order to better the socio-economic and political status of women. However, the most significant challenge that the framers faced in drafting the gender-related provisions of the Constitution was the lack of unanimous support from the general public on the issue of providing preferential treatment to women in different aspects of life. Rather, a formidable section of the society insisted on carrying forward the customary practices, rituals and traditions that had patently been injurious to the interests of women. In such a scenario, what seemed most plausible to the Constitution makers was to just indicate the mind of the Constituent Assembly on a given issue without going into the niceties of the matter because doing so would have galvanized the obscurantist elements of society to cast aspersion on the wisdom and prudence of the assembly. Hence, the gender-related question are primarily addressed in the Constitution in a more sober and subdued manner rather than the robust way as has been done in the case of other marginalized sections such as SCs, STs and OBCs. In spite of such mellowed tone of the Constitution, in the post independent times, taking hints from the constitutional provisions, a number of progressive measures have been initiated to improve the social, economic and political conditions of women. However, much still remains to be done if the cycle of social revolution is to move full circle in the country as per the vision of the Constitution makers.

Concluding observations

A constitutional design is built on certain specific politico-ideological ethos which are sought to be articulated in the text. Since the Enlightenment philosophy remains an important source of ideological inspiration for the founding fathers, majority of the 1950 constitutional provisions were drafted to imbibe its spirit. The aim of the Constitution makers was to develop a truly democratic system of governance, as they were persuaded to believe that it was the best option for governing an immensely diverse country like India. As the debate in the Constituent Assembly demonstrates, the 1950 Constitution was hardly a borrowed doctrine because it evolved out the intense debate among the members of the Assembly over a period little less than three years between 1946 and 1949. This section delves into those areas of India's Constitution which are clearly derivative of the ideological concerns of the founding fathers who strongly endorsed liberal constitutionalism while underplaying the Gandhian notion of *village swaraj*, which Gandhians supported as perhaps the only option for India's inclusive growth as a nation state.

As is evident, in the shaping of India's constitutional identity, the Enlightenment principles remain an important reference point. A perusal of the constitutional trajectory since the inauguration of the 1950 Constitution reveals that what the founding fathers upheld while contributing to the making of the Constitution continues to be as effective as it was then. It is true that given the fact that India's Constitution is neither extremely right nor whimsically flexible, it cannot be compared with the established liberal constitutions around the world. Here, the cautionary note of BR Ambedkar appears to be instructive. Babasaheb was not in favour of a rigid Constitution simply because it needed to be adapted to the rapidly changing socio-economic and political milieu; unless, this is admissible, a Constitution ceases to be organic to the society, it becomes a mere lifeless document comprising provisions without being effective. That it should be flexible should also be understood with reference to whether the amendment is absolutely necessary under the circumstances; and, it should be kept in mind that a change is allowed so long as it does not adversely affect the basic character of the Constitution. So, Ambedkar's caution helps us comprehend why India's Constitution is so distinctive among other functional constitutions. In the same vein, India's constitutional identity stands out since it draws on its equally distinctive texture and functioning which are, of course, linked with India's socio-economic and political circumstances. The analysis of selective, but fundamental, politico-ideological issues also shows the sagacity of the founding fathers who drafted the Constitution at a time when India was passing through perhaps the most tumultuous time of her past following the 1947 partition. It also confirms that for them, what was critical was to evolve an accepted format of constitutional governance which the 1950 Constitution provided. There were dissenting voices too when these issues were discussed in the Constituent Assembly; nonetheless, the majority opinion endorsed them which further confirms how democratic principles guided the discussion and also decisions in the Assembly. This is one part of the story; there is an equally important part which highlights that these issues provoke new debates in independent India, resulting in significant changes in the constitutional attitude towards religion and religious freedom, secularism, reservation and gender question. As shown in the relevant chapters, the changes are justified contextually which again substantiates the point that India's Constitution provides a mechanism to remain meaningful in the changed social, economic and political milieu. One example will suffice. The 2018 Triple Talaq, discussed in Chapter 6, is a remarkable judicial feat because by being appreciative of the Enlightenment values of freedom and equality, the apex court outlawed the prejudicial Triple Talaq, since it is contrary to the fundamental constitutional values governing the polity. Examples can be multiplied. What is critical here is to reiterate that (a) India's constitutional identity is sacrosanct because the basic values shaping its nature and also character cannot be allowed to be compromised, and (b) it is also constantly evolving, since there are instances when new ideas are introduced to make it contextually effective. With this conceptualization of constitutional identity, it is fair to argue that the above-discussed politico-ideological issues are an important area of concern for grasping the nature of India's constitutional identity primarily because they act as a bridge between what the founding fathers thought and what is required to be done in the present context to ascertain their contextual validity. This is useful presumably because it will allow newer conceptualizations by reference to the ongoing socio-economic and political metamorphosis without, of course, compromising on the foundational values on which India's constitutional identity rests.

Notes

1 S Radhakrishnan, *Indian Philosophy*, Vol. I, George Allen and Unwin, London, 1929, pp. 25–26.
2 TN Madan, 'Religion in India', *Daedalus*, Vol. 118, No. 4, Another India, Fall 1989, p. 115, accessed through www.jstor.org/stable/20025267 on 22 May 2018.
3 Granville Austin, *The Indian Constitution: Cornerstone of a Nation*, Oxford University Press, New Delhi, 1966, p. 54.
4 All Parties Conference, *Report of the Committee to Determine the Principles of the Constitution of India*, Chairman, Motilal Nehru, All Indian Congress Committee, Allahabad, 1928, p. 29.
5 ibid., p. 90.
6 Granville Austin, *The Indian Constitution: Cornerstone of a Nation*, Oxford University Press, New Delhi, 1966, p. 64.
7 *Rev. Stanislaus v State of Madhya Pradesh.*
8 HM Seervai, *Constitutional Law of India: A Critical Commentary*, Vol. 2, 4th edn, Universal Law Publishing, New Delhi, 2002, p. 1289.
9 S Radhakrishnan, *Recovery of Faith*, Hind Pocket Books, New Delhi, 1967, pp. 184–185.
10 ibid., p. 184.
11 Government of India, *Jawaharlal Nehru's Speeches*, Vol. 5, Publications Division, New Delhi, 1983, p. 59.
12 Rajeev Bhargava, 'Nehru against Nehruvians', *Economic and Political Weekly*, Vol. 52, No. 8, 25 February 2017, p. 48.
13 *Constituent Assembly Debates*, Vol. 10, Lok Sabha Secretariat, New Delhi, p. 440.
14 Ibid., p. 447.
15 TN Madan, *Modern Myths, Locked Minds*, Oxford University Press, New Delhi, 1997, p. 245.
16 Shefali Jha, 'Secularism in the constituent assembly debates: 1946–50', *Economic and Political Weekly*, Vol. 37, No. 30, 2 August 2002, p. 3180.
17 PM Bakshi, *The Constitution of India*, Universal Law Publishing, New Delhi, 2016, p. 4.
18 S Gopal, *Jawaharlal Nehru: An Anthology*, Oxford University Press, New Delhi, 1983, p. 327.
19 Marc Galanter, *Competing Equalities: Law and Backward Classes in India*, Oxford University Press, New Delhi, 1991.
20 *M. C. Valsala v State of Kerala*, AIR 2006, Ker I.
21 *Indra Sawhney v Union of India*, 1992 Supp (3), SCC 217.
22 *Ashok Thakur v Union of India*, 2008 6 SCC 1.
23 Vinay Sitapati, 'Reservations', in Sujit Chowdhary, Madhav Khosla and Pratap Bhanu Mehta (eds.), *The Oxford Handbook of Indian Constitution*, Oxford University Press, New Delhi, 2016, p. 730.
24 Radha Kumar, *The History of Doing: An Illustrated Account of Movements for Women's Rights and Feminism in India 1800–1900*, Kali for Women, New Delhi, 1993.
25 Granville Austin, *The Indian Constitution: Cornerstone of a Nation*, Oxford University Press, New Delhi, 1966, p. 54.

26 Ibid., p. 12.
27 Flavia Agnes, *Law and Gender Equality: The Politics of Women's Rights in India*, Oxford University Press, New Delhi, 2000.
28 Kamala Sankaran, 'Special provisions and access to socio-economic rights: women and the Indian Constitution', *South African Journal of Human Rights*, Vol. 23, No. 1, 2007, p. 277.
29 *Dattatreya Motiram More v State of Bombay*, AIR 1953 Bombay 311.
30 *Vishakha v State of Rajasthan*, AIR 1997 SC 3011.

4 Politico-ideological structures

Politico-structural designs

The Indian Constitution is an ideological response seeking to design governance in India in accordance with the fundamental ethos of liberal democracy of the Western variety. As a result, the 1950 Constitution was structured in a specific way to translate these concerns; a specific structure of governance was, in other words, created to fulfil the politico-ideological goals that the founding fathers so assiduously nurtured. This chapter pursues arguments to substantiate the claim that constitutional identity is hardly a fixed denomination, but is being regularly reinvented by democratic struggles and also judicial interventions while upholding the fundamental character of the Constitution and the concomitant constitutional practices. It is difficult to deal with each and every aspect of constitutional designs in a single monograph; hence only those parts shall be dealt with which are critical to the argument defending India's unique constitutional identity. Instead of providing a threadbare account of the system of constitutionalism that has evolved in India, this chapter concentrates on federalism and Article 370 of the Constitution for reasons connected with the articulation of constitutional identity in a specific manner. One of the reasons for discussing federalism and Article 370 in one capsule is to highlight the distinctive texture of India's democratic compact, which is not exactly derivative of the Western textual sources notwithstanding the critical importance of the Enlightenment philosophy in creating and sustaining its foundation. In their defence for federalism, the founding fathers harped on the unique nature of India's democracy, which was also rooted in the nationalist struggle against British colonialism. During their battle against an imposed authority, they appeared to have been inspired by the democratic ideals that had flourished in England and elsewhere in Europe; for them, they not only allowed them to conceptualize colonial rule as detrimental to India's progress as a democratic polity, but also helped them understand colonialism as repugnant to constitutional liberalism. It was easier for them to justify the adoption of constitutional democracy since it corresponded with the ideological priorities that they cherished and also pursed while challenging the British rule in India. An empowering ideological preference, constitutional liberalism, despite its alien roots, emerged as a natural choice among the nationalists largely because of ideological affinity that the latter had with the former; it was an affinity that evolved gradually in circumstances in which the struggle for freedom was also an endeavour at articulating a voice for change and transformation.

Besides dealing with the context in which constitutional liberalism was privileged, the chapter underlines the point that the distinctive texture of India's political tapestry needs to be understood contextually because a conventional reading of the functioning of contemporary federal polities will lead us nowhere which, all the more, emphasizes that a derivative mode of conceptualization shall not be adequate. Implicit here is also the contention that the nature of federalism is historically ordained, if not, governed, which is also supportive of the argument that federalism evolves, and it cannot be imposed. In the available literature, it is usually explained by suggesting that since federalism is also about a mindset, it does not evolve overnight, but unfolds gradually in a propitious environment. Here is a conceptual point: federalism is not merely a structure of governance in which the units are treated uniformly, but also a socio-psychological choice recognizing the units as equal partners for a common cause. Furthermore, what is important to remember is the fact that the mere parachuting of ideas will be futile unless they are upheld and nurtured in a context as the most appropriate system capable of creating and also sustaining a collectivity. The story of how federalism grew in India is illustrative here: the British government introduced federalism step-by-step strategically to defuse the nationalist onslaught; since it was also a design to devolve power to the Indian allies, federalism became an effective tool to project the colonial rule in a different fashion. So, federalism in India evolved as a mechanism of devolution of power which the British authority introduced in India during the course of its rule. The 1935 Government of India Act was the culmination of a process which had its ideological root in various other acts, supplemented by ideas in its support. For the nationalists who were involved in the framing of the 1950 Constitution, it appears to be an effective device to cement a political bond among the constituent provinces around a common template. Out of the debates in the Constituent Assembly, there had emerged a new design of federalism which neither corresponded to any of the existent federal countries nor was entirely different from what the classical theorists of federalism depicted. A unique form, Indian federalism can be said to have created a new genre of thinking in this regard. An analysis of Article 370, which the chapter strives to do, reveals how the 1950 Constitution constitutionalizes a peculiar mode of federalization to address equally peculiar political concerns that needed immediate attention due to the vivisection of the country. A new politico-ideological template was produced and constitutionally endorsed perhaps to take care of the contingent circumstances. With constitutional support, Article 370 recognized a semi-independent status to

Jammu and Kashmir, one of twenty-nine constituent units of federal India which the framers had accepted as they seem to have run out of choice.

The aim of this chapter is two-fold: first, since Article 370 shall be discussed within the wider framework of Indian federalism, what is thus needed is to lay out India's federal structure with reference to the constitutional provisions and also the judicial pronouncements redefining its character. Secondly, critical here is Article 370. The chapter is devoted to a detailed analysis of this article to demonstrate how the claim of a constituent Indian province is justified despite being a part of federal India. Primarily, the objective here is to understand and also conceptualize India's federalism as a constitutional design which continues to evolve in response to newer social, economic and political priorities. If this be so, India's constitutional identity is also being regularly reinvented. So, a critical scrutiny of India's federalism shall also help us comprehend the constantly changing texture of India's constitutional identity.

Federalism

India is a uniquely textured federal polity for a variety of reasons. The shape in which the Indian Constitution finally emerged has thus been a unique creation with a number of novel features underlining its concern for addressing the pressing issues and challenges facing the country. In other words, the final shape of the provisions on federalism emerged to be typically Indian with no parallel in any of the Constitutions in the world. Structurally, the Constitution definitely created a federal polity in the country, but the provisions were also made to create such a strong central government that the labelling of such a system as a federation would have appeared improper. The Constitution, therefore, branded India as a 'Union of States', instead of a federation, the technicality of which was explained by Ambedkar. He said that the Drafting Committee wanted to make it clear that though India was to be federation, the federation was not the result of an agreement by the states to join in a federation, and that the federation not being the result of an agreement, no state has the right to secede from it. The federation is a Union because it is indestructible. Moreover, operationally, as he explained, it would be a federal Constitution inasmuch as it establishes what may be called a dual polity. It will consist of the union at the centre and the states at the periphery, each endowed with sovereign powers to be exercised in the field assigned to them, respectively, by the Constitution. Still, the Constitution avoided the 'tight mold of federalism' in which the American Constitution was cast, so that it could become 'both unitary as well as federal according to the requirements of time and circumstances'. Thus, the Indian Constitution contained a number of asymmetrical provisions which otherwise are not considered desirable for a classical federal system. Prominent among them is the apparent mismatch between Article 1 of the Constitution of India and the actual unfolding of the spirit of federalism in governance.

Article 1 endorses the view that India, that is Bharat, is a union of states which clearly privileges the union over the states. The latter remain appendages to the union, at least, as per Article 1. This is strictly a legalistic interpretation which is, however, untenable if Article 1 is seen in conjunction with Seventh Schedule enumerating three lists that demarcated domains for the union and constituent provinces. Hence, India's Supreme Court stated, in a 1962 pronouncement, that

> the evolution of a federal or a quasi-federal structure necessarily involved in the context of the conditions then prevailing, a distribution of powers and a basic part of our Constitution relates to that distribution with the three legislative lists in the Seventh Schedule.[1]

There are two important points which this judgement endorses: federalism needs to be understood in a specific context; no rigid formulation will therefore work. Equally important is the idea that the Constitution of India, by categorically demarcating powers in three legislative lists, also lays out and justifies the foundation of a federal system. This further confirms that India's federalism defies the universal pattern that had emerged in the constitutional experiences elsewhere.

Perspective

Historically federations have been created in two ways. The first was the coming together of independent units in such a way that each unit surrendered its sovereign status to form a common union. The second path was the opening up of unitary systems, usually old imperial systems, in order to provide representation to territorially based social groups in an effort to create a consensual state system. The first path led to the creation of classical federations such as the US, Australia and Canada, while the latter could be said to include a wide variety stretching from the former Soviet Union to many post-war federations which emerged after decolonization.

There seems to be an inverse relationship between the constitutional arrangement propounding federal structure and its historical evolution. The US and Indian federal system shall be illustrative here. In the case of the former, despite the founding fathers' deliberate attempts to make a weak centre with strong states, the constitutional evolution led to the growth of a strong centre and consequently weak states. At present, the US federal government is perhaps the most powerful although the Constitution makers intended otherwise. The Indian situation follows the pattern, but in a different direction: after the British left, the Indian National Congress took over the administration which was British in tune and spirit. So the strong centre which was created and favoured by the British as an instrument for imperial control was allowed to stay with marginal changes. The government of independent India defended the strong centre in order to maintain national integrity, which was being threatened by fissiparous tendencies in the nascent free state.[2] Justification of a strong state seems logical and therefore understandable. The situation remained unchanged till Jawaharlal Nehru presided over India's destiny as its first premier. There were no dissidents and the centre-state relations were generally amicable. Four reasons are usually offered for such an amicable partnership: (a) the role of the Congress Party which won freedom in institutionalizing state-society relationship; (b) the national elite enjoyed high legitimacy largely because of their contribution to the freedom struggle; (c) despite elitist predisposition, there was moderation in the use of state power drawn partly out of self-confidence of those in power, partly out of relative trust and mutuality and partly out of the feudal bent of mind of the rulers and (d) the state was largely utilized as an instrument of social change. Since 1964, however, there were occasions when the constituent states openly challenged the centre. The process was articulated in 1967 when non-Congress government assumed power in different states which strengthened regional voice vis-à-vis the hegemony of the centre which continued to be ruled by the Congress Party till the capture of power by the Janata Party in 1977. Following the 1998 national elections, the situation has become more complex now with the dominant role of different regional parties in the formation and continuity of the Bharatiya Janata Party (BJP)-led coalition at the centre. With the demand for regional autonomy, the Union government of India is constantly being challenged and forced to succumb to pressure. This indicates, *inter alia*, the weakening of the centre and the gradual strengthening of the states[3].

What follows from above is that the Indian states are growing strong gradually and steadily. Not only have they articulated their demands effectively, but they also have on occasions become decisive in the policymaking. Politically, it seems to be a sign of 'adulthood of Indian states' which may create the US confederal-type polity with strong units and a centre as a mere monitoring instrument. The concept of adulthood of states does not endorse 'terrorism' at all to snatch statehood; instead, it is premised on a particular variety of 'political consciousness' favouring a strong and healthy India. There are instances which may be cited to substantiate that attainment of adulthood disrupts national integrity, but a thorough study of these 'disruptive movements' championing regional autonomy may reveal that the outcome would have probably been otherwise had they been dealt with more seriously at the outset. A critical scan of the functioning of the federal system in India reveals that as an organic arrangement reflective of the changing social, economic and political processes, Indian federalism is not, at all, static. There has been a clear shift from a predominantly parliamentary system during the heyday of the Congress system to a considerably federalized system under a multiparty system with coalition governments since 1989.

Evolution of the federal arrangement

As early as 1928, the Indian National Congress unanimously decided for regrouping of provinces 'on a linguistic basis [since] language as a rule corresponds with a special variety of culture of traditions and literature. In a linguistic area all these factors will help in the general progress of the province'. The second equally important consideration

> is the wishes of the majority of the people [because] people living in a particular area feel that they are a unit and desire to develop their culture . . . even though there may be no sufficient historical or cultural justification for their demand. . . . [A third consideration], though not of the same importance, is administrative convenience, which would include the geographical position, the economic resources and the financial stability of the area concerned. But the administrative convenience is often a matter of arrangement and *must as a rule bow to the wishes of the people*. (Emphasis added)[4]

What is striking in this 1928 Report is the fact that the pluralist character of the Indian polity was a significant determinant in devising a constitutional arrangement for the country. The Congress leadership seemed to be appreciative of this principle and thus endorsed regional grouping on the basis of distinct cultural traits, including language. Along with the importance of the regional grouping, the nationalists never lost sight of India's unity as a compact. It was evident when GB Pant, who played a critical role in articulating constitutional provisions for federalism in India, exhorted that

> the Constituent Assembly is resolved to set up a suitable republic for independent India. The recognition of the unity of India forms the cornerstone of this scheme. We do not know what will exactly be the subjects reserved for the Centre, but we know that the integrity and unity of India shall be preserved. The sentiment of unity will not be impaired in any way. That is first fundamental condition, as without it no constitution can be formulated and none can last for a day.[5]

So, the attempt was made to retain the distinctive sociocultural texture of the constituent units within the collective compact, called India. This was the perspective in which the provisions for federalism were conceptualized and drafted by the framers of the 1950 Constitution by being engaged in fierce debates in the Constituent Assembly for little less than three years between 1946 and 1949. There was hardly a doubt; the Assembly was unanimous in its support for transforming independent India into a federal 'union'. For BR Ambedkar, the choice was categorical since

> the draft constitution is a Federal Constitution in as much as it establishes . . . Dual Polity [with] the Union at the centre and the States at the

> periphery, each being assigned with sovereign powers to be exercised in the field assigned to them respectively by the Constitution. The States in our Constitution are in no way dependent upon the Centre for their legislative and executive authority. [T]he Centre and the States are co-equal in this matter. [I]t is therefore wrong to say that the States have been placed under the Centre.[6]

Ambedkar's clear preference for a specific type of federal polity did not match with the provisions of the 1950 Constitution, which heavily tilted in favour of the 1935 Government of India Act.[7] What probably conditioned the choice of those who presided over free India's destiny was a pragmatic consideration of converting India into 'a Union out of the patch work quilt of [British Indian] Provinces and Princely States'[8]. Given the large number of princely states which enjoyed paramountcy during the colonial rule, the task of bringing them under the union was difficult. Moreover, the decision of the Muslim majority provinces of British India to constitute themselves into Pakistan aroused the apprehension in the minds of the nationalist leadership in India that they might have to face further attempts at secession from a future Indian union. As a result of this fear, 'the Gandhian notion of a truly decentralised and federal India did not receive the serious attention in the debate on the Constitution which it otherwise deserved'.[9] However, the very apprehensions that produced a desire for stronger central authority also led to a counter-tendency in the form of demands from several states for greater autonomy. There were also members drawing inspiration from 'the Gandhian tradition for greater decentralization of institutions … down to the district and village level' who pressed hard for greater autonomy of the states as a precaution to the growth of an authoritarian centre.[10]

There is another distinctive feature that clearly separates Indian federation from its counterparts elsewhere. Indian federalism is a distinct case of 'asymmetrical' federalism that characterizes a federation in which some of the units are accorded weightage under the imperative of compelling historical or cultural factors necessitating 'special constitutional recognition'. One comes across four kinds of asymmetries in Indian federation: first, there is universal asymmetry with regard to the constituent provinces because they are represented in Rajya Sabha on the basis of their demographic strength unlike the American system, where each state has two members in the Senate regardless of the strength of population. Second, there are specific asymmetries as regards administration of tribal areas, intra-state regional disparities, law and order situation and fixing the number of seats, as per Article 371 of the Constitution, in states like Maharaṣhtra, Gujarat, Manipur, Assam, Andhra Pradesh, Arunachal Pradesh, Sikkim and Goa. Third, the areas identified as Union Territories, altogether seven in 2006 – enjoy special constitutional status. Finally, there is a stark asymmetry vis-à-vis Jammu and Kashmir, Nagaland and Mizoram. While Article 370 accords 'special status' to Jammu and Kashmir, Article 371 guarantees special privileges to Nagaland and Mizoram.[11]

As the discussion shows, Indian federalism, or for that matter any constitutional arrangement, is contextual and is thus relative to the polity in which it has evolved over a period of time. In the words of TT Krishmachari, federalism 'is not a definite concept; it has not got any stable meaning. It is a concept the definition of which has been changing from time to time'.[12] Hence, it is theoretically misleading and empirically wrong to characterize Indian federalism in simple straight-jacketed formula. As a constitutional format, federalism is constantly reinvented and the governing principles are thus regularly redefined. In recent times, the federalization process has been augmented by the more active role of the new incumbents of federal institutions – the President, the Election Commission and the Supreme Court of India. The President and the Election Commission have become more watchful to ensure that the rules of the game in their restrictive constitutional jurisdiction are respected by the political and administrative authorities.

Federalism in India

According to BR Ambedkar, 'the chief mark of federalism lies in the partition of the legislative and executive authority between the centre and units of the constitution', though the Constitution can be federal or unitary according to the requirements of time and circumstances. Yet, the Centre 'cannot by its own will alter the boundary of that partition. Nor can the judiciary … [because it] cannot assign to one authority powers explicitly granted to another'.[13] Generally speaking, whether a political system is federal is determined by these five criteria which are as follows:

> (a) dual or two sets of government – one at the centre, national or federal and the other at state or provincial levels; (b) written constitution – list of distribution of powers though the residuary powers generally rest with the federal government; (c) supremacy of the constitution; (d) rigidity of the constitution – the constitution can be amended 'by a special majority followed by ratification by at least half of the states', barring 'the basic structure' of the constitution and (e) the authority of the courts as regards the interpretation of the constitutional provisions.

In the light of the above criteria, there was no doubt that the founding fathers preferred federalism in its true spirit and yet what emerged after the deliberations in the Constituent Assembly was a unique form, adapted to the Indian context. As Ambedkar argued, the draft Constitution contained provisions that provide for both federal and unitary forms of government. 'In normal times, it is framed to work as a federal system', stated Ambedkar. But in times of war

> it is so designed as to make it work as though it was a unitary system. Once the President issues a Proclamation which he (sic) is authorized

> to do under the Provisions of Article 275, the whole scene can become transformed and the State becomes a unitary state.[14]

Ambedkar showed extreme caution while defending provisions for federalism. There was no doubt in his minds that Indian federalism was to be adapted to 'the local needs and local circumstances'. But this very diversity, 'when it goes beyond a certain point, is capable of producing chaos'. Hence '[t]he Draft Constitution has', argued Ambedkar, 'sought to forge means and methods whereby India will have Federation and at the same time will have uniformity in all the basic matters which are essential to maintain the unity of the country'. Three important means capable of holding the country together were thus identified: (a) a single judiciary, (b) uniformity in fundamental laws, civil and criminal and (c) a common All India Civil Service to important posts.[15]

As evidence shows, the founding fathers took ample care in creating a constitutional arrangement which is 'federal' in a very specific sense. The system that emerged in India was hardly comparable with any of the prevalent federations. What was critical in their vision was perhaps the fact that federalism is not merely a structural arrangement for distribution and sharing of power between the federal partners, but also a culture sustaining its very spirit. Its emergence and later consolidation in India is slightly paradoxical since it is the product of two conflicting cultures: one representing the national leaders' 'normative' concern for India's multicultural personality, shaped by its unique history and geography and other underlining their concern for unity, security and administrative efficiency. While the former led to the articulation of federalism, as laid down in the 1950 Constitution, the latter resulted in the retention of the very state machinery, which consolidated the colonial rule in India. The net result was the articulation of a semi-hegemonic federal structure that drew largely upon the 1935 Government of India Act. Nonetheless, the federal system that supported unwarranted centralization of power appeared to be the most suitable alternative for nation building in India. However, the situation radically changed following the articulation of new demands by hitherto peripheral sociopolitical groups. The aim here is to grasp the processes that contributed to this significant metamorphosis of India's federal system in the context of constantly changing domestic and global situation.

Parliamentary federalism and the basic structure of the constitution

Parliamentary federalism is a core value of the Constitution of India in two significant ways: *first*, by providing a definitive format in which governance is to be articulated, parliamentary federalism lays and sustains India's politico-administrative foundation. *Second*, despite apparent incompatibility of parliamentary form of governance with federalism, it emerged as perhaps the best possible structure in the context of the political situation arising out of the partition of the country and the integration of the states. Do they constitute 'the basic structure' of the Constitution? Given their politico-institutional importance is sustaining democratic structure in India, there is no doubt that they are critical to Indian polity. Constitutionally significant, ideologically critical and politically meaningful, these values seem to have grown stronger presumably because of India's pluralist character. In this sense, despite the imperial origin because parliamentary federalism was conceptualized (though in a different form) in the 1935 Government of India Act, the combination of two apparently contradictory constitutional tendencies acquired salience largely because of the peculiar social texture of Indian polity in which this constitutional format struck organic roots.

The Basic Structure debate that began with the 1973 Kehsavananda Bharati case redefined the constitutional discourse in India. In this oft-quoted case, the Supreme Court of India restricted the parliamentary domain with the argument that parliamentary power cannot be so exercised as 'to alter or destroy the basic structure of the Constitution'. This is a significant judgement in two respects: *first*, it reiterates the caution of the founding fathers that parliament in India is not as supreme as it is in the Westminster system of governance except during emergency. *Second*, the critical principles that hold the Constitution in its true spirit can never be sacrificed in any circumstances. Parliamentary supremacy is appreciated within the political format of parliamentary democracy which upholds 'federalism' as 'a life wire' of Indian polity. One can tinker with these foundational values of the Constitution only at the cost of its basic structure.

There is a serious problem of interpretation of what constitutes the basic structure because the Supreme Court itself stressed that 'the claim of any particular feature of the Constitution to be a basic feature would be determined by the Court in each case that comes before it'.[16] So, these basic features are not 'finite' although the Court identifies a number of features – like the supremacy of the Constitution, parliamentary democracy, the principle of separation of powers, the independence of judiciary and the limited amending powers of parliament – as basic features. The doctrine therefore amounts that there are some features in the Constitution that are more 'basic' or 'fundamental' than others. While the Constitution can be amended by following the stipulated procedures, these features which are basic to the Constitution can never be altered presumably because amendment to these radically alter the nature of the Constitution.

Two important points that emerge out of the discussion on the basic structure need to be addressed. First, the debate seeks to strike a balance between judiciary and parliament by redefining parliamentary supremacy as 'relative' to the circumstances. In no circumstances, the parliament is empowered to challenge the foundational values, since they are so integral to the evolution of India as a parliamentary democracy. Second, by seeking to provide a contextual interpretation of the basic structure, the apex court draws our attention to the organic nature of the Constitution that evolves in conjunction with the rapidly changing socio-economic and political circumstances. Conceptually, the idea of basic structure is not sacrosanct, but is not amenable to change if circumstances so require. An example will suffice here. Federalism that the founding fathers preferred was articulated as a scheme of distribution of power between two layers of government – one at the union level and other at the provincial levels. The 73rd and 74th Amendment Acts in fact altered the basic structure of the Constitution by introducing 'a third tier' besides the union and states and were therefore 'violative' of the basic structure. The introduction of a third tier is a striking distortion in the prevalent two-tier structure of governance because this change is 'in the direction of greater federalism' that what exists. However, these amendments were appreciated for having translated the notion of 'democratic decentralization' into practice and are thus reflective of the organic nature of the Constitution. Similarly, the introduction of the terms, like socialism and secularism (though the former considerably lost its salience with the adoption of the 1991 New Economic Policy) did not disrupt the basic structure simply because these changes evidently commanded 'general assent'. What is thus critical is the fact that the values or the constitutional structure that is considered 'basic' or 'fundamental' is not entirely sacrosanct, but is amenable to change if it is absolutely necessary to keep pace with the social, political and economic milieu.[17] Although basic structure doctrine creates a contentious space, it nonetheless has struck 'a balance, if an uneasy one, … between the responsibilities of parliament and the Supreme Court for protection of integrity of the seamless web [of constitutional democracy in India]'.[18]

Parliamentary federalism is not merely a constitutional structure, but also provides an ideological foundation to cement a bond among Indian constituent states which are diverse on various counts. In this sense, it is basic to the politico-constitutional structure that evolved in India since the Constitution was adopted in 1950. Especially in the coalition era, parliamentary democracy in India is redefined with the growing federalization that began with the decimation of Congress rule in various states in the 1967 state assembly election. The scene was completely different during the heydays of the 'Congress system' when the Congress Party controlled all the state governments and also the union. What was symptomatic in 1967 seems to be a well-entrenched pattern now with the clear political ascendance of the constituent provinces, governed mainly by parties with regional roots. The leading member of either of the major coalitions at the pan-Indian level can afford to ignore them only at their political peril. In India's changed political texture, parliamentary federalism seems to be a creative politico-constitutional response to a situation that is hardly comparable. Because of its historical roots, parliamentary federalism also provides perhaps the only mechanism that reconciles the seemingly contradictory tendencies between parliamentary and federal forms of government.

The 1994 SR Bommai judgement[19]

No discussion on India's federalism is complete without being engaged with the 1994 SR Bommai judgement of the Supreme Court of India. Opposing the Presidential proclamation, under Article 356 of the Constitution of India, for dismissal of state governments in Meghalaya, Nagaland, Madhya Pradesh, Rajasthan, Himachal Pradesh and Karnataka, the former Karnataka chief minister, SR Bommai challenged the validity of the decision, since it was contrary to the federal spirit of the Constitution of India. Two issues seem to have bothered the division bench of nine judges who, while deciding the justiciability of the dismissal, drew our attention to the increasing importance of the provinces in the federal compact: on the one hand, the division bench paid attention to the constitutionality of the proclamation which also led the apex court to assess its justiciability in the context of India's changing political texture in which states no longer remained mere appendages to the Union. Critical was the concern that the court had expressed in the light of the presidential decision to impose central rule by dismissing the duly elected state governments due to their purported failure to sustain constitutional governance. The basic concern was to make sure that the proclamation was meant to serve politico-ideological ends or constitutionally justiciable following the due process.

Legally speaking, the task of the court was made easier with the acceptance of the idea that federalism is part of the basic structure of the Constitution though the points, raised by the division bench, are useful to firmly establish the argument that federalism, being integral to the basic structure, cannot be fiddled with so easily. By drawing upon the conceptualization that AV Dicey had evolved in the Law of the Constitution, the bench addressed the concern by stating that

> Federalism is, therefore, a concept which unites separate States into a Union without sacrificing their own fundamental political integrity. Separate States, therefore, desire to unite so that all the member-States may share in formulation of the basic policies applicable to all and participate in the execution of decisions made in pursuance of such basic policies. Thus the essence of a federation is the existence of the Union and the States and the distribution of powers between them. Federalism, therefore, essentially implies demarcation of powers in a federal compact.[20]

India is a federal compact, argued the bench, in which the Union and the States are partners sharing identical concerns for the well-being of the polity. There is hardly a space for confrontation since 'the distribution of the legislative and executive power within limits and coordinate authority of different organs are delineated in the organic law of the land, namely the Constitution itself'.[21] With the demarcation of authority between the Union and the States, the Constitution created a healthy constitutional arrangement to govern healthy federal balances. Being aware of the peculiarities of India's federalism that evolved in a parliamentary form of governance in India, the bench also underlined that

> the organic federalism designed by the founding Fathers is to suit the parliamentary form of Government to suit the Indian conditions with the objective of promoting mutuality and common purpose rendering social, economic and political justice, equality of status and opportunity; dignity of person to all its citizens transcending regional, religious, sectional or linguistic barriers as complementary units in working the Constitution without confrontation.[22]

Supportive of hybridization of government, the apex court justified federalism as an appropriate mechanism to realize the constitutional goals that the Preamble enumerates. It was therefore forcefully argued to avoid confusion by saying that

> institutional mechanism aimed to escape friction to promote harmony, to set constitutional culture on firm foothold for successful functioning of the democratic institutions, to bring about matching political culture adjustment and distribution of the roles in the operational mechanism are necessary for national integration and transformation of stagnant social order into vibrant egalitarian social order with change and continuity economically, socially and culturally.[23]

In strict constitutional terms, there is hardly a threat to the federal compact because the founding Fathers, as the bench underlined, took ample care to create a balanced structure of governance for the fulfilment of the politico-ideological aims that they so assiduously nurtured during their confrontation with the alien rule. Nonetheless, there are provisions in the Constitution that privileged the Union over the States, which is clearly an impediment towards establishing federalism in its true spirit and form. For instance, the constitutional design of lodging

> in Parliament the residuary legislative powers, and in the Central Government the executive power of appointing certain constitutional functionaries including High Court and Supreme Court Judges and issuing appropriate directions to the State Governments and even displacing the State Legislatures and the Governments in emergency situations.[24]

While being aware that these features are likely to weaken the federal edifice of the Constitution, the bench defended its stance by suggesting that

> the extent of federalism ... is largely watered down [in India] by the needs of progress and development of a country which has to be nationally integrated, politically and economically coordinated, and socially,

> intellectually and spiritually uplifted, [and hence] ... the States cannot stand in the way of legitimate and comprehensively planned development of a country in the manner directed by the Central Government.[25]

That India's federalism is peculiar was, according to the apex court, contingent on the historical circumstances in which it had evolved. Being an example of pragmatic federalism, Indian federal structure cannot be conceptualized in the format of classical federalism of the American type. One has to take into account the historical antecedents and also the immediate sociopolitical instability following the 1947 partition of the country to meaningfully comprehend the so-called deviant features of India's federalism. The bench thus stated that 'federalism in the Indian Constitution is not a matter of administrative convenience, but one of principled outcome of our own historical process and a recognition of the ground realities'.[26] Be whatever it is, the bench however affirmed that the presidential proclamation for imposing emergency by dismissing the elected governments could not escape judicial scrutiny because

> federal principle, [along with] social pluralism and pluralist democracy which [forms] the basic structure of our Constitution [demands] that the judicial review of the Proclamation, issued under Article 356 (1) is not only an imperative necessity but is a stringent duty and the exercise of power under the said provision is confined strictly for the purpose and to the circumstances mentioned therein and for none also.[27]

Furthermore, seeking to scrutinize 'circumspectly the material on the basis of which the [presidential] power is exercised',[28] the bench reinforces the argument that under no circumstances, the federal structure cannot be allowed to be fiddled for partisan political gain. Dismissing the proclamation as *ultra vires* to the Constitution, the bench further affirmed that being integral to the basic structure, federal rights of the States could never be violated till all options were exhausted. Here, the judges drew on what BR Ambedkar suggested while defending the Emergency provisions. According to Ambedkar, the President, before suspending the administration of a province, was required to 'issue a mere warning to a province that has erred [and] ... things were not happening in the way in which they were intended to happen in the Constitution'.[29] This was the first step to be followed by holding election to the legislative assembly to provide an opportunity 'to the people of the province to settle matters by themselves'.[30] Once these endeavours yielded no results, the President was authorized to resort to powers, enshrined in Article 356. In the said case, the proclamation for dismissal was issued without exhausting the options that received the approval of the founding fathers. In view of the clear violation of the spirit of the Constitution, the presidential endorsement of the dismissal of the elected state governments was put to stringent judicial enquiry, which was justiciable in the light of the deliberate avoidance of the Union government to act as per the constitutional direction.

The 1994 SR Bommai judgement will go down the history as a landmark event in history of constitutionalism in India for three important reasons. First, by reiterating that the exercise of Emergency powers is permissible once the other constitutionally available options are exhausted. This has serious implications: on the one hand, it has now been made amply clear that the President does not have absolute power, but enjoys conditional power, which can be exercised if the situation so warrants. Second, the verdict emphasizes the limitations within which Article 356 needs to work. As per the apex court, the presidential power is to be exercised sparingly since it is the last resort in cases where it is manifest that there is a complete breakdown of the constitutional machinery in the concerned state. Third, by suggesting that the presidential proclamation is subject to judicial review, the court created a space for itself which is inviolable in this case that it concerned a basic structure of the Constitution of India. Under no circumstances, federal principles cannot be bypassed or ignored because they are integral to India as a federal compact, the court held. Hence, the 1994 SR Bommai judgement is a path-breaking decision in India's constitutional history.

India's federalism: a contextual response

What has emerged in India during the course of more than half a century does not correspond with any of the classical models of government. Indian political structure is neither strictly unitary nor purely federal; it is a form in which the elements of both are traced and evident. Distinct from the classical types for obvious reasons, Indian political system offers a unique model drawing upon both the British tradition of parliamentary sovereignty and the American federal legacy in which regions seem to be prior to the Centre. This is essentially a hybrid system of governance that has emerged due to a peculiar unfolding of sociopolitical processes in the aftermath of India's rise as a nation state. Parliamentary federalism is therefore not merely a structural device for distribution of powers between different layers of government, but also an articulation of a basic philosophy accommodating diverse regional interests in the name of a nation.

As a hybrid political system, India is neither fully parliamentary nor federal. The 1950 Constitution has devised an elaborate system of distribution of powers. So, it is federal following the principles, enshrined in the American Constitution. It is not federal because the Constitution has failed to acknowledge the need to make the central institutions of government fully federal through bicameralism. Instead, the Constitution is clearly in favour of 'an obsolescent' Westminster model of parliamentary government that is clearly 'unitary'. The political processes however have led to the gradual, but steady importance of intergovernmental agencies, like the National Development Council (NDC) and Inter-State Council (ISC). Identified as 'federal' agencies, these structures are clearly those with potentials for radically altering the governance format. However, at present, these institutions do not appear to be effective in the context of economic liberalization when there is a clear shift from 'inter-governmental cooperation' to 'inter-jurisdictional competition'. While there are institutions like the NDC or ISC to tackle the former, there is no formally constituted agency except the ad hoc conferences of chief ministers and the interstate Water Commission to grapple with the emerging tensions arising out of centre-state relations. New circumstances have emerged in which conventional conceptualizations do not appear to be relevant, for obvious reasons. In the light of the increasingly competitive patterns of federal relations, what is now needed is to devise contextual models which are not tuned to create a federal compact as inclusive enough to defend federal India and exclusive enough to scuttle the threat of the small states of being engulfed by the bigger ones.

India's political system is in constant flux. Parliamentary federalism is a unique form of governance that is context-driven. Adapting the colonial model of centralized governance designed to sustain 'a revenue-based-law-and-order federal structure',[31] independent India favoured a powerful centralized bureaucracy as critical for securing nation's unity and planned development. Yet, parliament is neither supreme nor sovereign as in the Westminster model of parliamentary democracy. The adoption of the federal principles seems to have 'tempered the unlimited power of Parliament'.[32] Yet, the ruling party, if it musters a stable majority in Parliament, can become an absolute authority under specific circumstances where the legislature will simply act as a ratifying agency. Supported by three major institutions – the Finance Commission, the Planning Commission and the All India Services – the Central Government may substantially alter the federal balance in its favour. Furthermore, under the changed circumstances of liberalization, the constitutionally guaranteed rights of the constituent States have been significantly eroded. One area that has created consternation among the member states of the Union is whether the Centre is constitutionally authorized to sign treaties with other countries without consulting the affected States.[33] This has become relevant at a time when trade and other international agencies – like those under the Uruguay Round of the General Agreement on Tariffs and Trade (GATT) – are being created in ways that national barriers and sovereignty of the nation state are being assailed. The new GATT is a special instance in question because it is not just concerned with trade in goods, but also services (General Agreement on Trade and Services), investment (Trade Related Investment Measures), intellectual property (Trade Related Intellectual Property rights) and various other aspects of the economy. Apprehending that GATT is likely to curb their power that has been guaranteed by the Constitution, three States, Tamil Nadu, Rajasthan and Orissa, have filed suits in the Supreme Court in 1994 against the Union of India 'raising a federal dispute that the new GATT affects their exclusive powers given to them by the Constitution and forces them to share power with the Union in ways that violate the basic structure of the Constitution'.[34] Though the Court verdict is not yet available, the step is indicative of a new trend where the provinces no longer remain the 'silent' observers. Whatever one may think of the desirability of GATT, a powerful argument can be made that it effectively redefines the Centre-State relations in context of mutual cooperation between the Centre and States vis-à-vis the imposed restrictions by the international agencies. This is one dimension of federalism in its new form. The other dimension is about the changing nature of Centre-State relations in the changed environment of the 1990s. For instance, the state governments are not dismissed the way they were in the 1970s and 1980s, but they have declined in a situation where the Centre has surreptitiously taken so many of states' powers. Whatever one may think of the desirability of India's signing the World Trade Organization (WTO), there is no doubt that it has tilted the balance in favour of the Union government because the Centre is authorized to endorse an economic treaty that affects things on the state list (taxation, agriculture) without serious consultation of the States. Nonetheless, the fact that in many cases, international organizations deal with state governments directly – at times bypassing the Union government – is indicative of the rising importance of states in federal India. A network with the global capital has thus contributed to the consolidation of 'a federal market economy' fast-replacing 'the Nehruvian centralized command economy in the country's economic imagination and practice'.[35] It is not therefore surprising that the World Bank negotiated separate structural adjustment packages with Andhra Pradesh, Karnataka and UP since 1998. The World Bank also recognized that 'a reorientation of its strategy' was necessary in view of the changing texture of federalism in India. Hence, it declared, '[w]hile continuing to support nation-wide programs in health and education, the Bank has reoriented its strategy to focus on reforming States'.[36] At an uncritical level, this was welcome and the World Bank support was well-appreciated. The World Bank showcase of Andhra Pradesh with its glitter of information technology-based industries was hailed as 'the brightest star' in skyline of 'shining India' campaign of the erstwhile National Democratic Alliance (NDA) government. There were constant reports in the media of the several suicides of indebted farmers, but the market-friendly policies of inviting foreign investment continued. With the electoral defeat of the incumbent state government, it became apparent that 'investment without a human face' might not be politically expedient. And a government, argues Amit Bhaduri, 'whose eyes and ears are turned to the market, fails to see the poor, and hear their voice' may not succeed in a situation where politics is constantly redefined.

Federalism is thus no longer a constitutional format of distribution of power, but a process that is being constantly reinvented in view of the rapidly changing social-economic and political circumstances in which it is rooted. The growing assertiveness of major political institutions holding the federal balance, such as the Supreme Court, the President and the Election

Commission, has radically altered the centre of gravity. In the famous 1994 Bommai judgement, the Supreme Court quashed the decision of the Union government to impose president's rule in Karnataka under Article 356 by underlining that

> [d]emocracy and federalism are essential features of the Constitution and are part of its basic structure. … States have an independent existence and they have as important role to play in the political, social, educational and cultural life of the people as the Union. They are neither satellites nor agents of the Centre.[37]

The unanimous judgement by the nine-judge constitutional bench held that any proclamation under Article 356 is subject to judicial review. The judgement further endorsed that Article 74(2) does not bar the court from summoning the material that guides the cabinet in deciding in favour of imposition of president's rule in a state. This path-breaking ruling radically altered the centre-state relations by 'the federal compact a new institutional force'.[38]

There is one final point concerning the gradually changing nature of the structure of governance, as it has emerged in India retaining the 'basic' structure of the 1950 Constitution. As a hybrid political system, India is neither fully parliamentary nor federal. The 1950 Constitution has devised an elaborate system of distribution of powers. So, it is federal following the principles, enshrined in the American Constitution. It is not federal because the Constitution has failed to acknowledge the need to make the central institutions of government fully federal through bicameralism.[39] Instead, the Constitution is clearly in favour of 'an obsolescent' Westminster model of parliamentary government that is clearly 'unitary'. Yet, the script of Indian federalism is being constantly rewritten, given the changing nature of its context. For instance, the radical departure from the established federal arrangement happens to be the recent local government amendments of 1992, which require the states to devolve power and resources permanently to the control of three-tier local *panchayats* from grass roots to district levels. Furthermore, the political processes however have led to the gradual but steady importance of intergovernmental agencies, like the NDC and ISC. Identified as 'federal' agencies, these structures are clearly those with potentials for radically altering the governance format.[40] However, at present, these institutions do not appear to be effective in the context of economic liberalization when there is a clear shift from 'inter-governmental cooperation' to 'inter-jurisdictional competition'. While there are institutions like the NDC or ISC to tackle the former, there is no formally constituted agency except the ad hoc conferences of chief ministers and the interstate Water Commission to grapple with the emerging tensions arising out of centre-state relations. In the light of the increasingly competitive patterns of federal relations, this absence creates 'a problem for the horizontal integration of the states in India'.[41]

There is no doubt that India's politico-constitutional structure has undergone tremendous changes to adapt to changing circumstances. Parliament continues to remain, at least constitutionally, supreme though the constituent states have become more powerful than before. Under the changed circumstances, what is evident is a clear shift of emphasis from the Westminster to federal traditions, more so, in the era of coalition politics when no single political party has an absolute majority in Parliament. For practical purposes, the scheme, the framers had adopted to bring together diverse Indian states within a single authority, was what is known as 'executive federalism' – a structure of division of powers between different layers of governmental authorities following a clearly defined guidelines in the form of 'Union', 'State' and 'Concurrent' lists in the Seventh Schedule of the Constitution of India. Due to compulsions of circumstances arising out of coalition politics, the constituent States do not remain mere instruments of the Union; their importance is increasingly being felt in what was earlier known as 'the exclusive' domain of the Centre. Although India has an executive-dominated parliamentary system, backed by a powerful all-India services dominating the over-centralized governance, a process seems to have begun towards 'legislative federalism' in which the upper chamber representing the units of the federal government is as powerful as the lower chamber. Drawn upon the American federalism where the Senate holds substantial power in conjunction with the House of Representatives, legislative federalism is an arrangement, based on an equal and effective representation of the regions. The decisions, taken at the union level, appear to be both democratic and representative, given the role of both the chambers in their articulation. In other words, legislative federalism in its proper manifestation guarantees the importance of both the chambers in the decision-making process that no longer remains 'exclusive' territory of the Lower House for its definite representative character. Not only will the upper chamber be an effective forum for the regions its role in the legislative process will also be significant and substantial. If properly constituted, it could be an institution that represented the regions as such, counterbalancing the principle of representation by population on which the Lower House is based. It will also be a real break with the past since India's politico-constitutional structure draws upon the Westminster model with a strong centre associated with unitary government.

Whether 'bicameralism' with a reconstituted Rajya Sabha enjoying equal authority with the Lok Sabha would be desirable is debatable. If the political climate undermines the spirit of coalition, it would increase governmental impotence because what is likely to govern the decisions of the parliamentarians is a design to stall the motions that may not have been inspired out of solicitude for State's rights. So, the changed composition of Rajya Sabha may not be a politically appropriate device to creatively fashion the federal balance in India, though there have been occasions when the Rajya Sabha has been tough with the Lower House. Its partisanship was, for instance, demonstrated during the brief Janata Party interlude (1977–80) when the

Congress-dominated Rajya Sabha thwarted a government-initiated constitutional amendment by refusing to endorse the move for which the support of two-thirds of house was required. The divide between the two houses has become more prominent of late. The Congress majority in the Rajya Sabha appears to have pre-empted several attempts to adopt legislations to fulfil the government's agenda, while in the days before 1967, the Rajya Sabha hardly played a significant role except to corroborate the views expressed in the lower house. Following the installation of non-Congress governments in various states since 1967, the upper chamber seems to have acquired a definite, if not completely new role in the governing processes.[42] The rejection of the Prevention of Terrorism Ordinance (POTO) in early 2002 is an example showing that the Rajya Sabha had asserted its independence by rejecting the Ordinance, already endorsed by the Lower House. In terms of its numerical strength, the upper chamber is not simply equipped to stall the acceptance of any bill when the Lok Sabha has adequate numbers to push whatever decisions it adopts. In the case of POTO, the ruling coalition openly challenged the Rajya Sabha that turned down the legislation, already approved by the directly elected representatives.

Parliamentary federalism is a unique hybrid system of governance in which the apparently contradictory tendencies are sought to be managed. What has emerged in India during the course of more than half a century does not correspond with any of the classical models of government. Indian political structure is neither strictly unitary nor purely federal; it is a form in which the elements of both are traced and evident. The fate of federalism in India is quite mixed. Federalism was eroded in the 1970s and 1980s and the imperatives of party politics seem to have strengthened it during the 1990s. Even during the heyday of the Congress rule during the single party dominance phase (1947–66), no state has ever been held responsible for 'fiscal' indiscipline. Indeed, the constitutional provision for declaring financial emergencies in states has never been used since independence despite appalling financial conditions in some states. What it means is that even during the heyday of 'centralization', the Centre was not able to exercise leverage over the States as much as we seem to think though the Centre intervened to change Chief Ministers and dismiss governments, which is certainly a significant dimension of centralization. Distinct from the classical types for obvious reasons, federalism in India thus evolves as a unique model drawing upon both the British tradition of parliamentary sovereignty and the American federal legacy in which regions seem to be prior to the Centre. This is essentially a hybrid system of governance that has emerged due to a peculiar unfolding of sociopolitical processes in the aftermath of India's rise as a nation state. Parliamentary federalism is therefore not merely a structural device for distribution of powers between different layers of government, but also an articulation of a basic philosophy accommodating diverse regional interests in the name of a nation.

Article 370

The tumultuous circumstances of the emergence of India as an independent nation and the challenges it faced in smooth accession of a number of princely states indeed set the tone of asymmetrical nature of federalism in the country. In this regard, J&K stands out as the classic case, in which it was established that negotiated accession to the Indian union would invariably be advantageous in terms of autonomy and other concessions for the acceding state. Interestingly, such tendencies became apparent during the processes of drafting the Constitution, therefore, asymmetry producing autonomy provisions could become part of the original Constitution itself. Thus, while Article 370 has been placed in the Constitution to grant special status to J&K, Article 371 is stipulated as the umbrella article under which as many subsections may be inserted from time to time as may be required to maintain the unity and integrity of the nation. At the same time, Schedules Fifth and Sixth impart a distinct character to the Constitution as they become the mainstay of the accommodation and protection of ethnic and cultural distinctions of the areas inhabited by numerous tribes in the northeast. In sum, thus, these asymmetries have probably become the saving mechanism through which the vast and varied diversities of the country have been managed, and formidable challenges to the unit and integrity of the nation have been warded off. Though the asymmetrical autonomy arrangements have not been able to resolve all the issues of national integration and peaceful coexistence in the country as problems such as in Kashmir and some parts of northeast still persist, they have indeed provided the most viable mechanism through which federalism in India has come to serve the purposes for which it has been envisaged since the colonial times. Instead of dwelling on each aspect of asymmetries in India's federal structure, this segment focusses on the distinctive nature of Article 370 that was included in the 1950 Constitution to take care of the distinct sociocultural and political interests, if not needs, of Jammu and Kashmir. The arrangement that this constitutional provision provides for the province is clearly concessional since it upholds its semi-independent status, at least legally, in the Indian polity. There were justifiable reasons for this when this provision was deemed to be appropriate. It was perhaps an innovative design, suggested and also approved by the founding fathers, to build a united India in a context of serious political turmoil following the transfer of power in 1947. It is also important to highlight here that Article 370 was 'a temporary provision' as per the Constitution, which perhaps shows that the framers felt that in course of time, the need for special protection for Jammu and Kashmir was to disappear. Their emphatic belief was drawn on their conviction that circumstances would change in independent India leading to the creation of a compact based on the Enlightenment values of benevolence, toleration and empathy. It was, therefore, not difficult for them to endorse Article 306A, which later became Article 370 in the 1950

Constitution of India despite containing conditions supportive of a clearly semi-independent status for Jammu and Kashmir. At one level, the willingness to endorse 'a distinct constitutional status' to a constituent unit in federal India was politically expedient given the exigency of the situation; at another level, the endeavour epitomized political sagacity of the framers who seem to have laid a solid ideological foundation for the young polity by privileging values and principles over narrow, if not partisan, concerns.

Historical antecedents[43]

The Constituent Assembly of India which framed the Constitution of India debated the issue. A perusal of the debate shows that this article was not as intensively debatable as other articles in the proposed Constitution. It was N Gopalaswami Ayyangar of Madras who held the forte against an equally feeble opposition, led by Maulana Hasarat Mohani of United Provinces. Nonetheless, it was an interesting chapter in the Constituent Assembly debates because it enables us to understand (a) how a special status to a state was justified by the dominant section in the Assembly and (b) how a discriminatory provision in India's federal Constitution helps build a strong political opinion in the state for merging with the Union.

While presenting Article 306A, which later became Article 370 in the Constitution of India, Gopalaswami Ayyangar, the minister without portfolio in the interim government, attributed the special nature of the Article to 'the special conditions' that existed in the state. Article 306A was, according to him, 'a discriminatory' constitutional design to enable the state to fully integrate with the Union of India in due course. While elaborating his argument for such a discriminatory constitutional provision, he further argued that 'the discrimination is due to the special conditions in Kashmir. This particular state is not yet ripe for this kind of integration. ... There are various reasons why this is not possible now'.[44] One of the important reasons was linked with the unusual and abnormal conditions in the state 'due to war' which resulted in 'the capture of part of the state by the rebels and enemies'. The other critical factor supportive of special provision for Jammu and Kashmir was India's commitment to the people of the state for

> an opportunity ... to decide for themselves whether they will remain with the Republic or wish to out of it. [The Indian State was] also committed to ascertaining this will of the people by means of plebiscite provided that peaceful and normal conditions are restored and the impartiality of the plebiscite could be guaranteed. [It was also] agreed that the will of the people, through the instrument of a constituent assembly will determine the constitution of the state as well as the sphere of the Union jurisdiction over the State.[45]

According to Ayyangar, the discriminatory status to Jammu and Kashmir is attributed to the difficult circumstances in which the local habitat was placed due to war and rebellion. And also, the state was allowed to go for a plebiscite to decide whether it would integrate with the Union or not; there was also a concession for creating a constituent assembly for the state to frame its own Constitution.

Being entirely politically expedient, the terms and conditions were clearly discriminatory. Interestingly, Ayyangar's defence of a clearly discriminatory Article 306A did not provoke any of the Assembly members to initiate debates except Maulana Hasarat Mohani who raised his voice by questioning the partiality that the Assembly had shown to the Maharaja of Kashmir at the cost of other princely states. 'Why do you make this discrimination about the Ruler [of Jammu & Kashmir]?', asked Maulana Hasarat Mohani who further argued that 'if you grant this concession to the Maharaja of Kashmir you should also withdraw your decision about [the merger of other princely states] with the Union of India'.[46] The special status clause was questioned for being discriminatory; it was unwarranted, as Mohani strongly felt, because it amounted to a serious compromise to India's suzerainty as an independent polity. For him, this concessional provision was thus not justified since no constituent units in federal India had the authority of having either a plebiscite or an independent constituent assembly to frame its own Constitution, especially when the Constituent Assembly was already in the process of making one for the Union.

Mohani had hardly had supporters, and Article 306A which later became Article 370 in the 1950 Constitution was approved without a single dissent. Ayyangar thus concluded that

> the effect of this article is that the Jammu and Kashmir State which is now a part of India will continue to be a part of India, will be a unit of the future Federal Republic of India and the Union Legislature will get jurisdiction to enact laws on matters specified either in the Instrument of Accession or by later addition with the concurrence of the Government of the State. And steps have to be taken for the purpose of convening a Constituent Assembly in due course to frame a constitution for the state.[47]

Justifying that concessions were absolutely 'temporary' since the Assembly agreed to have a plebiscite to ascertain 'the will of the people' and also the formation of a constituent assembly to devise a Constitution for the state. That Article 306A was approved without discussion confirms that the proceedings of the Assembly were state-managed. As the available media sources suggest that when Article 306A was placed for discussion before the Congress Parliamentary Party, it provoked fierce debates and there was hardly a consensus among the members, given the discriminatory nature of Article 306A. Nobody in the meeting could digest the discriminatory treatment that was meted out to the state. Vallabhbhai Patel was reported to have been in accord with the discordant opinion though he hardly spoke since it meant a betrayal to the Congress pledge.[48] Jawaharlal Nehru and

Vallabhbhai Patel persuaded the recalcitrant colleagues by saying that the concessional Article 306A was likely to mobilize global opinion in India's favour in the light of Pakistan's counter claim for the entire Kashmir.

Article 370 thus became integral to the Constitution of India. In the light of the assurances, given in the Assembly, the Article guaranteed that the power of Parliament to make laws for the state shall be limited to

> (i) those matters in the Union List and the Concurrent List, which, in consultation with the Government of the State, are declared by the President to correspond to matters specified in the Instrument of Accession governing the accession of the State to the Dominion of India as the matters with respect to which the Dominion Legislature may make laws for that State; and (ii) such other matters in the said Lists as, with the concurrence of the State, the President may by order specify.

The second part of the Article is a further endorsement of the distinct constitutional status for the state. As it stipulates,

> notwithstanding anything in the foregoing provisions of this article, the President may, by public notification, declare that this article shall cease to be operative or shall be operative only with such exceptions and modifications and from such date as he may specify [p]rovided that the recommendation of the Constituent Assembly … shall be necessary before the President issues such a notification.

Article 370 though titled as 'Temporary Provisions', and included in Para XXI entitled 'Temporary, Transitional and Special Provisions' is a permanent feature of the Constitution of India which embodies the conceptual framework of relationship between the Union of India and Jammu and Kashmir, and also lays down broad features of special status granted to the State. This is constitutionally guaranteed. In a 2015 judgement on reservation in government jobs, the Jammu and Kashmir High Court articulated its response in categorical terms. Very explicit in its articulation, the judgement underlines: (a) the State of Jammu and Kashmir retained limited sovereignty and did not merge with the Dominion of India, like other Princely States, which signed Instrument of Accession with the Union. The state continues to enjoy special status to the extent of limited sovereignty retained by the state. The limited sovereignty or special status guaranteed under Article 370 of the Constitution – only provision of the Constitution that applied to the State *ex-propriovigore* or on its own. Except Article 1, no other provision of the Constitution would be applicable to the State except, by Presidential order in consultation with the State in case the provision is akin to subjects delineated in Instrument of Accession and with concurrence of the State; and (b) it is beyond amendment, repeal or abrogation, inasmuch as Constituent Assembly of the State before its dissolution did not recommend its amendment or repeal. As per Article 370, the President is conferred with power to extend any provision of the Constitution to the State with 'such exceptions and modifications' as may be deemed fit subject to consultation or concurrence with the State government.[49]

As the judicial pronouncement confirms, Article 370 cannot be abrogated. The Division Bench of Justice Hasnain Masoodi and Janak Raj Kotwal categorically states that it is 'beyond amendment, repeal or abrogation' as the mechanism provided under clause 3 of the Article is no longer available with the dissolution of the State Constituent Assembly, which was the only authority, endowed with powers to recommend abrogation or amendment in the Article. For the court, the Article does not seem to be an exception because Kashmir had 'limited sovereignty' when the Kashmiri ruler agreed to sign the Instrument of accession following India's independence from colonialism.

An Article which was accepted because of the exigency of the situation gradually became an integral part of the existence of Jammu and Kashmir as a constituent province of the Union of India with all the special constitutional privileges. With a specific constitutional embargo, the President of India is restrained to act, according to Article 370, without 'consultation' and concurrence of 'the government of the state'. Moreover, the authority of Indian parliament is further curtailed by clause 3 of Article 370, which makes the recommendation of the State Constituent Assembly mandatory in case this Article is sought to be changed or repealed.

Constitutional implications notwithstanding, the effort towards abrogating Article 370 will have serious internal political repercussions with global ramifications since strife in Jammu and Kashmir will create a constituency for those anti-democratic forces which are reportedly drawing sustenance from operators, located in different countries. Furthermore, it may not be politically useful for the NDA government in Delhi to antagonize its alliance partner, People's Democratic Party (PDP) that is ruling the state of Jammu and Kashmir because (a) it will allow the opposition to characterize any move towards that as anti-secular and (b) it is likely to alienate the people in the state, especially in the Kashmir valley who always view any attack on Article 370 as debilitating for their identity. So, any kind of fiddling with the Article may mean playing with fire. Neither the NDA nor the PDP can afford to lose out on this count since both these political outfits had to struggle a lot to be in the saddles of power after a long political hibernation. For those living in Jammu and Kashmir that had suffered terribly due to the consolidation of terrorism-engineered anti-democratic forces, Article 370 is no longer as important an issue as in the past simply because it has become part and parcel of their being. There are important socio-economic issues, like poverty, hunger and unemployment that need immediate attention. An opinion seems to have gained momentum highlighting the fact that involvement in the campaign for abrogation of Article 370 will lead Kashmiris nowhere except fomenting trouble and creating instability in the state.

For the rest of India, the campaign for the abrogation of Article 370 will garner support for the NDA's leading partner, BJP, because of its discriminatory nature while in the Kashmir valley, in particular, it will create a fissure between two coalition partners at the cost of those who are fighting for political stability and consolidation of democratic processes at any cost. By highlighting the constitutional validity of Article 370, the Jammu and Kashmir High Court has raised an issue that cannot be addressed as easily as is construed, given its obvious implications on what the country stands for.

An accommodative design for building (and also consolidating) a collective compact

Article 370 is a source of discontent, if not, serious resentment since it constitutionalizes imbalances, or asymmetries, in India's federal arrangement. It is also a puzzle because Article 370 does not seem to have been grounded on the fundamental principles of federalism; instead, it justifies a constitutional arrangement supportive of a confederal system of government. Whether it is plausible in today's context cannot be decided so easily in view of the specific historical context in which Article 370 was incorporated in the 1950 Constitution of India. There is no doubt that the special treatment that was constitutionally guaranteed for Jammu and Kashmir despite being included in federal India may not appear to be justified in the changed political milieu. An easy option to address this constitutional anomaly is an amendment to the Constitution which, however, does not seem to be plausible given the adverse political implications in the province and elsewhere in the country. A precarious situation has thus emerged in which neither of the options – abrogation of Article 370 or its acceptance – provides an acceptable solution. A careful reading of the debates in the Constituent Assembly also shows that the founding fathers seem to have faced the same dilemma which was evident in their support for making Article 370 a temporary provision; this means that the Article was to be withdrawn if it was needed. As history has shown, it was a hope that dissipated soon due to a peculiar unfolding of socio-economic and political circumstances in the province. In fact, the idea was shelved and Article 370 became an integral part of India's federal arrangement in which the state of Jammu and Kashmir was allowed to retain its semi-independent constitutional identity.

In the constitutional discourse, Article 370 is a new conceptual intervention in the sense that by constitutionalizing the terms and conditions of the accession treaty between India and the erstwhile ruler of this princely state, it contributes to a persuasive argument in favour of autonomy within a federal structure of governance. Here, the argument draws on the principle of accommodation and reconciliation, whereby a federal system is both constructed and consolidated. This further confirms that federalism cannot be understood, let alone conceptualized, merely as 'a constitutional design', but also 'a political arrangement' which is hardly static. This is a significant conceptual formulation in two complementary ways: on the one hand, it endows us with persuasive theoretical inputs to enable us to understand the consolidation of federal practices in a socioculturally diverse polity; it also helps us understand, on the other, the importance of the political will in the shaping of constitutional norms, values and principles in support of an arrangement which is not ordinarily endorsed within the available discursive tools of analysis for federalism. By being deviant from the conventional understanding of federalism as a 'holding together' mechanism, Article 370 is thus a unique constitutional experiment which is academically refreshing, ideologically innovative and politically decisive.

On a surface reading of India's constitutional designs, one may be persuaded to argue that Article 370 stands in contradiction with India's federal polity though an in-depth reading of her constitutional practices reveals that this is not, at all, an aberration, but an obvious offshoot of the processes leading to conceptualizing India's constitutional identity in consonance with the historical context in which such a uniquely textured constitutional design prospered and also nurtured in independent India due to a peculiar unfolding of her socio-economic and political circumstances. The most significant of the aspects happens to be the basic structure doctrine which is not only unique but also an innovative constitutional intervention by the judiciary; it is a design that has in a very creative manner redesigned constitutional identity in circumstances when the threat to the democratic governance does not seem to be imaginary but real!

Concluding observations

A careful analysis of growth and consolidation of India's constitutional polity confirms the claim that the 1950 Constitution is a living organism. Perhaps the most elaborate written Constitution, it is also most adaptive to the rapidly changing socio-economic milieu in which the Constitution is being constantly reinvented within, of course, accepted constitutional parameters that the framers had set out by being devoted to the Enlightenment values. So, there are certain well-defined foundational principles which can never be sacrificed; they can be discarded only to the detriment of the Constitution's fundamental character. At the same time, being organic to the prevalent socio-economic and political circumstances, the Constitution needs to be regularly reinvented; otherwise, it becomes a sterile document of set of rules and regulations. Implicit here are two claims: on the one hand, it reaffirms that changes in the Constitution does not necessarily affect the constitutional identity since they are admissible so long as they remain compatible with the core values. It also implies, on the other, that amendment is a device to adapt the Constitution to the changing environment, which also recognizes the legitimate roles of the executive and legislature in this regard. The final arbiter is, of course, the judiciary. This combined trio thus remains critical in upholding (and, also re-conceptualizing, if needed) constitutional identity by being sensitive of the core values on which it rests and also the newer demands supportive of the former. In other words, since Constitution is a journey, there are ample scopes for the Constitution to refashion within, of course, the fundamental values and ethos in which it is grounded. So, constitutional identity is not, at all, static, but, at the same time, not flexible enough to dilute the core values shaping its nature and also character.

The above discussion is directional in the sense that it helps us understand how the changing nature of India's federalism is not an aberration but complementary to the democratic polity that the founding fathers so assiduously endeavoured to build. As argued above, India's federal compact was neither derivative nor exactly indigenous, but a creative amalgamation of both. The trajectory of federalism also shows that it has metamorphosed as history progresses; at the dawn of India's independence, in view of the contingent circumstances, it was understood more as a constitutional principle which was largely ornamental, given the need of the newly emerged polity for a strong state. There was hardly a demand for state autonomy. The assumption of power by the Indian National Congress that fought for independence at both the union and provincial levels helped build an atmosphere of bonhomie between the national- and state-level leaders. The scene had undergone a sea change once the Congress lost power and non-Congress parties assumed charges at the state level. In the changed scenario, the demand for autonomy gained momentum and the process started for the consolidation of a compact drawing on the true spirit of federalism. As argued above, there were campaigns for more autonomy for the states which received an approbation by the Supreme Court of India in its many pronouncements, including the 1994 SR Bommai judgement. It is now established that the Union government is not authorized to whimsically apply the constitutional provisions to undermine state autonomy for partisan aims. The Bommai verdict is one of those decisions of the apex court that reiterates that the constituent states are an integral part of the federal compact, and hence, their interests need to be protected. Besides highlighting the importance of the provinces, the judgement is also a deterrent to the rise of the Union government as a big brother at the cost of the units; it is also an impediment to the consolidation of tendencies towards 'unhealthy paternalism',[50] which is constitutionally a serious aberration not only because it privileges the centre over the states, but also because it creates an atmosphere of subservience in which the states are expected to be pliant partners. In a clearly worded pronouncement, India's apex court left no ambiguity in conceptualizing federal relations between the union and the states by stating that

> in evolving an integrated [federal compact in India], our Constitution-makers seem to have kept in mind three main considerations: first, in the larger interest of India, there must be free flow of trade, commerce and intercourse, both inter-State and intra-State; second, the regional interest must not be ignored altogether, and third, there must be a power of intervention by the Union in case of crisis to deal with particular problems that may arise in any part of India.[51]

An unambiguous conceptualization of federalism, the above articulation is explicit enough to identify the distinctive features of India's federalism; the founding fathers' aim was to create a compact of cooperative federal units. This is one side of the story; the other side is epitomized by Article 370, which guarantees special privileges for Jammu and Kashmir, one of the twenty-nine Indian provinces. The framers had agreed to bestow privileges to one of the constituent states in the federal union largely due to contingent circumstances. Despite occasional murmurs, it has now been accepted as a fait accompli; perhaps there is no constitutional-legal option within the constitutional framework that the 1950 Constitution sets out though it is not correct to say that Article 370 is sacrosanct because it was a politico-ideological design that was preferred at a particular juncture of history, and there is no guarantee that the same set of political preferences remain valid in the days to come. Changes are welcome to translate the states' aspirational urges. The 1994 SR Bommai judgement is illustrative here. Similarly, the adoption of the Seventy-Third and Seventy-Fourth Amendment Acts (1992) heralded a new genre of thinking in so far as democratization of governance is concerned though the framers were not persuaded to incorporate panchayati raj governance in the justiciable parts of the Constitution. Fundamental here is the point that constitutional arrangements are hardly permanent since they undergo metamorphosis in response to newer challenges and demands. Changes are admissible so long as they do not adversely affect India's constitutional identity or the core politico-ideological values on which the Constitution rests. By drawing our attention to 'the basic feature/structure of the constitution', the 1973 Kesavananda Bharati judgement of the Supreme Court reaffirmed that 'the Constitution is a precious heritage, [and, therefore, neither the executive nor legislature] can destroy its identity'.[52] Those constitutional values which are deemed sufficiently fundamental cannot be fiddled with under any circumstances. So, India being a union of states, as Article 1 characterizes the polity, needs to be conceptualized with reference to the core values which the founding fathers instilled and the judiciary nurtured over time. Here lies the conceptual validity of constitutional identity which not only acts as a determinant of whether a legislative design or an executive feat is tenable, but also reinforces the claim that unless it is protected the principles which informed the 1950 Constitution would cease to be meaningful in no time!

Notes

1 https://indiankanoon.org/doc/304499/, The Supreme Court judgement in the Automobile Transport versus the State of Rajasthan, 1962, accessed on 21 May 2018.

2 India attained freedom in 1947 through a negotiated act of transfer of power. Following the well-entrenched 'two nation theory' of the Muslim League, two independent dominions, India and Pakistan, were created on a principle of 'religious minorities'. There were at least 865 princely states over which the colonial

rulers exercised paramountcy without actually incorporating them into the provinces of the British India. Through negotiation and persuasion, most of the princely states agreed to join the union with a major exception of Junagadh, Bhopal, Jammu and Kashmir and Hyderabad, which were brought under the Indian dominion by military interventions.

3 On the growing importance of states as the epicentre of Indian politics, see Atul Kohli, 'Power and powerlessness: Indian's democracy in a comparative perspective', in Joel Migdal et al. (eds.), *State Power and Social Forces: Domination and Transformation in the Third World*, Cambridge University Press, Cambridge, 1995.

4 *All Parties Conference, 1928* (report of the committee appointed by the conference to determine the principles of the Constitution of India), All India Congress Committee, Allahabad, 1928, pp. 62–63.

5 Govind Ballabh Pant's convocation Address at Allahabad University on 21 December 1946, *Selected Works of Govind Ballabh Pant*, Vol. 11, Oxford University Press, New Delhi, 1998, p. 425.

6 *CAD*, Vol. XI, p. 976.

7 India's federal system presents some peculiarities and adaptations of a well-known form of government. Although politics in India are more regionalized than in any other federal polity reflecting the unrivalled cultural diversity of the country, the system has more unitary features than most federal systems, including the US, Canada and Australia. For details, see Paul Brass, *The Politics of India since Independence*, Cambridge University Press, Cambridge, 1990, pp. 59–63.

8 Mahendra Ved, 'Honouring Sardar Patel: Bismarck of India', *The Times of India*, New Delhi, 22 August 1998.

9 Ravinder Kumar elaborated this point in his 'Securing stability: no cause for constitutional reforms', *The Times of India*, New Delhi, 15 September 1998.

10 Paul Brass, *The Politics of India since Independence*, Cambridge University Press, Cambridge, 1990, p. 63. Underlining the various counter veiling tendencies within what eventually emerged as India's federal system, this argument is a pointer to the future direction of Indian polity following the disintegration of the Congress Party as an umbrella organization.

11 This discussion is drawn on Rekha Saxena and MP Singh, *Indian Politics: Shifts without a Paradigm*, Orient Longman, New Delhi (forthcoming).

12 TT Krishmachari's address to the Constituent Assembly, 25 November 1949, *CAD*, Vol. 12, p. 950.

13 *CAD*, Vol. XII, p. 976.

14 *CAD*, Vol. 7, pp. 34–35.

15 This discussion is drawn on BR Ambedkar's address to the Constituent Assembly on 4 November 1948. *CAD*, Vol. 7, pp. 36–37.

16 Somnath Chatterjee's foreword in Pran Chopra (ed.), *The Supreme Court Versus the Constitution: A Challenge to Federalism*, Sage, New Delhi, 2006, p. 13.

17 This discussion drawn on Ramaswamy R Iyer, 'Some Constitutional Dilemmas', *Economic and Political Weekly*, Vol. XLI, No. 21, 27 June 2006, pp. 2066–2068.

18 Granville Austin, *Working a Democratic Constitution: The Indian Experience*, Oxford University Press, New Delhi, 1999, p. 652.

19 This discussion has partly appeared in my *Indian Constitution: Text, Context and Interpretation*, Sage, New Delhi, 2017, chapter 13 (pp. 214–230).

20 The Supreme Court judgement in the SR Bommai versus Union of India, 1994, judgement delivered on 11 March 1994, available in https://indiankanoon.org/doc/60799/, accessed on 21 May 2018, para 14.

21 ibid., para 169.

22 ibid., para 174.

23 ibid., para 174.

24 ibid., para 56.
25 ibid.
26 The Supreme Court judgement in the SR Bommai versus Union of India, 1994, judgement delivered on 11 March 1994, available in https://indiankanoon.org/doc/60799/, accessed on 21 May 2018, para 276.
27 ibid., para 106.
28 ibid.
29 BR Ambedkar's defence in the Constituent Assembly, 4 August 1949, *Constituent Assembly Debates*, Book No. 4, p. 177 – cited in The Supreme Court judgement in the SR Bommai versus Union of India, 1994, judgement delivered on 11 March 1994, para 106, available in https://indiankanoon.org/doc/60799/, accessed on 21 May 2018.
30 ibid.
31 Rajeev Dhavan and Rekha Saxena, 'Republic of India', in Katy Ke Roy and Cheryl Saunders (eds.), *Legislative, Executive and Judicial Governance in Federal Countries*, MeGill-Queen's University Press, London and Ithaca, 2006, p. 179.
32 LI and SH Rudolphs, *In Pursuit of Lakshmi: The Political Economy of the Indian State*, The University of Chicago Press, Chicago, 1987, p. 105.
33 Under economic liberalization policies, there have been no fundamental changes in the state or central power. The impact on the states of centre's treaty-making power has always been there. Only in the US and Canadian constitutions, there is a constitutional bar on the role of the state vis-à-vis treaty making, while in the Australian constitution, no such embargo is evident.
34 Rajeev Dhawan and Geetanjali Goel, 'Indian federalism and its discontents', in Gert Kueck and others (eds.), *Federalism and Decentralization: Centre-State Relations in India and Germany*, Mudrit, New Delhi, 1998, p. 54.
35 LI and SH Rudolphs, 'The iconization of Chandrababu: sharing of sovereignty in India's federal market economy', *Economic and Political Weekly*, 5 May 2001, p. 1546.
36 The World Bank report entitled 'Bolstering state reform programs for faster growth and poverty reduction in India' – quoted in Aseema Sinha, 'The changing political economy of federalism in India: a historical institutional approach', *India Review*, Vol. 3, No. 1, January 2004, p. 50.
37 The Supreme Court judgement in the SR Bommai versus Union of India, 1994, judgement delivered on 11 March 1994, para 106, available in https://indianka noon.org/doc/60799/, accessed on 21 May 2018.
38 Aseema Sinha, 'The changing political economy of federalism in India: a historical institutional approach', *India Review*, Vol. 3, No. 1, January 2004, p. 32.
39 Rajni Kothari suggests for a Pradesh Sabha to make the second chamber more effective in governance. According to him,

> the central Parliament should consist of a directly elected Lok Sabha and an indirectly elected Pradesh Sabha, to which each state electoral college consisting of elected representatives of the district councils and the state legislature elect an equal number of representatives. Unlike the Rajya Sabha which has become a tame replica of the Lok Sabha, the function of the Pradesh Sabha should be to represent the interests of the lower rungs of the political structure in national deliberation and, at the same time, act as a channel and a training ground for regional cadres in national affairs. A convention should be established that only those who have had experience in district or state bodies should contest the election to the Pradesh Sabha. They would thus bring a fund of experience to bear upon parliamentary deliberations.

Rajni Kothari, *Democratic Polity and Social Change in India: Crisis and Opportunities*, Allied Publishers, Bombay, 1976, p. 83.

40 The forums and agencies that constitute the life line of the process of federalization in India are: (a) inter-governmental agencies, namely NDC, ISC and ministerial- and secretarial-level meetings and (b) federal agencies having implications for States as well. For instance, the Finance Commission, the Planning Commission, a number of independent regulatory authorities in sectors such as electricity, telecommunications, Central vigilance Commission, Central Bureau of Investigation, Central Reserve Police Force, etc., and (c) inter-state conferences of Chief Ministers, either all of them or those from one particular or political persuasion. Apart from these agencies, there is also National Integration Council, created by Jawaharlal Nehru in the wake of the 1962 war with China, which is another inter-governmental device involving also the important personalities from all walks of life apart from those associated with the functioning of the government machinery at both the central and state levels. For a detailed description of these agencies, see Rekha Saxena, 'Role of inter-governmental agencies', *The Hindu*, 29 January 2002.

41 Lawrence Saez, *Federalism without a Centre: The Impact of Political and Economic Reform on India's Federal System*, Sage, New Delhi, 2002, p. 158.

42 The rise of the regional parties in several states has radically altered the composition of the Rajya Sabha. In other words, parties other than the ruling party at the centre are being able to send more representatives to the Rajya Sabha. As a result, ruling parties have invariably fewer members in the upper house than before. There have been occasions when the ruling party has failed to muster the required two-thirds majority in the Rajya Sabha to pass constitutional amendments, as was the case with the Forty-Third and Forty-Fourth constitutional amendments.

43 Part of this discussion is drawn on my *Indian Constitution: Text, Context and Interpretation*, Sage, New Delhi, 2017, chapter 15 (pp. 252–256).

44 N Gopalaswami Ayyangar (Madras), 17 October 1949, *Constituent Assembly Debates*, Book No. 5, p. 424.

45 ibid.

46 Maulana Hasarat Mohani (United Provinces), 17 October 1949, *Constituent Assembly Debates*, Book No. 5, p. 428.

47 N Gopalaswami Ayyangar (Madras), 17 October 1949, *Constituent Assembly Debates*, Book No. 5, p. 427.

48 LK Advani, 'When the Congress Party opposed Article 370', *The Indian Express*, 17 February 1992.

49 http://judis.nic.in/Judis_Jammu/list_new2_Pdf.asp?FileName=1843, Ashok Kumar and Others versus the State of Jammu and Kashmir, 2015, accessed on 30 November 2016.

50 https://indiankanoon.org/doc/161666/, The Supreme Court judgement in the Kerala Education Bill versus unknown, 1958, accessed on 21 May 2018.

51 https://indiankanoon.org/doc/304499/, The Supreme Court judgement in the Automobile Transport versus the State of Rajasthan, 1962, accessed on 21 May 2018.

52 https://indiankanoon.org/doc/257876/, the Supreme Court judgement in the 1973 Kesavananda Bharati versus the State of Kerala, accessed on 21 May 2018.

Part C

Reinforcing constitutional identity

Judicial intervention

Constitutions articulate an ideologically governed voice which means that they draw on deliberately chosen sociophilosophical predispositions. A careful dissection of the functioning of constitutions shall confirm the statement. For instance, a liberal Constitution derives its philosophical sustenance from the philosophy of Enlightenment, whereas for a Marxist Constitution (that evolved in the erstwhile Soviet Union, for instance), it will invariably be Marxism-Leninism (in its most expansive form) that consolidates its philosophical foundation. The core ideas that inform a Constitution are articulated in the design of governance that it seeks to establish; they also help develop a supportive mindset to ensure its existence and continuity. The former is easily understandable while the latter does not seem to be an easy task because the creation of an appropriate mindset is both time-consuming and necessitates the formation of suitable set of institutions in its favour. This is also a complex process. Nonetheless, history abounds with examples demonstrating the dialectical interconnectedness between the Constitution and institutions which are meant to articulate and also translate the constitutional provisions in spirit and texture. There are two interrelated points here: on the one hand, it is argued that the adoption of a Constitution by itself may not be enough to form a Constitution-driven polity; instead, what is required is also to create conditions for generating a fitting mindset for its survival and strength. Furthermore, there is also the point, on the other, about the critical importance of the institutions which are considered to be the beacon of the relevant constitutional values and also the shield in case there are threats and also doubts about their viability. Here comes the immensely significant role of executive, legislature and judiciary and other agencies which are supportive of the Constitution that seem to have created an environment for those values, ethos and ideas which form its kernel. For constitutional identity to strike roots, these institutions and agencies play a formidable role. Drawn on the core values, the executive executes the legislative acts, approved by the legislators while the judiciary by being engaged in post-mortem exercises ascertains whether these acts do conform or otherwise to the foundational politico-ideological priorities of the Constitution. In other words, while the legislature and executive act in tandem, since they are involved in the making and executing laws the judiciary can be said to reinforce (or otherwise) them, provided they are constitutionally justified. In doing so, the court of law seeks to ascertain whether these laws are consistent with the core constitutional values and also their interpretations by the lawmaking, law-executing and law-adjudicating agencies. The task for the judiciary does not seem to be an easy one, since it involves careful understanding and exact (or near-exact) comprehension of values shaping, if not determining, constitutional identity of a Constitution in question. Implicit here are two ideas which are interlinked: on the one hand, the judiciary, by being constitutionally empowered to offer interpretation/reinterpretation of the laws, discharges a great responsibility in defending and also protecting the specific constitutional identity of a Constitution; as a custodian of the Constitution, the judiciary, on the other, also shoulders the responsibility of reinforcing the foundational values without which the Constitution loses its identity. On the whole, this Part is drawn on the argument that constitutional identity needs to be reinforced; otherwise, the widely accepted conceptual claim that it is not merely a description, but is being constantly reworked shall be vacuous.

The aim of this Part is thus to understand and also conceptualize the role of Indian judiciary as a constitutionally guided institution which is meant to uphold India's constitutional identity by being true to the core values on which the 1950 Constitution of India rests. In order to perform its role as a watchdog of India's constitutional democracy as efficiently as it is expected, the judiciary needs to be absolutely independent of control by any of the organs of the government to which the founding fathers paid adequate attention. As history has shown, an independent judiciary is a *sin qua non* in a democratic polity drawing its sustenance from the rule of law. In other words, the Constitution remains a reference point for the judiciary to function as a watchdog of democracy. As is argued above, the Constituent Assembly members took ample care to ascertain independence to judiciary although they were aware that independence in its absolute sense was illusive because it could hardly be immune from the contextual compulsions. What they meant by independence of judiciary was that it was free from executive or legislative control; otherwise, they would be constrained to objectively test the constitutional validity of the decisions, taken by the executive or legislature. This is the crux of the argument in favour of judicial independence which was most eloquently articulated by an eminent jurist, Krishna Iyer J, in his pronouncement in the Union of India versus Sankalchand Himmatlal Sheth case of 1977. According to him,

> in a dynamic democracy, with goals of transformation set by the Constitution, the Judge, committed to uphold the founding faith and fighting creeds of the nation set forth, has to act heedless of executive hubris, socio-economic pressure, and die-hard obscurantism. This occupational heroism, professionally essential, demands the inviolable independence woven around the judiciary by our Constitution.[1]

Independence of judiciary is guaranteed once the judges avoid being influenced. This is easier said than done because judges are also the product of specific socio-economic and political circumstances. Neither constitutional guarantee nor statutory provisions can ever be an effective means because 'the best guarantee of judicial independence is the character of the person holding the office' and hence judicial independence is argued to be 'directly proportional to the value attached by the citizens of the country and the judges to that signal virtue'.[2] Virtues do not fall from heaven; instead, they are nurtured in our worldly existence which confirms the importance of the context in their conceptualization. In the ultimate analysis, judicial independence is thus context-specific and hence it cannot be universally formatted since situation varies from one context to another.

In two interrelated chapters, the Part delves into the issues, in a rather selective way, by reference to selective sets of judicial pronouncements which are critical in sustaining and protecting India's constitutional identity amidst attacks and threats. A perusal of the judgements reveals that while ascertaining the constitutionality of the legislative acts and designs, the judiciary is primarily governed by the foundational ideas, values and ethos of the 1950 Constitution of India and the concomitant constitutional practices. By dwelling on the verdicts threadbare, these two chapters also confirm how India's constitutional identity is being reinvented by being true to the fundamental ideological priorities that the Constitution-makers upheld. As the discussion follows, Chapter 5 dwells on how the concern for retaining the fundamental characters of the 1950 Constitution led to the conceptualization of the Basic Structure Doctrine, while Chapter 6, by offering an analytical account of selective judgements, recently delivered by the courts, reconfirms the contention that India's constitutional identity of being a constitutional democracy reigns supreme despite challenges and threats.

5 Challenges to Constitutional identity

The doctrine of basic structure of the Constitution*

Constitutional identity is hardly static since it is constantly being refashioned in the light of newer social issues and demands. The judiciary is certainly a powerful instrument in articulating the ideational transformations reflective of changes in the public mood. The purpose here is to assert that a Constitution survives, since it is accommodative of inputs which are critical for the continuity of the system of governance that it upholds. Implicit here is an assumption suggesting that a Constitution is both sensitive to the foundational politico-ideological values on which it rests and receptive to the ideas emanating from the prevalent socio-economic circumstances. As history has shown, there were occasions when the basic constitutional values and mores are seriously threatened and judiciary acts as a shield against these endeavours. While discharging its role as a custodian of the Constitution, judiciary re-establishes its supremacy by reiterating that under no circumstances, fundamental values from which a Constitution derives its sustenance can be undermined or discarded. The idea that is being suggested here is that a Constitution has a basic structure, and even mere tinkering with the edifice has devastating consequences. One of the important designs that the Indian judiciary has contributed to is the basic structure of the Constitution that, in view of being integral to the 1950 Constitution of India, needs to be respected to sustain the democratic polity that has evolved in the aftermath of India's decolonization in 1947. In the constitutional parlance, the basic structure of the Constitution entails those distinctive features which form the core of the Constitution. Once they are compromised, it would be detrimental to the fundamental character of the Constitution. In view of their critical importance in conceptualizing the foundational values on which the Constitution rests, these features remain inseparable and can never be belittled for the sake of sustaining its basic ideological thrust. This is usually understood in two complementary ways: on the one hand, the Constitution evolves out of certain fundamental values and principles which are articulated in the provisions or conventions that

* Part of the chapter appeared in my earlier works.

also flourish along with specific constitutional practices; there are also, on the other, significant sociopolitical and economic inputs arising out of the prevalent context with which the Constitution is organically linked. Fundamental here is the idea that the doctrine of basic structure of the Constitution can never be conclusively defined independent of the context since it is an offshoot of a dialectical interconnection with the context; as a consequence, it cannot thus be articulated as something that is sacrosanct which further means that the features of the basic structure need to be constantly reinvented in response to the demands of the time and space. One has to factor in, in other words, the rapidly transforming socio-economic context to pinpoint what constitutes the basic structure at a particular juncture of India's existence as a democratic polity.

The doctrine of basic structure is conceptually empowering since it also enables us to grasp the foundational basis of democracy. Broadly speaking, in the liberal conceptual mould, there are two major forms of democracy, which draws its sustenance from the demos. On the one hand, there is the Westminster form of parliamentary democracy in which it is the parliament which reigns supreme and everything else is subservient; the parliamentary authority is, in principle, unrestrictive and shackle-free, of course, within the ideological boundaries that have set by the constitutional practices and conventions. The American system of governance provides, on the other, another form of democracy where it is neither the Congress nor the President who holds sovereign authority, but the Constitution which remains supreme in so far as the polity is concerned. The idea is very simple: the only source of authority is the Constitution and all other institutions of governance derive their constitutional right in governance from the Constitution. The Indian Constitution does not follow either of these formats of governance in its undiluted form. Instead, by creatively blending these two unique constitutional experiences, it articulated a third alternative, namely a parliamentary democracy in which Constitution is made the supreme authority though it took a while to establish that the Constitution cannot be bypassed by any of the institutions of political authority. In such a context, basic structure doctrine assumes tremendous constitutional significance.

In the articulation of the doctrine of basic structure, the Indian judiciary has played a very critical role. Not only has the Indian judiciary acted as a guardian of constitutional democracy in India, it has, by creatively interpreting the constitutional provisions in the context of the changing socio-economic circumstances, evolved a new area of jurisprudence drawing on the 'due process of law' doctrine. The interpretation is not exactly drawn on 'the procedure established by law' which the Constitution of India upholds in Article 21, but on the basis of those values emanating from the social compact epitomizing new politico-ideological concerns. Being a proactive player in India's constitutional democracy, the Supreme Court of India has not only created a new domain of its functioning, it has also initiated significant processes of change by privileging the Constitution over the executive and legislature. A new era in India's constitutional democracy has ushered in whereby judiciary does not merely seem to be an interpreter of the legislative acts and executive feats, but also provide powerful inputs to the policymakers. The doctrine of basic structure is therefore a watershed in India's constitutional democracy. With the recognition of the doctrine, it is now established beyond doubt that constitutional supremacy can be relegated under no circumstances. Parliament, despite being the voice of the people, is subservient to the Constitution which sets out the parameters for its functioning. In other words, the parliament has to function within the boundary demarcated by the Constitution. This has not been readily accepted by the parliament, and judiciary, as history has shown, had to confront the legislature, on a number of occasions, for being respectful to the basic structure of the Constitution.

The aim of this chapter is to acquaint the readers with the basic structure doctrine with reference how it emerged in India's constitutional discourses with reference to the major judicial pronouncements since the inauguration of the 1950 Constitution. This is a narrative of judicial ascendancy in India. An offshoot of creative jurisprudence, the doctrine delineates a critical role for the judiciary which is also constitutionally authorized to ascertain whether parliament is within its limits while discharging its obligation to the governed. Given the massive significance of basic structure in constitutional governance in India, by drawing on some of the major judicial verdicts which are pertinent here, this section thus concentrates on how it evolved in India's democratic practices with reference to its integral features.

Historical antecedents

The root of the basic structure debate can be traced back to the debates in the Constituent Assembly it pondered over the choice between 'the procedure established by law' and 'due process of law', which the US Constitution upholds. The founding fathers favoured the former on the basis of the advice given by Justice Felix Frankfurter of the US Supreme Court to BN Rau; they were persuaded to believe that 'the due process law' was likely to be a deterrent to the independent functioning of the parliament which was, in their views, not justified in democratic governance where parliament represented the voice of the people; the judiciary being authorized to ascertain the constitutionality of parliamentary acts in accordance with the due process of law would then overpower the parliament weakening, thereby the foundation of constitutional democracy in India. The decision provoked fierce debates. Kazi Syed Karimuddin of Central Provinces and Berar, for instance, did not seem persuaded, since he felt that if the Constitution incorporated

> the procedure established by law, instead of due process of law, there will be very great injustice to the law courts in the country because as

> soon as a procedure according to law is complied with by a court, there will be an end to the duties of the court and if the court is satisfied that the procedure has been complied with, the judges cannot interfere with any law which might have been capricious, unjust or iniquitous. ... As soon as the procedures is complied with, there will, [in other words] be an end to everything and the judges will be only spectators. The clause, as it stands, can [thus] do a great mischief in a country which is a storm centre of political parties and where discipline is unknown. Let us guarantee to individuals inalienable rights in such a way that the political parties that come into power cannot extend their jurisdiction in curtailing and invading the Fundamental Rights laid down in the Constitution.[3]

An apprehension loomed large because it was felt that parliament was to gag individual freedom, since political parties might not be sensitive enough of their obligation to the values of constitutional democracy. Sharing the concern, Krishna Chandra Sharma (United Provinces), also argued that

> the term 'without due process of law' has a necessary limitation on the powers of the State, both executive and legislative. ... What this phrase means is to guarantee a fair trial both in procedure as well as in substance. The procedure should be in accordance with law and should be appealable to the civilized conscience of the community. It also ensures a fair trial in substance, that is to say, that substantive law itself should be just and appealable to the civilized conscience of the community.[4]

Here, the argument for parliamentary supremacy was being questioned by reference to the apprehension that it was likely to be missed in future, which was not entirely unfounded as the 1975–77 Emergency experiences demonstrate. Despite forceful arguments, the clause, due process of law, was not finally accepted since it was believed that 'the clause may serve as a great handicap for all social legislation [and] would allow the judiciary a free hand in devising major policies'.[5] Such an understanding also reveals that 'the Drafting Committee, ... in suggesting "procedure" for "due process of law" was possibly guilty of being apprehensive of judicial vagaries in the moulding of law'.[6] BN Rau's warning that due process was an impediment for parliament to act, without shackles, for fulfilling mass democratic aspirations seemed to have conclusively settled the issue; and the Constitution incorporated 'the procedure established by law' in Article 21.

It is true that Indian judiciary is constrained to go beyond the constitutional mandate of following the procedure established by law while looking into the justiciability of the policy preferences of the executive and legislative feats. Nonetheless, with the growing acceptance of the idea of basic structure of the Constitution which can never be violated, the court seems to have carved an independent space in constitutional governance in India.

The doctrine of basic structure does not provide the judiciary with the authority that the US Supreme Court possesses because of the constitutional guarantee of due process; it, however, creates a definite space for the judiciary to act in case the parliament undermines the fundamental constitutional values and principles for the fulfilment of partisan goals and desires. In the changed socio-economic environment leading to the consolidation of democratic ethos and values, the basic structure doctrine further constitutionalizes judicial intervention in areas which are considered to be critical for sustaining constitutional democracy in India.

The basic structure doctrine

As is mentioned above, the basic structure doctrine is rooted in the processes leading to democratization of governance in India. With the growing public disenchantment with the executive and legislature, the judiciary seems to have emerged as a messiah for constitutional democracy. The beginning of the doctrine is usually traced back to the judicial concern for misuse of power by the parliament as per Article 368 of the Constitution. With the constitutional guarantee, can the parliament amend any part of the Constitution for the socio-economic causes? This was the question that the judiciary was asked to respond. According to Article 368, parliament 'may, in exercise of its constituent power, amend by way of addition, variation or repeal any provision of this constitution in accordance with the procedure laid down in this article'. The founding fathers did not seem to have restrictions on parliament's authority in amending the Constitution. For instance, Jawaharlal Nehru argued that

> while we want this Constitution to be as solid and as permanent a structure as we can make it, nevertheless, there is no permanence in constitutions. There should be certain flexibility. If you make anything rigid and permanent, you stop a nation's growth. So, when you pass this Constitution, . . . you will . . . lay down a period of years . . . during which changes to that constitution can easily made without any difficult process. . . . We should not make a Constitution such as some other great countries have, which are so rigid that they do and cannot be adapted easily to the changing conditions. . . . Therefore, while we make a constitution which is sound and as basic as we can, it should also be flexible and for a period we should be in a position to change with relative facility.[7]

Nehru was keen to make the Constitution flexible to keep pace with the changing world while insisting on making it as 'basic' as was possible under the circumstances. This means that the Constitution is to have a basic character in politico-ideological terms which can never be compromised. The basic character needs to be sustained. The idea that Nehru offered was made clearer by BR Ambedkar who, while elaborating the procedure for amendment to the Constitution, clarified that by eliminating the proviso that the Constitution could only be amended by 'a decision, adopted in a convention or referendum', the Constitution was made flexible which means that legislature, central and provincial, is empowered to revise the Constitution by following simple procedures. This is one aspect of the amendment procedure. The other aspect relates to 'the amendment of specific matters' for which 'the ratification of the State Legislatures is required' along with the condition that 'such an amendment shall be done by majority of not less than two-thirds of the members of each House present and voting, and a majority of the total membership of each House'. He also apprehended that future parliament, being elected on adult suffrage, could be tempted 'to alter the fundamental character of the Constitution . . . by acting as partisans seeking to carry amendments to facilitate the passing of party measures'.[8] The idea is crystal clear, namely, there are some values which hold the substance of the Constitution and they need to be protected and cannot be allowed to be bypassed under any circumstances. Nehru too endorsed the point by suggesting that there were 'specific areas' in the Constitution that could be amended by following a rigid procedure.

Two basic points that had emerged in the Assembly seem to have contributed to the formulation of the basic structure doctrine: first, Indian Constitution has certain distinctive features which allow it to be distinguished as a democratic Constitution; these features are integral and cannot be fiddled with; second, since these are core to the Constitution, they cannot be allowed to be sacrificed by the parliamentarians for the sake of fulfilling their partisan aims.

Conceptual roots

In conceptual terms, basic structure entails those values and principles which form the core of a Constitution. The doctrine is about certain characteristics which are essential since they define the nature of the Constitution and, once they are separated, the Constitution, by implication, loses its identity. The crux of the argument is that given their critical importance in shaping the politico-ideological characteristics of a Constitution, they can never be divorced from the Constitution. Although the idea has philosophical roots in some of the classical texts on democracy, federalism and republicanism, it was very clearly articulated in a commentary on the Weimer Constitution in the context of the early phases of Nazism in Germany in the early 1930s. Ernest Rudolf Huber, who is infamous for his support to the Nazi regime since it came to power through election, underlined the importance of constitutional norms in governance which, if bypassed, would lead to the collapse of the constitutional structure in no time. In a very categorical way, he thus argued that

> every constitution consists of such principles, which determine the totality of the constitutional order and make up 'the spirit of the constitution'. There is no equality of rank among the numerous provisions of a written constitutional document. The main principles of the common order have clear priority; the remaining legal precepts are derived from them. . . . One can say of a constitution that it is valid only so long as his core of the constitution maintains its existence. If the core of the constitution is destroyed, then the entire constitution is wiped out, even if individual constitutional precepts of inferior rank continue to be legally valid.[9]

The argument provides us with three important conceptual inputs to articulate the basic structure doctrine: (a) no amendment is permissible if it effectively alters the basic essential principles of the Constitution since it means a stark departure from the purpose for which it was framed; (b) if the amendment destroys the foundation values of the Constitution, it is unconstitutional and thus uncalled for; and finally (c) if the amendment undermines the basic values of the Constitution, it has no intention of revising the Constitution, but desire to eliminate the Constitution. Hence, it is argued that 'if certain fundamental principles, values and norms . . . are seriously altered, the life of the constitution actually comes to an end; from its ashes, a new political regime emerges'.[10] What is explicitly stated here is that once the core values of a Constitution are altered, it results in a complete breakdown of the edifice on which the Constitution rests which means that the Constitution is no longer the same as it was in the past in its original form.

In India, the idea of basic structure is a judicial invention and is attributed to MK Nambyar, a lawyer who pleaded before the Supreme Court in the IC Golaknath versus the state of Punjab in 1967. Nambyar owed this idea to Dietrich Conrad, an academic from Germany who delivered a speech in Banaras Hindu University, entitled 'implied limitation of the amending power' in February, 1965. According to Conrad, 'any amending body organized within the statutory scheme, howsoever verbally unlimited its power, cannot by its very structure change the fundamental pillars supporting its constitutional authority'.[11] The idea was further expanded when he argued that

> Could a constitutional amendment abolish Article 21, to the effect that forthwith a person could be deprived of his life or personal liberty without authorisation by law? Could the ruling party, if it sees its majority shrinking, amend Article 368 to the effect that the amending power rests with the President acting on the advice of the Prime Minister? Could the amending power be used to abolish the Constitution and reintroduce, let us say, the rule of a moghul(sic) emperor or of the Crown of England? I do not want, by posing such questions, to provoke easy answers. But I should like to acquaint you with the discussion which took place on such questions among constitutional lawyers in Germany in the Weimar

> period – discussion, seeming academic at first, but suddenly illustrated by history in a drastic and terrible manner.[12]

What Huber had apprehended in the 1930s had resonated in Conrad's assessment of the situation. He also felt that there were certain features in the Constitution that could never be abrogated; Conrad also warned that if the parliament was allowed to undertake such an exercise, it would finally contribute to the growth of an authoritarian state, as it happened in Germany following the disintegration of the Weimer republic.

Judicial pronouncements

As argued above, the basic structure doctrine evolves in India in the course of a series of judicial verdicts, especially since the 1967 Golaknath case. In the history of constitutional laws in India, the idea of basic structure was mooted in the 1964 Sajjan Singh versus the state of Rajasthan. While endorsing the right to property, P Gajendragadkar raised a question by saying

> whether the basic features of the Constitution under which we live and to which we owe allegiance are to endure for all time – or at least for the foreseeable future – or whether the yard no more enduring than the implemental and subordinate provisions of the Constitution.[13]

In his note of dissent, JR Mudholkar, another member of the bench, also referred to the concept by stating that

> it is a matter of consideration whether making a change in a basic structure of the Constitution can be regarded as an amendment or would it be, in effect, rewriting a part of the Constitution; and, if the latter, would it be within the purview of Article 368?[14]

This is the beginning of the unfolding of the conceptual-legal journey of the basic structure doctrine which passes through a series of judicial pronouncements. The purpose here is not to provide a detailed account of the verdicts, but to highlight the points that India's apex court made while laying out the foundation of the doctrine and its essential features by reference to the major court judgements in this regard.

One of the first significant judicial steps in this regard was the 1967 Golaknath case in which the Supreme Court contributed to the articulation of the doctrine. The primary question that the Supreme Court had raised was whether

> in the exercise of the power of amendment the fundamental structure of the Constitution may be changed or even destroyed or whether the

> power is restricted to making modification within the framework of the original instrument for its better effectuation.

The answer is equally unambiguous: characterizing the fundamental rights as 'transcendental and immutable or inviolable', the majority of the judges in the bench held the view that

> (1) the constitution is intended to be permanent and therefore it cannot be amended in a way which would injure, maim or destroy its indestructible character; (2) the word 'amendment' implies such an addition or change within the lines of the original instrument as will effect an improvement or better carry out the purpose for which it was framed and it cannot be so construed as to enable the parliament to destroy the permanent character of the Constitution; (3) the amending power cannot be used to abolish the compact of the Union or destroy the democratic character of the Constitution teeing individual and minority rights; and (3) the fundamental rights are a part of the basic structure of the Constitution and, therefore, the said power can be exercised only to preserve rather than destroy the essence of these rights.[15]

In clear terms, the court held that fundamental rights being a part of the basic structure of the Constitution cannot be abrogated. So, the parliament does not have unrestricted authority to amend any of the rights enshrined in Part III of the Constitution. There was a dissenting note too; Justice Wanchoo of the bench felt that the court's insistence on the basic structure could be an impediment to social progress, as the members of the Constituent Assembly had apprehended. He was thus categorical in asserting that no limitation should be implied on the amending power of the Parliament under Article 368 and

> basic structure would lead to the position that any amendment made to any article of the Constitution would be subject to the challenge before the Courts on the ground that it amounts to the amendment of the basic structure.[16]

Nonetheless, the decision that basic structure cannot be challenged was carried forward as the majority of the bench endorsed the argument. It was now settled that fundamental rights were a part of the essential features of the Constitution that needed to be protected and upheld unconditionally. A revolutionary judgement, it, for the first time in India's recent political history, established that parliament was subservient to the Constitution which remained supreme and its authority to amend the Constitution was also absolute. The parliament took the verdict as an infringement in its constitutional rights for being the voice of the people, and hence it adopted legislations to re-establish its absolute authority in lawmaking. The result was the enactment of the Twenty-Fourth, Twenty-Fifth and Twenty-Ninth Amendment Acts in 1971. While the Twenty-Fourth Amendment Act was meant to abrogate the Golaknath ruling of the court to restore parliament's unconditional authority in amending the Constitution the Twenty-Fifth and Twenty-Ninth Amendment Acts evolved separate legal tools of safeguarding compulsory acquisition statutes from being struck down for violating fundamental rights.

These amendments were put to test for the first time in the 1973 Kesavananda Bharati case in which the Supreme Court, with its full bench of thirteen jurists, probed into the constitutional validity of the Kerala Land Reforms Act, 1963, as amended by Kerala Land Reforms (Amendment) Acts, 1969 and 1971. The decision challenging the Twenty-Fourth Amendment Act was clinched by a majority of seven judges as against six; the court ruled that Article 368 does not enable Parliament to alter the basic structure of the Constitution; there are three different expressions, basic structure, basic elements and basic features which figured in the judgements. Although the jurists did not conclusively define what constituted the basic structure, they left enough inputs to identify those essential characteristics which, according to them, constituted 'the basic structure'. That the apex court avoided defining the basic features categorically was presumably due to the fact that it was not exactly needed and it was also not possible to enumerate them since they were context-driven. The court also held that because 'a particular concept of law cannot be rigidly defined, it does not cease to be a concept of law; principles of natural justice and negligence also cannot be rigidly defined still they are effective concept of law'.[17] In order to further strengthen the argument, the court advanced the point by saying that

> the ultimate purpose of the Constitution is the conservation of utility and integrity of the nation and also the dignity of the individual. This can be assured only by promoting fraternity. Any principle of law which, if taken away from the Constitution, would result into a loss of fraternity and unity and integrity of the nation and dignity of the individual would be considered to be an essential feature of the Basic Structure.[18]

The amending power of the parliament was conditional and subject to judicial scrutiny to probe whether it had affected the basic structure. While exercising its constituent power under Article 368, the parliament cannot, the court held, 'damage, emasculate, destroy, abrogate, change' the basic structure or the fundamental framework of the Constitution. The argument was persuasively justified by Justice SM Sikri of the bench that supported the basic structure doctrine by saying that

> our Constitution is not a mere political document. It is essentially a social document. It is based on a social philosophy and every social philosophy like every religion has two main features, namely basic and

> circumstantial: the former remains constant but the practices associated with it may change. Likewise, a Constitution like ours contains certain features which are so essential that they cannot be changed or destroyed.[19]

This was a powerful argument in defence of the basic structure doctrine. Being essentially a product of consensus, the 1950 Constitution of India was also an offshoot of a bargain by which the diverse groups constituting the Indian polity came together to form the Union. So, it became a social compact which emerged out of processes in which differences were resolved through dialogues and deliberations without fear or coercion. The founding fathers devoted a great deal of energy to consolidate the social compact by way of reconciliation, accommodation and agreements among the socio-economically diverse groups. And, the basic features evolved out of such intensive dialogues among groups holding contrasting points of view. The idea was captured in its true spirit by Justice Khanna who held that

> amendment of the Constitution necessarily contemplates that the Constitution has not to be abrogated but only changes have to be made in it. The word 'amendment' postulates that the old Constitution survives without loss of its identity despite the change and continues even though it has been subjected to alterations. As a result of the amendment, the old Constitution cannot be destroyed and done away with; it is retained though in the amended form. . . . Although it is permissible under the power of amendment to effect changes, however important, and to adapt the system to the requirements of the changing conditions, it is not permissible to touch the foundation or to alter the basic institutional pattern. The words 'amendment of the Constitution' with all their wide sweep and amplitude cannot have the effect of destroying the basic structure or framework of the Constitution.[20]

There was a unanimity among the seven of thirteen judges of the bench that engaged in the Kesavananda Bharati case. The minority view, articulated by a group of six jurists, led by Justice AN Ray held that all parts of the Constitution were essential, and the distinction between essential and non-essential did not seem to be constitutional; they also endorsed the Twenty-Fourth Amendment Act and agreed to the view that parliament was empowered to amend any part of the Constitution.

The majority verdict in Kesavananda Bharati case upheld the view that there were features which constituted the core of the Constitution and could never be abrogated though there was hardly a compact list of basic features; each of the seven judges gave their own lists of essential features which, of course, are fundamental to the Constitution. The lists are exhaustive, as the following shows:

In Justice Sikri's conceptualization, the list should include:

- Supremacy of the Constitution;
- Republican and democratic form of government;
- Secular character of the Constitution;
- Separation of powers between the legislature, executive and the judiciary;
- Federal character of the Constitution.

According to Justice AN Grover and Justice SJ Shelat, the following two are important:

- The mandate to build a welfare state contained in the Directive Principles of State Policy (Part IV of the Constitution);
- Unity and integrity of the nation.

Justice KS Hegde and Justice SN Mukherjea incorporated the following:

- Sovereignty of India;
- Democratic character of the polity;
- Unity of the country;
- Essential features of the individual freedoms secured to the citizens;
- Mandate to build a welfare state.

Justice Jaganmohan Reddy listed the following:

- Sovereign democratic republic;
- Provisions for social, economic and political justice;
- Liberty of thought, expression, belief, faith and worship;
- Equality of status and opportunity.

These are aspects of the basic structure of the Constitution. By identifying the fundamental politico-ideological values and also institutions for constitutional democracy, the court prepared an exhaustive list. In the 1975 Indira Gandhi versus Raj Narain case, the court devised a principle to characterize the basic structure. Justice KK Mathew argued that whether a particular feature forms part of the basic structure needed to be determined on the basis of the specific provisions of the Constitution. According to him,

> 'to be a basic structure it must be a terrestrial concept having its habitat within the four corners of the Constitution'. What constitutes basic structure is not like 'a twinkling star up above the Constitution. For instance, the Preamble enumerates great concepts embodying the ideological aspirations of the people, but these concepts are particularised

> and their essential features delineated in the various provisions of the Constitution. It is these specific provisions in the body of the Constitution which determine the type of democracy which the founders of that instrument established; the quality and nature of justice, political, social and economic which aimed to realise the content of liberty of thought and expression which they entrenched in that document and the scope of equality of status and of opportunity which they enshrined in it. These specific provisions enacted in the Constitution alone can determine the basic structure of the Constitution. These specific provisions, either separately or in combination, determine the content of the great concepts set out in the Preamble. It is impossible to spin out of any concrete concept of basic structure out of the gossamer concept set out in the Preamble. The specific provisions of the Constitution are the stuff which the basic structure has to be woven'.[21]

These are very useful inputs to conceptualize basic structure. There are two important aspects that appear to be critical in capturing the core of the doctrine. On the one hand, instead of pinpointing specific characteristics, the court in this instance preferred to identify basic features in terms of the values that inform them – which means that in the conceptualization of basic structure, the supportive constitutional values and principles remain significant. The court also preferred, on the other, to be indecisive possibly because what constitutes fundamental is also context-dependent – which denotes that the list cannot be conclusive presumably because it needs to be revised in accordance with the prevalent socio-economic priorities.

Following the Kesavananda Bharati judgement, the Congress government, led by Indira Gandhi enacted the Forty-Second Amendment Act in 1976 to dilute the basic structure doctrine. The court intervened again and reaffirmed the basic structure in the 1980 Minerva Mills versus the Union of India. Striking down the authority of the parliament to repeal any of the features, identified as part of the basic structure, the court ruled that 'parliament cannot, under Article 368, expand its amending power so as to acquire for itself the right to repeal or abrogate the Constitution or to destroy its basic and essential features'.[22] Reiterating the parliament has conditional authority of amendment, the apex court further argues that

> it has no inherent power of amendment of the Constitution and being an authority created by the Constitution, it cannot have such inherent power but the power of amendment is conferred upon it by the Constitution and it is a limited power which is conferred. Parliament cannot in exercise of this power to amend the Constitution as to alter its basic structure or to change its identity. Now, if, by constitutional amendment, Parliament was granted unlimited power of amendment, it would cease to be an authority under the Constitution, but would become supreme over it because it would have power to alter the entire

> Constitution, including its basic structure and even to put an end to it by totally changing its identity. Therefore, the limited amending power of parliament is itself an essential feature of the Constitution, a part of its basic structure for if the limited power of amendment was enlarged into an unlimited power, the entire character of the Constitution would be changed.[23]

The Minerva Mills case reaffirms the limited authority of parliament in so far as amendment is concerned. The court defended the argument by saying that this was likely to change the fundamental identity of the Constitution. As Justice YV Chandrachud of the Supreme Court bench argued, in a rather poetic language, that

> the theme song of . . . Kesavananda Bharati is: amend as you may even the solemn document which the founding fathers have committed to your care, for you know best the needs of your generation. But, the Constitution is a precious heritage; therefore, you cannot destroy its identity.[24]

What is emphasized here is the sanctity of the Constitution that can never be compromised, which means that the Indian system of governance is neither exactly the Westminster form of democracy nor its US counterpart, but a creative blending of the two.

The limited nature of the amendment power is now an established constitutional principle. And, the parliament has to respect the basic structure while seeking to enact an amendment to the Constitution. Hence, it is argued that 'since the power to amend the Constitution is not unlimited, if changes brought about by amendments destroy the identity of the Constitution, such amendments would be void'.[25] In order to pursue the argument, Justice YK Sabharwal Singh who wrote the judgement for the IR Coelho (dead) versus the State of Tamil Nadu (2007) thus adumbrated that

> the existence of the power of parliament to amend the Constitution at will, with requisite voting strength, so as to make any kind of laws affecting rights, enshrined in Part III including power of judicial review under Article 32 is incompatible with the basic structure doctrine. Therefore such an exercise, if challenged, has to be tested on the touchstone of basic structure as reflected in Article 21 read with Article 14 and Article 19, Article 15 and the principles thereunder.[26]

Here too, the parliament is told again that it does not have the absolute power of amending the Constitution at will; it has to be respectful to the essential features of the Constitution which the Supreme Court has upheld in a series of its pronouncements. The doctrine of basic structure has now become 'an axiom [which] is premised on the basis that invasion [by parliament] in areas, recognized as the basic structure, is not, at all, permissible [because] it is constitutionally *ultra vires*'.[27] The court prevailed over the parliament and the validity of the basic structure doctrine was ascertained beyond doubt. Whether it undermines representative democracy is an issue that cannot be settled so easily though there is no doubt that by privileging its role as a reliable custodian of constitutional values and principles, the court tilted the balance in its favour. Whatever may have been the consequences of court prevailing over the elected representatives, the fact remains that it was possible for the apex judiciary to overturn a series of executive decisions presumably because of the public trust-deficit in the political authority, which cannot be brought back so quickly.

Summarizing the argument

Out of the tussle between the judiciary and executive emerged the basic structure doctrine. It has also evolved largely due to the judicial concern for sustaining the sanctity of the Constitution, which is being violated by the executive as and when opportunity arises. The judiciary is not unanimous, of course, in its assessment of the situation as the majority pronouncements show that on most occasions, the judiciary was divided, and the decision was endorsed by the majority opinion. The only major exception is 2007 IR Coelho (dead) versus the State of Tamil Nadu, where the apex court approved the contention without being split in their opinion. Nonetheless, in view of its growing importance in reviewing the constitutionality of the executive feats, the basic structure doctrine can be said to have become 'the bedrock of constitutional interpretation in India'.[28] The judiciary-executive interaction has thus become far from being amicable, with each trying to over-smart the other as soon they get a chance.

Despite the disagreement between the judges on what constitute the basic structure of the Constitution, the idea that the Constitution has a core has always been upheld in the judicial discourse. As the trajectory of the doctrine shows, there was hardly a fixed list of 'essential' features; the court keeps on adding to the list. Of course, the jurists while deciding the 1973 Kesavananda Bharati case provided an exhaustive list of items which, they felt, should be the core of the Constitution and were thus to be protected. In its judgement in the 1980 Minerva Mills case, the court privileged the non-justiciable Directive Principles of State Policy, since they

> nourish the roots of our democracy, provide strength and vigour to it and attempt to make it real participatory democracy which does not remain merely a political democracy but also becomes social and economic democracy with Fundamental Rights available to all irrespective of their power, position and wealth. The dynamic provisions of the Directive Principles of State Policy fertilize the static provisions of the

> Fundamental Rights [which] cannot be considered in isolation from the socio-economic structure in which it is to operate.[29]

So, despite not being enforceable, the court held that the rights enshrined in Part IV of the Constitution are relevant in the changed context of massive democratization of governance. By establishing an obvious link between Part III (Fundamental Rights) and Part IV (Directive Principles of State Policy), the court seems to have been governed by the Forty-Second Amendment Act (1976), which privileged Part IV rights as they were considered to be effective politico-ideological tools for bringing about the required socio-economic changes for the establishment of 'a socialist republic', which the Preamble to the Constitution announces. This was pursued further in the 1994 SR Bommai judgement of the apex court. Reiterating that

> 'the Indian Constitution, being a social document, contains the ideals expected by the nation', the apex court while delivering the verdict, underlined that 'federalism, social pluralism and pluralist democracy . . . form the basic structure of our Constitution, [and] . . . if the fabric of pluralism and pluralist democracy and the unity and integrity of the country are to be preserved, judiciary in the circumstances is the only institution which can act as the saviour of the system and of the nation'.[30]

Here too, the basic structure doctrine was expanded to include some of the major socio-economic ideals that are pertinent to effect visible socio-economic transformations. It also implies that the executive did not seem to have paid adequate attention to the goal that the Constitution laid out. What is interesting to note that the court set aside the presidential decree for dismissal of the Karnataka state government not on procedural grounds but on certain constitutional values which represented the basic structure.

In carving out a specific constitutional position for the basic structure doctrine, the judiciary seems to have upheld two important issues which are critical in parliamentary democracy: one substantive and another institutional.[31] Substantively, the rivalry between judiciary and executive has established that the former retains 'inherent power' to review the parliamentary feats to ascertain whether they are constitutionally justiciable. By implication, it means that the parliamentary supremacy is not absolute and subject to judicial review because the court is not only the final interpreter of the Constitution, but also its saviour. The growing ascendancy of the court has serious institutional implication as well. As the scan of the multiple judgements reveal, the court has both won and asserted its institutional rights by challenging the parliament 'in constitutional matters through the basic structure doctrine'. There was hardly a significant opposition as it was believed that the court 'rescued the democracy strand of the seamless web from those who would have sacrificed it to genuine or pretended social revolutionary intentions'.[32] Nonetheless, it is difficult to arrive at a definite conclusion, since the tussle is far from over which is evident in a series of counterattacks by the executive intending to undermine the judicial supremacy in India's constitutional democracy.

Critiquing the doctrine

The basic structure doctrine seems to have put the two major organs of governance in a collusion mode. The court has appropriated powers which ordinarily belong to the parliament since it represents people. The minority bench in the Kesavananda Bharati case, led by Justice AN Ray, endorsed the view that being people's voice, the parliament remained supreme in India's constitutional governance which, by implication, means that it was authorized to enact legislations in accordance with what was required to fulfil the politico-ideological mission that the elected representatives had. By striking down the parliament's decision as it is contrary to the basic structure, the Supreme Court appears to have assumed 'a veto power on all constitutional amendments'.[33] Instead of interpreting the amendment clause, the court has, in effect, become the arbiter by suggesting that it will decide whether to permit the legislature to amend the Constitution. The basic structure creates an environment in which 'the constituent power gets transferred from the elected representative of the people to the judges of the Supreme Court', which is a serious threat to constitutional democracy.[34] Highlighting this aspect of the judicial overreach, HJ Kania, the first Chief Justice of India thus remarked that 'in a democratic country, the people make the laws through their legislature. It is not the function of the court to supervise or to correct the laws passed by the legislature as an overriding authority'.[35] In the name of protecting the Constitution, the judiciary through its 'self-invented doctrine of basic structure' appears to have 'destroyed the most basic feature of Indian polity, namely the primacy of the people and democracy being a government of the people, by the people and for the people'.[36] The argument is based on a fundamental principle of democracy privileging elected representatives, since they articulate people's voice and remain accountable to them whereas the judiciary is neither accountable nor institutionally equipped to capture people's voice; it does not seem to be constitutionally justified because it creates an arrangement contrary to the spirit of parliamentary democracy by allowing concentration of unfettered power in one institution which, incidentally, is not an elected body. This is an endeavour to replace the duly elected representatives by a small, often-divided set of appointed judges to devise policy preferences.[37] Hence, the basic structure doctrine is charged with being an alibi to tread into an area which, from the point of view of democracy, belongs to parliament. In a nutshell, the basic structure doctrine is being challenged as 'an illegitimate infringement on majority rule, an attempt to infuse India's constitutional scheme with judicial supremacy'.[38] Being a parliamentary democracy in the Westminster format, the judicial ascendance is ideologically debilitating since it puts hurdles to the elected representatives when they seek to bring about revolutionary socio-economic changes by way of innovative legislations. So, the basic structure doctrine is a retarding means in India's constitutional democracy which is ideologically restrictive and constitutionally contrarian.

Concluding observations

Conceptually, the basic structure doctrine is justified given the fact that the Indian Constitution clearly 'adopted the American model of constitutionalism with limited government and strong judicial review'. Though some elements of the British parliamentary system were 'adapted to the Indian constitution – the composition of the higher executive and effective collective cabinet responsibility' – it is difficult to accept that it entails 'the doctrine of parliamentary sovereignty'.[39] Despite strong critiques, the basic structure doctrine is being continuously expanded and appears to have created a wave in its favour around the world, especially in South Asia. In a 1989 judgement on Anwar Husain versus Bangladesh, Justice BH Chowdhury while emphasizing the importance of basic structure argued that

> call it by any name – basic structure or whatever, but that is the fabric of the Constitution which cannot be dismantled by an authority created by the Constitution itself, namely, the Parliament. . . . Because the amending power is but a power given by the Constitution to Parliament, it is a higher power than any other given by the Constitution to Parliament, but nevertheless (sic) it is power within and not outside the Constitution.[40]

The basic structure doctrine has also been appreciated by the Supreme Court in Pakistan. In Al-Jehad Trust versus the Federation of Pakistan (1996), the court ruled that in order to resolve a conflict between a constitutional provision and a later amendment, the Constitution has to be interpreted as a whole, taking into account 'the spirit and basic features of the Constitution'.[41] This was further pursued in a 1997 judgement when the Supreme Court reiterated that the Pakistan Constitution has salient features – federalism, parliamentary form of government blended with Islamic provisions – 'which are beyond the amendment power'.[42] Although the basic structure doctrine did not become integral to Pakistan's constitutional law as in India, these are important judgements which created a space for the doctrine more or less on the same arguments which were offered by the Indian Supreme Court.

Notwithstanding the obvious conceptual limitation of the arguments supportive of the doctrine in a parliamentary democracy, there is a powerful defence when it is shown to be an effective means for preventing parliament from being a self-engineered institution of governance. In the Indian context, the doctrine was conceptualized when the executive resorted to constitutional amendments rather indiscriminately to fulfil its political agenda seemingly at the cost of constitutional propriety. The doctrine that had emerged in the context of the challenges to the validity of constitutional amendments was thus hailed as a panacea which applied brakes; otherwise, 'the engine of amending power would soon', it was apprehended, 'overrun the constitution'.[43] By insisting on the basic structure, the Supreme Court thus acts as a brake which is required to sustain a healthy balance among the organs of the government. Besides imposing limits on parliament's amending power, the doctrine also acknowledges that the Constitution can be radically changed by the people themselves; it thus emphasizes simultaneously the importance of the elected representatives and 'the democratic pedigree earned by non-representative institutions', including judiciary. The trajectory of the basic structure doctrine confirms that it evolves and gets consolidated when the representative institutions fail to 'maintain democratic essentials' of the country.[44] Hence, the importance of the doctrine cannot be so easily dismissed; in fact, it has gained credibility to the extent of being part and parcel of constitutional democracy in India.

It is true that the Basic Structure Doctrine evolved with the intervention of the judiciary in opposition to the executive's interference in domains which are constitutionally integral to India's existence as a democratic polity. So, at one level, it is essentially a judicial intervention; at another far more perceptive level, it was made possible in view of the sustained democratic struggles in which the demos involved to retain the constitutional fabric upholding the liberal polity in India. Hence, the argument attributing the doctrine to judicial endeavour alone shall obviously be imperfect since it does not allow us to capture the popular movements involving various strata of people for sustaining the 1950 Constitution. Besides individual initiatives (discussed above), one of the major impetus for the Basic Structure Doctrine was certainly the long-drawn campaign against the imposition of Emergency in 1975. It was also felt then that by drawing on the constitutional provisions of Part XVIII of the Constitution (Emergency provisions), the incumbent ruling authority may easily destroy the democratic structure that is ingrained in the Constitution. Allowing the government to appropriate powers due to combat threats to the very existence of the polity, these provisions act as a conduit for extraordinary authority. A careful reading of the provisions of this Part of the Constitution (Articles 352–360) confirms the contention that the 1950 Constitution of India has ingredients to contribute to the rise and consolidation of what I call 'constitutional authoritarianism'. So, the 1975–77 Emergency was clearly constitutional, which was justified by the provisions, incorporated in Part XVIII of the Constitution. That Emergency was not allowed to continue is also indicative of the critical role that anti-Emergency popular campaigns had played in forcing the ruling authority for its withdrawal in 1977. The Forty-Second Amendment Act of 1976 enabling the parliament to amend any part of the Constitution was a wake-up call for those working hard to consolidate India's constitutional identity as a democratic polity. It was reversed by the Forty-Fourth Amendment Act in 1978, as it was contrary to the foundational values and principles on which the 1950 Constitution rests. This was also set aside by the Supreme Court in the 1980 Minerva Mills underlining that the parliament cannot abrogate the fundamental rights since they constitute basic structure of the Constitution. Examples are plenty to substantiate the claim that what India's judiciary did in fulfilling its constitutional obligation of being a custodian of the Constitution does not seem to have been exclusively its own initiative; instead, it is fair to argue that the apex court translated the popular resilience in the form of diktats for safeguarding those democratic values making the 1950 Constitution an epitome of liberal-constitutional-democracy.

In the final analysis, the basic structure is not merely a judicial decision, but a political intervention in governance which was likely to be derailed due to specific sociopolitical context reportedly leading to the consolidation of anti-democratic and authoritarian forces, especially in the mid-1970s. By raising concerns, the judiciary seems to have created an environment for 'fostering a democratic dialogue around key constitutional principles between the institutions of government',[45] which not only confirms the importance of the principles of checks and balances in constitutional governance, but also consolidates democracy as a collective venture. In principle, the doctrine is thus an important aid for keeping the executive within a limit; in practice, however, the judicial intervention through the doctrine of basic structure does not seem to be as fundamental as is construed which Justice Khanna (who was superseded when his turn to become the Chief Justice of India probably due to his dissenting note in the 1976 Habeas Corpus case) articulated by saying that

> there is no modern instance, it is said, in which any judiciary has saved a whole people from the grave currents of intolerance, passion and tyranny which have threatened liberty and free institutions. The attitude of a society and of its organized political forces rather than of its legal machinery, is the controlling force in the character of free institutions. The ramparts of defence against tyranny are ultimately in the hearts of the people. The Constitution, the courts and the laws can act only as aids to strengthen those ramparts; they do not and cannot furnish substitute for those ramparts. If the ramparts are secure, any who dares to tamper with the liberties of the citizens would do so at his own peril. If, however, the ramparts crack down, no convention, no court would be able to do much in the matter.[46]

This is the crux of the matter; no matter how strong the judiciary is while stream-rolling its diktats, its authority can be effective so long as it is held by the people as an effective instrument for fulfilling some of their cherished socio-economic goals. So, in the ultimate analysis, the basic structure doctrine, by itself, does not seem to be an empowering device; that it has acquired the status of being a significant shield against the trespassing by the executive of its constitutionally recognized boundaries clearly authenticates the critical role of the *demos* in charting out definite courses for institutions of governance in a democratic polity. In conceptual terms, the basic structure doctrine helps us understand what is basic to India's constitutional practices which can, under no circumstances, be violated. This is also doctrine, impregnated with significant conceptual imports, which is also a powerful impetus for ideologically challenging endeavours at undermining the foundational values that the Constitution-makers upheld while drafting the 1950 Constitution of India. Basic here is the point that in consolidating India's constitutional identity as a vibrant constitutional democracy, the role of judiciary is no less significant, as various judgements unambiguously demonstrate. In that respect, it is a powerful aid to the concern of the demos for sustaining and also strengthening the foundational framework of India's democratic polity. And, the Basic Structure Doctrine thus stands out as an important milestone in the series of endeavours that judiciary has undertaken in recent years in creating a politico-ideological ambience in support of India's constitutional identity as a resilient democracy.

Notes

1 Cited in BN Srikrishna, 'Judicial independence', in Sujit Choudhury, Madhav Khosla and Pratap Bhanu Mehta (eds.), *The Oxford Handbook of the Indian Constitution*, Oxford University Press, New Delhi, 2016, p. 349.
2 BN Srikrishna, 'Judicial independence', in Sujit Choudhury, Madhav Khosla and Pratap Bhanu Mehta (eds.), *The Oxford Handbook of the Indian Constitution*, Oxford University Press, New Delhi, 2016, p. 366.
3 Kazi Syed Karimuddin (Central Provinces and Berar), 6 December 1948, *Constituent Assembly Debates*, Book No. 2, p. 843.
4 Krishna Chandra Sharma (United Provinces), 6 December 1948, *Constituent Assembly Debates*, Book No. 2, p. 850.
5 Alladi Krishnaswami Ayyar (Madras), 6 December 1948, *Constituent Assembly Debates*, Book No. 2, p. 854.
6 ibid.
7 Jawaharlal Nehru, 8 November 1948, *Constituent Assembly Debates*, Book No. 2, pp. 322–323.
8 The quoted parts of the sentences are taken from the speech that BR Ambedkar made in the Constituent Assembly on 4 November 1948, *Constituent Assembly Debates*, Book No. 2, pp. 43–44.
9 Ernest Rudolf Huber, 'Constitution', in Arthur J Jacobson and Bernhard Schlink (eds.), *Weimer: A Jurisprudence Crisis*, 2002, p. 328 – cited in Yaniv Roznai, *Unconstitutional Constitutional Amendments: A Study of the Nature and Limits of Constitutional Amendment Powers*, Unpublished PhD dissertation, London School of Economics, 2014, p. 119.
10 Eivind Smith, 'Old and protected: on the supra-constitutional clause in the constitution of Norway', *Law Review*, Vol. 44, 2011, p. 369 – cited in Yaniv Roznai, *Unconstitutional Constitutional Amendments: A Study of the Nature and Limits of Constitutional Amendment Powers*, Unpublished PhD dissertation, London School of Economics, 2014, p. 119.

11 www.frontline.in/static/html/fl1809/18090950.htm, AG Noorani, 'Behind the basic structure doctrine: on India's debt to a German jurist, Professor Dietrich Conrad', *Frontline*, Vol. 18, No. 19, 28 April–11 May 2001, accessed on 18 December 2016.
12 ibid.
13 https://indiankanoon.org/doc/1308308/, Sajjan Singh versus the state of Rajasthan, 1964, accessed on 18 December 2016.
14 ibid.
15 https://Indiakanoon.org/doc/129358/, IC Golaknath versus the State of Punjab, 1967, accessed on 18 December 2016.
16 ibid.
17 https://Indiakanoon.org/doc/25786, Kesavananda Bharati versus the state of Kerala, 1973, accessed on 18 December 2016.
18 ibid.
19 ibid.
20 ibid.
21 https://indiankanoon.org/doc/1569395/, Indira Gandhi versus Raj Narain, 1975, accessed on 18 December 2016.
22 https://Indiakanoon.org/doc/1939993, Minerva Mills Limited and others versus the Union of India, 1980 accessed on 18 December 2016.
23 ibid.
24 ibid.
25 https://indiankanoon.org/doc/322504/, IR Coelho (dead) versus the State of Tamil Nadu (2007), accessed on 18 December 2016.
26 ibid.
27 ibid.
28 Granville Austin, *Working a Democratic Constitution: A History of Indian Experience*, Oxford University Press, New Delhi, 1999, p. 258.
29 https://Indiakanoon.org/doc/193993/, Minerva Mills and others versus the Union of India, 1980, accessed on 19 December 2016.
30 https://indiankanoon.org/doc/60799/, SR Bommai and others versus the Union of India, 1994, accessed on 19 December 2016.
31 The idea is drawn on Granville Austin, *Working a Democratic Constitution: A History of Indian Experience*, Oxford University Press, New Delhi, 1999, pp. 258–276.
32 Granville Austin, *Working a Democratic Constitution: A History of Indian Experience*, Oxford University Press, New Delhi, 1999, p. 258.
33 Subhas C Kashyap, *Indian Constitution: Conflicts and Controversies*, Vistara Publications, New Delhi, 2010, p. 246.
34 ibid., p. 247.
35 *Hindustan Times*, New Delhi, 21 May 1950.
36 Subhas C Kashyap, *Indian Constitution: Conflicts and Controversies*, Vistara Publications, New Delhi, 2010, pp. 247–248.
37 NR Madhava Menon, 'Basic structure after 30 years', in Pran Chopra (ed.), *The Supreme Court Versus the Constitution: A Challenge to Federalism*, Sage, New Delhi, 2006, p. 62.
38 Madhav Khosla, *The Indian Constitution*, Oxford University Press, New Delhi, 2012, p. 155.
39 Sudhir Krishnaswamy, *Democracy and Constitutionalism in India: A Study of the Basic Structure Doctrine*, Oxford University Press, New Delhi, 2009, pp. 218–219.
40 The judgement is cited in Yaniv Roznai, *Unconstitutional Constitutional Amendments: A Study of the Nature and Limits of Constitutional Amendment*, Unpublished PhD dissertation, London School of Economics and Political Science, 2014, p. 59.
41 ibid., p. 61.

42 ibid.
43 Upendra Baxi, Courage, *Craft and Contention: The Indian Supreme Court in the Eighties*, NM Tripathi, Bombay, 1985, p. 68.
44 Sudhir Krishnaswami, *Democracy and Constitutionalism in India: A Study of the Basic Structure Doctrine*, Oxford University Press, New Delhi, 2009, p. 221.
45 ibid., p. 215.
46 Cited in Michael Henderson, 'Setting India's democratic house in order', *Asian Survey*, Vol. XIX, 1979, pp. 955–956.

6 Constitutional constructivism and justiciable designs of governance

Rearticulating constitutional identity

Constitutional identity is a politically contrived designing device. Implicit here is the idea that constitutional identity is neither permanently fixed nor inflexible nor extremely fluid, but is reinvented in response to newer social, economic and political demands. One has to add a caveat here because change in the identity is admissible so long as the basic principles on which it rests remain unaffected. The argument is thus made at two levels: at the level of conceptualization, it is accepted that constitutional identity is precious and it needs to be protected. This part of the argument defends the point to the extent of suggesting that constitutional identity is almost sacrosanct and therefore it cannot be fiddled with under any circumstances. At the level of mundane politics, there is contention that constitutional identity undergoes changes in conformity with those core values upholding a specific structure of constitutional governance. In other words, what is identified as change does not seem so because it draws on those basic ideas which are immanent to the Constitution itself. What is argued here is the point that since constitutional identity evolves contextually in liberal democracies it cannot be completely independent of sociopolitical changes which are derivative of those fundamental values supportive of one kind of constitutional identity. The point is simple: drawn on the philosophy of Enlightenment, India's constitutional identity is articulated around the concerns for benevolence, compassion and empathy. The 1950 Constitution of India confirms the claim. It was possible because (a) the founding fathers were appreciative of liberal constitutionalism, driven by the Enlightenment values, and (b) those who presided over India's destiny following decolonization shared similar ideological predilections and commitments. This is perhaps one of those critical factors which explain why India's constitutional identity remains unaltered despite occasional threats when efforts were made to radically transform its very nature and also texture. There is no dearth of examples to substantiate the argument that India's democratic polity is resilient enough to successfully combat the contrarian forces. The chapter thus makes two major arguments. First, keeping in view the resilience that Indian democracy has so far evinced, one is confident to argue that regardless of occasional challenges, it is too strong to be crippled so easily. It has emerged as a system with adequate institutional backup and a supportive environment. A vibrant system of governance which is also participatory, India's constitutional democracy by being receptive to newer demands and concerns creates space for democratic debates, discussions, contestations, bargaining and negotiations. Second, the role that the institutions, both governmental and otherwise, had played in independent India is no less insignificant in consolidating her democratic polity. A cursory examination of the debates in India's parliament reveals that except during the 1975–1977 Emergency, the parliamentary proceedings did not generally deviate from the well-established principles of constitutional democracy. With these two arguments in mind, the chapter focusses on how judiciary contributes to the reinvention of India's constitutional identity, of course, in consonance with those fundamental ethos and values upholding constitutional liberalism in India. To be precise, the chapter is an elaboration of how judiciary shields India's constitutional identity from being vitiated by fulfilling its role as a true custodian of India's constitutional democracy. There are many endeavours that the Indian apex court undertook to protect the liberal constitutional fabric that the founding fathers so assiduously nurtured both during their battle against colonialism and its aftermath. To substantiate the argument that the Indian judiciary always remains a critical player as a defender of liberal values, this chapter concentrates on those four important judicial pronouncements, the Triple Talaq judgement and the right to privacy judgement, the judgement decriminalizing homosexuality and the Sabrimala judgement allowing women entry to the Sabrimala temple in Kerala, which epitomized its role as a defender of India's identity as a constitutional democracy. Of all the verdicts which are said to have critically influenced India's Constitution identity, the basic structure judgement (discussed in Chapter 5) is most fundamental in the sense that not only has it set in motion a process privileging the core values of constitutional democracy, but has also contributed to the creation of an environment for democratic principles to flourish and also generation of an equally powerful zeal among the citizenry for their protection. The other two judgements concerning the right to divorce and alimony to the Muslim women and the right to privacy for all are no less insignificant because they are immensely critical to the consolidation of India's constitutional identity epitomizing the core values of the philosophy of Enlightenment. These judgements are thus useful in conceptualizing constitutional identity as an evolving phenomenon on the basis of those important principles and values which form its core. Implicit here is another vital aspect of constitutional identity that underlines the fact that changes in the Constitution are welcome so long as they do not override the foundational values on which it rests. In a nutshell, the purpose of this chapter is to emphasize the point that being drawn on the Enlightenment values constitutional identity remains unaltered. By analytically dissecting these major judgements of the Supreme Court of India, the chapter further argues that it is possible presumably because of the consolidation of a mindset in support of constitutional democracy in India. That the Supreme Court is conscious of its role as a custodian of India's democratic fervour and ethos is a testimony to its claim of being a key player in retaining India's identity as a constitutional democracy in the liberal mould amidst occasional threats and challenges.

The Triple Talaq judgement (2018)

As shown in Chapter 5, what the basic structure doctrine seeks to do is to firmly establish the point that fundamentals of the fundamental can never be fiddled with since they uphold India's constitutional identity. The Preamble to the Constitution is both a pointer and also an endorsement of those critical constitutional values, which remain integral to India's constitutional democracy. Primarily, there are three major ideological pillars: liberty, equality and fraternity, insofar as India's constitutional identity is concerned. Being critical to India's democratic polity, these pillars chart out specific politico-ideological directions which, once analysed, help us comprehend the basic nature of her constitutional identity. With the articulation of the basic structure doctrine, the Indian judiciary, as argued above, played a significant role in conceptualizing what constitutional identity means in the Indian context. A perusal of many judicial pronouncements since the adoption of the doctrine in the 1973 Kesavananda Bharati verdict reveals how critical it gradually became in shaping constitutional democracy in India in a particular fashion. Two claims are implicitly made here: on the one, that the judiciary has a major role to play in the rise and consolidation of democracy in India is now established beyond doubt; along with the legislature and the executive, the courts have also been recognized as legitimate partners in the processes leading to India's democratization. The Kesavananda Bharati judgement also shows, on the other, that Indian judiciary, especially the apex court, can be proactive as well, which is little novel since, according to classical jurisprudence, it is usually reactive. By setting out the broad principles for governance, the Supreme Court of India creates a space for the fundamental ethos of democracy, liberty, equality and fraternity, to flourish.

The apex court's main concern, as the Kesavananda Bharati case demonstrates, was to uphold those complementary values and also those supportive institutions with a view to designing a polity drawing on the Enlightenment principles. There are many illustrative judgements. The purpose here is not to dwell on each and every judgement; instead, we will focus on one of the most widely discussed pronouncements in recent times. It was a verdict which, by outlawing the Shariat-based divorce of Muslim women, sought to translate into reality equality in its substantial sense. A dimension, which is not exactly new, was added to India's constitutional discourse by seeking to establish the point that Shariat laws stand in contradiction with the idea of equality that the Constitution upholds. That equality in its unalloyed form is integral to India's constitutional identity has already been firmly established since the acceptance of the 1973 Kesavananda Bharati judgement. The 2016 Supreme Court verdict in the Shayara Bano versus the Union of India is a further elaboration of its concern for substantial equality by knocking out the age-old practices of Triple Talaq, being practised by the Muslim men to divorce their legally wedded wife. The principle that constitutional equality and Triple Talaq can never coexist since they are contrary to each other was sought to be established when the court was asked to adjudicate in 1985 when a Muslim woman, Shah Banu Begum was denied alimony by her husband, Mohammad Ahmad Khan, who resorted to Triple Talaq to divorce here. The Supreme Court decision of supporting Triple Talaq was politically conditioned in the sense the then ruling party, the Congress, felt that a contrary decision was likely to alienate its Muslim voters. So, an opportunity was lost in the quagmire of vote-politics.

That equality was integral to India's constitutional identity was, however, proved in 2016 first in a judgement of Allahabad High Court, which more or less reverberated in the 2016 Supreme Court verdict. According to Allahabad High Court, Triple Talaq in its presently practised form, known as instant Triple Talaq has no religious sanction and is basically a cultural practice. Hence, it is contrary to the spirit of the fundamental scripture, Quran. Instead of drawing on the claim that Triple Talaq is antithetical to equality, the court justified its viewpoints by referring to the Quranic instructions. The court thus observes that 'divorce is permissible in Islam only in case of extreme emergency [because] the parties may proceed to dissolution of marriage by Talaq . . . only when all efforts for effecting reconciliation have failed'.[1] So, even in Quranic terms, divorce does not seem to be so easily possible. On this basis, the court builds its argument by further saying that

> the view that the Muslim husband enjoys an arbitrary, unilateral power to inflict instant divorce does not accord with Islamic injections. It is [thus] a popular fallacy that a Muslim husband enjoys, under Quranic law, unbridled authority to [annul] the marriage [since] the whole Quran expressly forbids a man to seek pretexts for divorcing his wife, so long as she remains faithful and obedient to him.[2]

So, as per Quran, Talaq is both a distortion of the fundamental Quranic principles and an attempt to justify a partisan design in its name. This was articulated by the court most unambiguously in its statement underlining that

> Islamic law gives to the many primarily the faculty of dissolving the marriage, if the wife, by her indocility or her bad character, renders the married life unhappy; but, in the absence of serious reasons, no man can justify a divorce, either in the eyes of religion or law.[3]

The argument that the court develops justifies the contention that Triple Talaq does not seem to be embedded in Quran; it evolved as a cultural practice. Although the court defended its argument by reference to Quranic instructions, it had its root in its concern for gender equality, which the Constitution advocates. By linking one of the fundamental constitutional principles, the principle of equality, with a Quranic canon, the court not only justified, but also raised one important point suggesting that the religious dictum did not always stand in contradiction with the constitutional directions. The 1950 Constitution's insistence on equality corresponded with the Quranic commands, and hence the court decided accordingly. There are two points that need attention here: on the one hand, it is clear that the Allahabad High Court was persuaded to endorse the claim against Triple Talaq, since Quran provides a clear direction to the contrary; the judgement was not exactly based on the religious dictum since the court also draws, on the other, on India's well-defined constitutional identity underlining equality regardless of gender, ethnicity or region. The judgement also represented an effort on the part of the court of creatively blending the available cultural practices with the constitutional concerns for absolute equality which was not allowed to be vitiated by any other considerations. This has two serious politico-ideological implications for collective human life: (a) the judgement has shown that the judges remain sensitive to the prevalent religio-cultural perspective, which plays a critical role in shaping human response; this is quite obvious since, in individual socialization, the importance of religion cannot be undermined; and (b) this verdict is also an endeavour to argue that the 1950 Constitution, by contending that equality remains an aspired goal for independent India, conforms to one of the basic Quranic principles. It was one of the most intelligent ways of addressing perhaps one of the vexed socio-economic and political issues confronting India, as history has shown.

While Allahabad High Court outlawed Triple Talaq, because it was in contradiction with Quran, the Supreme Court of India dismissed the same by arguing that it is contrary to the right to equality and freedom, enshrined in Articles 14 and 15 respectively, of the Constitution of India. In its 2016 landmark verdict, India's apex court in the Shayara Bano and others versus Union of India set aside the practice of Triple Talaq which justified divorce of Muslim women by their legally wedded husbands instantaneously and irrevocably, since it violated the Constitution of India.[4] Unlike the Allahabad High Court judgement which was also a definite step towards ascertaining gender equality, the Supreme Court pronouncement was drawn on the fundamental constitutional provisions upholding those individual rights which are inalienable as the case details show. When she was divorced through Triple Talaq, which permits men to arbitrarily and unilaterally effect instant and irrevocable divorce by pronouncing the word Talaq three times at once in oral, written or, more recently, electronic form, Shayara Bano challenged before the apex court by arguing that the Islamic practices of Triple Talaq, polygamy and *nikah halala* (the practice allowing women to divorce and marry another man so that her previous husband can remarry) were unconstitutional. These Islamic practices, she further elaborated, were violating Article 14 (right to equality), Article 15 (right to freedom), Article 15 (1) prohibiting discrimination including on the ground of gender, Article 21 (right to life) and Article 25 (right to freedom of religion). The majority judgement held the view that Triple Talaq was unconstitutional under Article 14, as the court stated that 'an action that is clearly arbitrary, must necessarily involve negation of equality'. This was also a negation of the right to equality since Triple Talaq provided that 'the marital tie can be broken capriciously without any attempt at reconciliation so as to save it', which is also illustrative of the violation of Article 14. In its operative part, the judgement highlights the point by forcefully stating that

> given the fact that Triple Talaq is instant and irrevocable, it is obvious that any attempt at reconciliation between husband and wife by arbiters from their families . . . which is essential to save the marital life, cannot ever take place. . . . This being case, it is clear that this form of Talaq is manifestly arbitrary in the sense that the marital tie can be broken capriciously and whimsically by a Muslim man without any attempt at reconciliation so as to save it. This form of Talaq must, therefore, be held to be violative of the fundamental right contained under Article 14 of the Constitution of India.[5]

By strictly applying the constitutional canons, the majority of the judges privileged the rule of law over the prevalent Islamic cultural practices. The minority view, however, supported the contention that since Triple Talaq, or for that matter, matters of personal laws, remained outside the purview of the Constitution. The argument was defended, as an analyst adumbrates, by suggesting that

> triple talaq was a matter of faith affirmed and anointed by 1,400 years of uninterrupted and open practice and belief and there it was not open to the Court to interfere with it, although the legislature in its capacity as a reformer could do so.[6]

Denying the court of law of any rights, the analyst further argues that

> under Muslim Personal Law, the religious heads of imams are called upon to decipher the teachings of Quran and Hadith (record of the traditions and sayings of the Prophet Mahammad, revered and received as a major source of religious law and moral guidance, second only to the authority of Quran), in particular conflicts. The imams resolve these conflicts not by deciding what the correct course of action is, *suo motto*,

> but by reading the sources, that the Holy Quran and the Hadith, and deciphering the correct interpretation /meaning of the same.[7]

The judges representing the minority opinion seemed persuaded and were reluctant to intervene in an area of human life which is exclusively private. According to them, religion was a matter of faith and not logic, and hence the court, under normal circumstances, lacked jurisdiction to govern personal private life. As per Article 25 of the Constitution, the court was bound to protect and preserve the cultural distinctiveness of a religious community. So, the judges concluded, it was not within the court's domain to decide whether Triple Talaq was contrary to individual rights, protected under Articles 14, 15, 21 and 25. Articulating the minority opinion, Justice J Kurian took onto himself the responsibility of ascertaining whether 'what is bad in theology is good in law, especially after the Saariat (sic) laws were accepted as primary insofar as personal laws are concerned'.[8] Aware that Triple Talaq was contrary to Quran, he was not willing to intervene, since it had evolved in India as a cultural practice, which he stated by saying that

> commentators on the Quran have rightly observed – and this tallies with the law now administered in some Muslim countries like Iraq – that the husband must satisfy the court about the reasons for divorce. However, Muslim law, as applied in India has taken a course contrary to the spirit of what the Prophet or the Holy Quran laid down and same misconception vitiates the law dealing with the wife's right to divorce.[9]

For Kurian, religious dictum is privileged primarily because the rule of law has no jurisdiction in individual personal matter. It is true, as he admitted, that the Indian customary practices differed from the established religious practice that does not allow the judiciary to intervene in a domain which is strictly private. While defending this line of thinking, Kurian most eloquently put his views by saying that 'what is held to be bad in the Holy Quran cannot be good in Shariat and, in that sense, what is bad in theology is bad in law as well'.[10] In his well-thought-out views, interference is legally not tenable though Kurian was not in favour of status quo because he also felt that if the legislature thought so an appropriate law could be enacted. As he argued,

> when issues of such nature come to the forefront, the discourse often takes the form of pitting religion against constitutional rights. I believe that a reconciliation between the same is possible, but the process of harmonizing different interests is within the powers of the legislature. Of course, this power has to be exercised within the constitutional parameters without curbing the religious freedom guaranteed under the Constitution of India. However, *it is not for the Courts to direct any legislation*. (Emphasis added)[11]

From the point of view of constitutional identity, Kurian appears to have prioritized the importance of religious dictum and practices in individuals' personal/private life. Drawn on a fundamental tenet of constitutional liberalism, the argument was further defended that under no circumstances, cultural practices of a multitude could never be fiddled with since it undermined one of the fundamental means of its self-actualization. In other words, for sustaining the compact of multitudes, which India was, the minority of the judges views India's constitutional identity as one which drew on a specific highlighting the inviolability of absolute groups rights. This is defensible only to the extent it does not harm the compact comprising many groups with distinct rights supported by religious-cum-cultural practices. Here is an important point of view which seems to have persuaded the majority of the judges, led by the Chief Justice of India, Justice JS Khehar, who settled the case by outlawing Triple Talaq. It was explicit when he forcefully argued that

> despite the views expressed by those who challenged the practice of [Triple Talaq] being able to demonstrate that the practice transcends the barriers of constitutional morality (emerging from different provisions of the Constitution), we have found ourselves unable to persuade ourselves, from reaching out in support of the petitioners' concern. We cannot accept the petitioners' claim, because the challenge raised is in respect of an issue of 'personal law' which has constitutional protection. . . . Till such time as legislation is considered, we are satisfied in injuncting Muslim husbands from pronouncing [Triple Talaq] as a means of severing their matrimonial relationship.[12]

There are two interrelated aspects which merit attention here: on the one hand, being attentive to major constituent features of India's constitutional identity, namely equality and freedom, the majority of the judges knock down the practice of Triple Talaq. They were not persuaded, on the other, to accept the arguments supportive of exclusive rights for one community and not another. For them, it is travesty, if not complete denial of justice, to those being affected as a result of protecting the right to Triple Talaq to only the Muslim men. Not only was this indefensible, it was a clear violation of the core values of liberal constitutionalism which evolved in India after protracted struggle both during colonialism and its aftermath. The judiciary was expected to uphold these principles; otherwise, the constitutional democracy that has struck roots in India over the years is likely to crumble. By quoting the Justice J Khanna's judgement in the State of Punjab v. Khan Chand, (1974), Justice Khehar further argued that

> it would be wrong to assume that there is an element of judicial arrogance in the act of the Courts striking down an enactment. The Constitution has assigned to the Courts the function of determining as to

> whether the laws made by the Legislatures are in conformity with the provisions of the Constitution. In adjudicating the constitutional validity of statutes, the Courts discharge an obligation which has been imposed upon them by the Constitution. The Courts would be shrinking their responsibility if they hesitate to declare the provisions of a statute to be unconstitutional even though those provisions are found to be violative of the Articles of the Constitution.[13]

This is an unambiguous statement defending that the courts had an inherent domain to intervene if a legislative act is ultra vires to the codified rules of the Constitution. What is not acceptable is judiciary being indifferent even in the face of flagrant violation of core constitutional provisions. The idea is stunningly clear: judiciary is endowed, in a liberal constitutional democracy, with an authority to look into the constitutionality of the legislative enactments. There is another aspect which Justice Khehar referred to while passing his judgement on an issue of personal law which is not only a politically sensitive matter but also the Constitution does not seem to be very categorical in providing a direction as per its written provisions. In this respect too, he drew on Justice J Khanna's historical pronouncement in the State of Punjab v. Khan Chand, (1974) in which it was stated that

> hesitation or refusal on the part of the Courts to declare the provisions of an enactment to be unconstitutional, even they are found to infringe the Constitution because of any notion of judicial humility would in large number of cases have the effect of taking away or in any case eroding the remedy provided to the aggrieved parties by the Constitution. Abnegation in matters affecting one's own interest may sometimes be commendable by abnegation in a matter where power is conferred to protect the interests of others against measures which are violative of the Constitution is fraught with serious consequences. It is as much the duty of the courts to declare a provision of an enactment to be unconstitutional if it contravenes any article of the Constitution as it is theirs to uphold its validity in case it is found to suffer from no such infirmity.[14]

The court's duty was to protect the right of those who were deprived of their fundamental rights because of the prevalence of a cultural practice which hardly had constitutional sanction. For the majority of the judges, it was a constitutional obligation, as Justice Khanna stated, to proactively act in favour of individual citizens who approached the court for protecting their legitimate individual rights. Here abnegation of responsibility by the court was tantamount to abdicating its role as constitution's custodian. Hence, they were persuaded to support the arguments of Shayara Bano when she brought before the Supreme Court for adjudication of her claim whether Triple Talaq was constitutionally justified since it was a clear infringement of one's fundamental rights.

There were detractors to the judgement suggesting that the court surpassed its domain; it has intervened in a domain which is exclusive to the legislature though the Indian judiciary claims to have been circumspect in going into matters that are essentially within the purview of the parliament and executive. The court is constitutionally empowered to intervene to check the uncontrolled exercise of judicial and executive powers. However, in performing such a role, the court should not, argues Salman Khurshid,

> be eager to subsume the powers it seeks to check. The Court should refrain from legislating afresh in the guise of commenting upon the constitutional validity of Personal Law. The Court should thus refrain from commenting on issues such as the institution of a Uniform Civil Code, which would fall within the ambit of the legislature.[15]

According to Khurshid who also appeared in the Triple Talaq case before the apex court, the court had no jurisdiction since it is exclusively a matter of private/personal domain. Furthermore, it had been a long cultural practice that prevailed in India and judiciary had no constitutional authority to intervene; its role was just to interpret in the light of the practices that had acquired legitimacy since they were justified by religious dictum. So, under no circumstances, the court could usurp the authority which, in a constitutional democracy, belonged to the legislature and executive. It was an effort to set the ball rolling for uniform civil code, apprehends Khurshid which he articulated by stating that 'the real intent is clearly to chip away at personal laws to bring in the uniform civil code, . . . for which there should be at least an honest debate in the country'.[16] Whether this monumental judicial decision will lead to the establishment of uniform civil code is a difficult question to respond though it can persuasively argued that this judgement is one of those verdicts which created a space for discussion on this vexed social issue. As argued above, India's Constitution is a compact in which discrimination of any kind is an anathema. Hence, the discriminatory system of divorce depriving Muslim women of their basic constitutionally guaranteed fundamental rights is, under no circumstances, justified. The point that long-standing personal laws cannot be abrogated unless the religious experts endorse so does not seem to be persuasive since they are protective of the Muslim men. This is, at best, a technically perfect argument, with, of course, no substance because gender-prejudiced customs or practices are clearly undemocratic and conceptually biased for being discriminatory against one section of the community. With the articulation, by the apex court, of the basic structure doctrine which is now integral to India's constitutional identity, the arguments, however persuasive they are in the technical sense, do not seem to be tenable.

The Triple Talaq judgement may not have been adequate in meaningfully addressing the concern for gender parity; nonetheless, it has put, in the public domain, the issue which requires wider attention. Equality or freedom, the important features of India's constitutional identity, remains ornamental in character so long as gender discrimination is justified and happily practised. There is no denying that women are disadvantaged due to their gender identity. A blanket legal stipulation may be a necessary, but not sufficient, shield against gender discrimination because the degree of suffering is also contingent on their social location, which is conceptually sought to be articulated by the notion of intersectionality. As a result, besides being disadvantaged as women, they are socially deprived due to their social and ethnic identity. In other words, in order to address gender inequality and discrimination, one need to take into account several other sources which conjointly work to contribute to social exclusion. For instance, women belonging to rural areas, or those who are Muslims or Dalits, are naturally underprivileged given the ingrained sectional social prejudices. These women are subject to accumulative dominance which is historically justified and sustained by appropriate socio-economic and political mechanisms. The voice that is raised against the visible sources of gender discrimination is thus rather easily gagged. So, the zeal for uniform civil code of, for that matter, designs for gender empowerment, does not seem to completely eradicate sources of gender inequality or ensure women empowerment in substance unless one is sensitive of the intersectional aspect of women deprivation because of the prevalent mindset in support of prejudices against gender parity. In that sense, a legal step, which is a mere diversional therapy, does not seem to be as effective as it is surmised so long as those who are responsible for implementation hold onto such prejudices.[17]

The above elaborate discussion on the judiciary's effort towards seeking to ensure gender parity is complementary to the larger point of concerns for equality and freedom. This is what constitutes the core of India's constitutional identity. As argued in the book, the 1950 Constitution, being drawn fundamentally on the Enlightenment principles, upheld equality and freedom as the main objectives of independent India's polity. At the dawn of India's freedom, these principles acted as the basic guiding politico-ideological devices. This was not a mean achievement especially in the context of bloodbath that followed India's partition. In an atmosphere which was not exactly in favour of constitutional democracy of the liberal mould, to establish a system drawing on the principle of equality and freedom was an arduous task. As Orini Shani argues,

> creation of a [constitutional] democracy had to be achieved in the face of myriad social divisions, widespread poverty and low literacy levels, factors that have long been thought by scholars of democracy to be at odds with the supposedly requisite for successful democratic nationhood.[18]

Notwithstanding the visible difficulties, India rose as a democratic polity and the 1950 Constitution is a testimony to the endeavour that the founding fathers had undertaken to install a structure of governance drawing on the fundamental values of the philosophy of Enlightenment. It was a Constitution with a difference which became a unifying tool as far as Indians were concerned. Prominent among the reasons was the ready acceptance of those values, which helped build a strong edifice for liberal democracy in India. A natural outcome of this was also the endorsement of reservation in public jobs and in educational institutions for the socially segregated sections of the population. Reservation was thus considered legitimate to ascertain a level playing for all the communities; no community shall be deprived of the opportunities which are available to everybody regardless of caste, ethnicity, clan or kin. The argument was accepted by the founding fathers, and the Scheduled Castes (SCs) and Scheduled Tribes (STs) received reservation in public employment and other facilities, which are deemed to be pertinent for their blossoming as citizens of free India. Being integral to the nation-building processes, the 1950 Constitution is thus said to have 'structured the relative stability at the core wherein aspirations (of castes and communities) emerging from within (the cultural, regional ethnic and linguistic) fault lines merge successfully into constitutional discourses of affirmative action'.[19] By following proportional reservation, SCs were given 15 per cent reservation, while the share of STs was 7.5 per cent in public jobs and in higher education. In regard to SCs and STs, there are twelve separate articles (Articles 15, 16, 46, 164, 330, 332, 334, 335, 338, 341, 342 and 366) in the Constitution of India. Of these articles, Article 15 seems to be most fundamental in the sense it ensures guarantee of reservation without shackles by stating that

> nothing . . . shall prevent the State from making any special provision for the advancement of any socially and economically backward classes of citizens or for the Scheduled Castes and Tribes.

There are also complementary provisions in Part XVI of the Constitution which provides reserved seats to the SCs and STs following the principle of proportional representation. As Article 330 stipulates, the state shall reserve seats in the legislature for the SCs and STs; the number of seats for them

> shall bear, as nearly as may be, the same proportion to the total number of seats allotted to that State or Union Territory . . . as the population of the Scheduled Castes in the State or Union Territory or of the Scheduled Tribes in the State or Union Territory.

The arrangement is total, and the Constitution leaves no space for confusion. The scheme for reservation continued for fifty years which was later, with the adoption of the Seventy-Ninth Amendment Act in 1999, expanded for sixty years. In an attempt to erase socio-economic differences, the Constitution creates an adequately equipped mechanism for the marginalized groups of people who remain at the bottom of the pyramid because of being born with a specific caste tag or in a tribal family. Politically forward-looking and ideologically empowering, these articles are a watershed in the unfolding of India's blossoming as a constitutional democracy.

The Constitution thus evolved as a mechanism which also gradually became a cementing device presumably because it represented a design whereby Indians, despite being diverse culturally and otherwise, created a politico-ideological template of togetherness. It was possible because the Constitution was believed to be a binding ideological force. As James Madison very eloquently put, the constitutional identity was not merely a set of values, but also about a well-entrenched and philosophically justified 'keenness' to uphold them. According to him, 'a reverence for the laws would be sufficiently inculcated by the voice of an enlightenment reason'.[20] A very perceptive comment, it suggests that unless one is persuaded ideologically, the constitutional values seem to be vacuous. In other words, mere codification of laws, despite being highly enlightening, does not necessarily create a space in which they are readily acceptable. Jacobsohn explicates the implications by saying that implicit in Madison's belief was the claim that

> a constitution however reasonable and clear in its articulation of rules and principles, can only succeed in translating word into deed (and thereby establish a discernible identity) if fundamental continuity in basic law and actual constitutional practice are seen as two sides of the same coin.[21]

Unless and until the basic laws are compatible with the prevalent constitutional practices, the Constitution shall hardly be a device for creating and also sustaining a compact of individuals. In case of Indian Constitution, the Enlightenment principles seem to have laid a foundation in the wake of colonialism which flourished as India matured as a democracy. These values became, in other words, part and parcel of India's constitutional laws and the resultant practices. There were hardly sources of dissonance. As the text demonstrates, the constitutional ethos, supplemented by supportive constitutional practices, was upheld by the judiciary when it was asked to ascertain whether specific parliamentary/legislative interventions for changing the Constitution were justiciable or in conformity with India's constitutional identity. It has been amply shown that with the articulation of the basic structure doctrine, the jurists left no ambiguity that no legislative design was appropriate if that violates the core principles on which the 1950 Constitution rested. The 2016 Triple Talaq judgement was a continuity with the past in the sense that it also corroborated the basic contention that discriminatory social designs, as Talaq was, were prejudicial to the constitutional guarantee of the right to equality and freedom; so it was repugnant to what was held as fundamental to India's constitutional identity. It was a titanic decision with path-breaking implications for this judicial pronouncement set in motion processes of significant changes in gender relations, which are generally governed more by archaic social mores and practices and less by constitutional rules and regulations. Being based on a specific interpretation of Shariat to justify India-centric (and not Quranic) cultural practices, Talaq defies the fundamental rights, right to freedom and equality, which are enshrined in the Constitution of India. For the first time, the Indian apex court came out with a judgement which corresponds with India's constitutional identity supportive of unalloyed enjoyment of freedom and equality for her citizens regardless of religion, ethnicity and region. The pronouncement is path-breaking in character since it firmly establishes the claim that since discrimination and liberal democracy are ideologically incongruent, the former cannot be allowed to be practised in India drawing on those fundamental Enlightenment principles that inform constitutional-liberal-democracy. Being citizens, the Muslim women are also entitled to be treated equally just like their counterparts in other religious groups. Under no circumstances, distinctive cultural practices which are argued to have been drawn on Shariat have no legitimacy, since they stand in contradiction with the fundamental constitutional values of equality and freedom. Hence, the argument that Talaq is legitimate since it is being practised in India over centuries is immediately discarded because it is not constitutionally justified. In a nutshell, the judgement is a reinforcement of India's constitutional identity supportive of those core politico-ideological values upholding constitutional liberalism in contrast with political systems in which the Constitution does not seem to be as critical as it is in the former. And, the fact that the Constitution is revered also confirms that the values from which it draws its sustenance seem to have developed organic roots largely due to (a) historical processes leading to India's rise as liberal democratic polity in the aftermath of decolonization in 1947, and (b) consolidation of complementary constitutional practices strengthening the liberal edifice that evolved first out of a long-drawn ideological battle that the nationalists had waged against the colonizers, and later due to its unfolding as organically linked with India's rise as democratic polity in the aftermath of the British withdrawal. In other words, liberal democracy had emerged due to the peculiar texture of British colonialism, which also encouraged processes of constitutionalization in phases as perhaps an effective means of consolidating British colonial rule, which was also unique if it is judged with reference to other European colonial powers. What is also striking is that constitutional democracy struck deep roots in India though it failed elsewhere in South Asia which also remained under British colonialism. This perhaps shows that constitutionalism cannot be instilled, but needs to be inculcated by encouraging complementary constitutional practices to grow and support, which also means that once they are in place, they create a specific kind of constitutional identity leading to conceptualizing Indian polity strictly in liberal democratic terms and also in its format. In other words, what is emphasized here is the importance of processes whereby adequately nurtured constitutional practices are privileged to evolve conditions helping liberal constitutionalism to grow and strike roots. This is a two-way traffic as history of constitutional democracy has shown: a fine-tuned liberal Constitution ceases to be effective unless it is nurtured by generating those practices which are integral to liberal constitutionalism. The Triple Talaq judgement is, in that respect, a significant step towards building and also consolidating a system seeking to creatively blend text and context of constitutional democracy in India.

The right to privacy judgement

As argued above, in the formation of a constitutional identity, constitutional practices which are supportive of liberal constitutionalism play a critical role. History is replete with examples showing that constitutional identity is a one-shot phenomenon, but an outcome of intricate processes which unfold in unique ways. A careful analysis of the trajectory of Indian democracy confirms that while the Enlightenment values laid the foundation that they gradually blossomed naturally is attributed to those nationalist leaders and also the invisible opinion makers who played an immensely important role in creating and sustaining an environment in which constitutional morality prevailed. The scene was hardly different in independent India: constitutional democracy continues to remain inspirational. Amidst challenges and threats, institutions of governance stand out in pursuing activities complementary to India's constitutional democracy. The role of the Supreme Court of India is immensely significant, as the past shows. In a 2017 path-breaking judgement, India's apex court reconfirms that individual is the core of constitutional governance in India, which can be undermined only to the detriment of the foundational values on which it is based. The case in question involves a petition before the apex court filed by a retired Justice KS Puttaswamy[22] who, in 2012, challenged the constitutional validity of the Indian biometric identity scheme, Aadhaar, on the ground that it violates the right to privacy which was, he further emphasized, a fundamental right under the Constitution. The judgement has wider ramifications because 'if privacy is to be construed as a protected constitutional value', argues DY Chandrachud, one of the members of the nine-judge bench, 'it would redefine in significant ways our concepts of liberty and the entitlements that flow out of its protection'. The judgement is a culmination of a constitutional battle that had begun in 2015 when the Attorney General of India defended the plea that the Constitution did not guarantee any fundamental right to privacy. Given the import of the issue, the three judges hearing the case put the matter to a larger bench of five judges which, in turn, referred it further to the nine-judge bench. The judgement is an endorsement of the right to privacy as a fundamental right. The final order thus stated that 'the right to privacy is protected as an intrinsic part of the right to life and personal liberty under Article 21 and as a part of the freedoms guaranteed by Part III of the Constitution'. With this pronouncement, the right to privacy was made integral to Article 21 protecting the right to life and liberty. It has two serious implications: at one level, it is validation of the Enlightenment concern of individuals being primary in governance; at another far more perceptive level, the verdict sets out a boundary for the state beyond which trespassing is not allowed.

Unfolding of the design

The 2017 judgement is both a continuity and break with the past: continuity because the apex court rearticulated its arguments in defence of the right to privacy in consonance with the Right to Freedom, and biometric identity clearly undermines individuals' fundamental rights. The Indian Constitution may have been silent; but a common sense interpretation of the Right to Freedom entails that an intervention in the individuals' personal domain is tantamount to taking away of their right to freedom. This is also a departure from the past because this judgement is contrary to what the Supreme Court itself decided earlier in 1954 and reconfirmed in 1962 in two famous cases of MP Sharma versus Satish Chandra and Kharak Singh versus State of Uttar Pradesh, respectively. Despite a gap of eight years, Indian apex court was unanimous in arguing that the right to privacy was not a fundamental right. In the 1954 MP Sharma case, the Supreme Court rejected the plea, since in the Constitution, there were no clear statements in its favour. The bench further argued that given the absence of such a declaration in the Constitution, the endorsement of the right to privacy as a fundamental right was contrary to the spirit of Article 21, emphasizing the importance of the procedure established by law in decoding the meaning of a particular constitutional provision. Once its attention is drawn to the US constitutional practices, especially the Fourth Amendment,[23] which recognized the right to privacy as part and parcel of individuals' fundamental rights, the bench defended the argument by saying that Indian Constitution neither endorses nor implies any such right in any of the provisions. The Court further argued that since the judges in the MP Sharma case did not get into the question whether 'a constitutional right to privacy is protected by other provisions contained in the Fundamental Rights, including among them, the right to life and personal liberty under Article 21', the issue remained unresolved. For the Supreme Court, the endorsement of the right to privacy thus neither rejected nor helped build its own argument on the basis of its earlier judgement; it was an attempt to review the concern afresh by being sensitive to the spirit in which the Right to Freedom was incorporated in Part III of the Constitution. The idea is clear: the concern for the right to privacy needed to be addressed not in isolation, but in conjunction with Right to Freedom which, by emphasizing that 'no person shall be deprived of his life or personal liberty except according to procedure established by law', recognized the right to privacy. The 1962 Kharak Singh case was also evasive because the judges did not look into the right to privacy per se. It is true that, as the 2018 Supreme Court bench argued, the 1964 judgement abrogated a police regulation that allowed for nightly domiciliary visits because it was 'an unauthorized intrusion into a person's home and a violation of ordered liberty'. Here too, the apex court avoided looking into the plea for the right to privacy with the same justification that it was not guaranteed under the 1950 Constitution though the dissenting judge, Justice Subba Rao, raised a point by saying that although the right to privacy was not expressly stated as a fundamental right, it was 'an essential ingredient of personal liberty under Article 21'. Although Rao failed to persuade his colleagues in the bench, in the Puttaswamy case, his views were hailed since they 'represent the exposition of the correct constitutional principle'. In three specific ways, the argument is justified: first, fundamental rights emanate from the basic notion of liberty and dignity of individuals, which form the core of constitutional democracy that flourished in India. Second, whether a law is valid or not needs to be judged not by 'state action', but by ascertaining whether it affects the enjoyment of freedom, guaranteed by the Constitution. Third, the constitutional endorsement of Article 14 suggesting that 'state action must not be arbitrary and must fulfill the requirement of reasonableness' is a shield vis-à-vis fundamental rights protected in Part III of the Constitution.

There were two important issues that the court looked into for deciding whether the right to privacy is a fundamental right. What triggered court intervention was the petition that endeavour at preparing citizens' biometric data was violative of the right to privacy. It was an important issue especially since the apex court in the past was persuaded to believe that the right to privacy was not integral to the Part III rights since it was not constitutionally endorsed. In the first place, the court was asked to determine whether, in view of the 1954 and 1962 judgements, it was constitutionally valid to claim that this right needed to be constitutionally protected; second, if the right to privacy was a constitutionally protected right, whether this had the character of an independent fundamental right or whether it arose from within the existing guarantees of protected rights such as life and personal liberty.

The task was difficult because (a) the Supreme Court had conclusively decided otherwise in the past, and (b) it was asked to arbitrate in a new context when the ideas of freedom and justice had acquired new dimension given the large-scale democratization of political processes and also the availability of electronic devices and tools to intrude into individuals' private domain. For the court, 'privacy . . . allows each human being to be left alone in a core which is inviolable'. This was likely to be infringed, the court apprehended, in the digital world which, at one level, connected individuals immediately, at another, makes easier for the state or any other non-state agencies to gain access to information which was otherwise not available. So, Internet was a double-edged device: on the one hand, it empowered individuals by making them being connected with one another in a virtual world; it, on the other, provided state and other agencies with a tool to gain access to information which was exclusively private in nature. What provoked the apex was the endeavour that the state undertook to link the AADHAR card with citizens' mobile phone and bank accounts. This was simply not acceptable because it was an intervention in individuals' private domain. In a liberal democratic set-up, as individuals remain the core of activities, it is an attack on the fundamental principle on which the liberal edifice stands. Hence, the endeavour of linking the AADHAR card with the basic facilities that citizens are entitled to enjoy stands contrary to liberal constitutionalism that was assiduously nurtured by the founding fathers and also those who presided over India's destiny following independence. This is one aspect of the argument which was made to disallow the Union Government to proceed further in this direction; but there is another aspect which cannot be completely wished-away, namely the growing dependence on technology, especially ICT (Information and Communication Technology) that cannot, at all, be ignored because of immanent advantages. It was endorsed by the apex court when it suggests that

> information technology together with the internet and the social media and all their attendant applications rapidly altered the course of life in the last decade [and] . . . today's technology renders models of application of a few years ago obsolescent.

Juxtaposed with this concern, the court also underlines the fact that the Constitution

> possesses the resilience necessary to ensure its continued relevance [which] . . . lies precisely in its ability to allow succeeding generations to apply the principles on which it has been founded to find innovative solutions to intractable problems of their times.

So, at one level, the court is aware that technology is welcome; but, at another level, it also refers to the cardinal constitutional principles that need to be upheld. The choice was therefore not so difficult since the values which the Constitution represents cannot be sacrificed under any circumstances. Implicit here are two basic points that merit attention: on the one hand, it was admitted by the court that so long as technology did not infringe in the domain which was considered to be critical for the Constitution to remain as it was, it should not concern; this is, however, not to suggest, on the other, that technology was a complete anathema to the court. While making up its mind, the court however drew on BR Ambedkar's warning that liberal constitutionalism needs to be guarded; otherwise, the entire constitutional structure will break down in no time. It was evident when the court expressed its views by categorically suggesting that the right to privacy was inviolable because the Constitution guarantees fundamental rights which are inviolable. Hence, the submission that claim for connecting AADHAR card with citizens' mobile phone and bank accounts

> betrays the lack of understanding of the reason why rights are protected in the first place as entrenched guarantees in a Bill of Rights or, as in the case of the Indian Constitution, as part of the fundamental rights. . . . Furthermore, elevating a right to a position of a constitutionally protected right places it beyond the pale of legislative majorities.

This was an unambiguous statement which clearly privileges rights under all circumstances. They are inviolable and, if there is an attempt in undermining the enshrined fundamental rights, it should immediately be stopped.

So far as the court is concerned, the right to privacy cannot be infringed as it is integrally connected with the realization of individuals' own being as a free entity. This is the crux of liberal constitutionalism, which cannot be undermined because, according to the judgement, 'right to privacy has been held to be a fundamental right of the citizen being an integral part of Article 21 of the Constitution of India'. Illegitimate intrusion into privacy of a person is, the court further agues,

> not permissible as right to privacy is implicit in the right to life and liberty guaranteed under our Constitution, [and] . . . in the view of this Court, privacy and dignity of human life have always been considered a fundamental human right of every human being like other constitutional values such as free speech.

The statement leaves no doubt that the right to privacy is primary to individual existence in a liberal democratic set-up. A careful reading of the concerns that the court had shown reveals that the right to privacy appears to be one of the cardinal guarantees for citizens to flourish as free agencies, of course, within the lawful constraints. Besides adequate legal protection, fundamental rights are likely to be jeopardized if the citizens are not alert or discharge their responsibility as true citizenry of a democratic polity. Hence, the court also insists on building a strong mindset in support of efforts towards infringing any of these fundamental rights. While identifying the philosophical basis of the argument, the court thus adumbrated by stating that

> the best decision on how life should be lived are entrusted to the individuals. They are continuously shaped by the social milieu in which individuals exist. The duty of the state is to safeguard the ability to take decisions . . . [and] not to dictate those decisions.

Here the responsibility is vested in the state which is expected to build an adequately strong system of governance which will protect individuals' freedom in case it is violated. This does not seem to be unusual, as history has shown by drawing our attention the fact that 'the struggle between liberty and power is eternal [and] . . . vigilance is the price that we like every other democratic society has to pay to safeguard the democratic values enshrined in our Constitution'. Apart from emphasizing the importance of evolving an alert mindset, the Court was equally sensitive to the possibility of denial of freedom and rights to the citizens by the state, which is generally prone to being an instrument of arrogating power to itself. It was made clear when, in the Puttaswamy judgement, it was mentioned that 'even the best of the Governments are not averse to have more and more power to carry out their plans and programmes which they may sincerely believe to be in the public interest'. This cannot be allowed under normal circumstances because 'a freedom once lost is', the Court exhorts, 'hardly ever regained except by revolution [and] . . . every encroachment on freedom sets a pattern for further encroachments'. The apprehension does not seem to be unfounded. As history has demonstrated, absence of opposition and challenge leads to the unfolding of tendencies which are not conducive for democratic governance; instead, it contributes to the consolidation of designs which are neither pro-freedom nor politico-ideologically supportive of liberal constitutionalism.

The Puttaswamy judgement is a powerful statement in favour of the right to privacy, which was justified in two complementary ways: first, by referring to the doctrine of basic structure of the Constitution, the division bench defended the argument that being fundamental to constitutional democracy in India, the right to privacy is to be upheld unconditionally within the constraints of a constitutionally recognized lawful living. The state is therefore responsible to 'secure its citizens the rights mentioned in the Constitution'. There cannot be 'any implicit meaning' in the guarantee because it is impossible 'to accept that the makers of the Constitution would have [incorporated provisions] to snatch the rights that have already been guaranteed in the Constitution'. Even the elected parliament has no power to abrogate the provisions bestowing rights on the individuals exactly for the same reason, namely it is tantamount to destroying the very foundation of India's constitutional democracy. Fundamental here is the idea that right to privacy cannot be taken away as it helps build constitutional democracy in its true form and spirit. Second, the Indian apex court also draws on the US constitutional precedents to justify its argument in favour of the right to privacy. By quoting extensively the 1886 US Supreme Court judgement supportive of the Ninth Amendment Act, the Indian counterpart argues that

> the established doctrine is that this liberty [the right to privacy] may not be interfered with, under the guise of protecting the public interests, by legislative action which is arbitrary or without reasonable relation to some purpose within the competency of the State to effect.

The argument that is offered here is a reiteration of the point relating to the inviolability of individual rights that cannot be interfered with by the whimsical state for its partisan desire. Interference is permissible provided it is justified beyond doubt. There are two aspects which need attention here: on the one hand, rights are general sacrosanct; they can be suspended, on the other, in case that is required for a well-defined purpose for ensuring the well-being of the democratic polity. This point was reinforced in a judgement of 1928 in which the US apex court again held views against unwarranted intrusion. As the judgement runs,

> the makers of our Constitution undertook to secure conditions favourable to the pursuit of happiness. They sought to protect Americans in their beliefs, their thoughts, their emotions and their sensations. They conferred, as against the Government, the right to be let alone – the most comprehensive of rights, and the right most valued by civilized men. To protect that right, every unjustifiable intrusion by the Government upon the privacy of the individual, whatever the means employed, must be deemed a violation of the Fourth Amendment. Whatever the power of the state to control public dissemination of ideas inimical to the public morality, it cannot constitutionally premise legislation on the desirability of controlling a person's private thoughts. . . . If the right of privacy means anything, it is the right of the individual . . . to be free from unwarranted governmental intrusion into matters so fundamentally affecting his/her being.

Significant here are three critical ideas which are useful in comprehending the right to privacy. First, the right to privacy was implied in the discussion that led to drafting and also acceptance of the 1789 US Constitution. The founding fathers were aware that privacy was essential to the unfolding of individuals as effective citizens of a democratic polity. Second, the right to privacy is also implicit in the Fourth Amendment Act, which prohibits 'unreasonable searches and seizures'. Part of the Bill of Rights, the Fourth Amendment Act is pioneer in the sense that it also contributed to the enactment of provisions in various democratic Constitution across globe for guarding individual basic citizenry rights. Right to privacy if it is infringed will amount to 'unreasonable' interference in a domain which no right-conscious individual shall permit. Finally, the right to privacy needs to be guarded to avoid unwarranted governmental intrusion, which is an anathema in a constitutional democracy. These rights cannot be absolute which is understandable because one's enjoyment of right should not cause difficulty for others. This is a now fairly established idea in a democratic system because rights come along with duties and the government interference is allowed, provided it is justified beyond doubt that it is of utmost necessity.

The 2017 Puttaswamy judgement stands out in India's journey as a constitutional democracy. It has established rather firmly the idea that the Constitution is not a document 'for fastidious dialectics but the means of ordering the life of a people; it has roots in the past; its continuity is reflected in the present and it is intended for the unknown future'. Implied here is the idea that the Constitution is a constantly evolving system of rules and regulations which, if violated, shall strike at its foundation. These are rules which are non-discriminatory. They exist for

> the common man, for the poor and the humble, for those who have businesses at stake, for the butcher, the baker and the candlestick maker; it lays down for this land a rule of law as understood in the free democracies of the world.

This judgement shall remain distinctive in the history of jurisprudence because it has emphasized, besides streamlining the government institutions created for protecting individual rights and freedom, the importance of creating a conducive mindset favouring the fundamental principles and values of constitutional democracy. It is evident when the judgement underlines that

> life and liberty are not granted by the Constitution. Constitution only stipulates the limitations on the power of the State to interfere with our life and liberty. Law is essential to enjoy the fruits of liberty. It is not the source of liberty and emphatically not the exclusive source.

So, at a rather fundamental level, the judgement privileges the importance of a mindset which gains credibility, if not strength, once it is constitutionally endorsed. In other words, mere constitutional guarantee may not be adequate unless there exists a supportive mindset for individual rights and freedom as essential for constitutional democracy to strike roots. Thus, within a broad conceptual framework, the judgement, at another perceptive level, elaborates the arguments for the right to privacy. According to the bench, 'privacy is the condition or state of being free from public attention to intrusion into or interference with one's acts or decisions [which, in common parlance means] "the right to be let alone"'. What is thus essential to privacy is 'the power to seclude oneself and keep others from intruding it in any way'. This is instinctive of human beings, feel the bench. Hence, it is mentioned that 'the right to privacy has its foundation in the instincts of nature [which is] . . . recognized intuitively'. It is an important conceptualization which is further expanded by suggesting that

> the existence of zones of privacy is felt instinctively by all civilized people, without exception. The best evidence for this proposition lies in the panoply of activities through which we all express claims to privacy in our daily lives. We lock our doors, clothe our bodies and set passwords to our computers and phones to signal that we intend for places, persons and virtual lives to be private.

Here, the justification is couched in a common language. Privacy is instinctive to human beings. In such circumstances, it is incumbent on the state to uphold privacy. This is fundamental to liberal democracy in which individual reigns supreme. Hence, the court insists that

> all liberal democracies believe that the State should not have unqualified authority to intrude into certain aspects of human life and the authority should be limited by parameters constitutionally fixed. Fundamental rights are the only constitutional firewall to prevent State interference with those core freedoms constituting liberty of a human being [and] . . . the right to privacy is certainly one of the core freedoms.

Persuaded by the argument that the right to privacy can never be belittled, the court sets out an agenda for freedom against state's unwarranted interference in areas which should be kept away from its control. As Court believed, the scheme of linking AADHAR with citizens' bank details and cell phone is not only repugnant with democratic ethos, it is also an attack on individual freedom and rights. Hence, the apex court emphatically declared that

> let the right to privacy, an inherent right, be unequivocally a fundamental right embedded in Part III of the Constitution of India, but subject to the restrictions specified, relatable to that part. This is the call of today. The old order changeth, yielding to new.

In the history of Indian jurisprudence, the 2017 Puttaswamy judgement does not seem to be a complete break with the past for a variety of reasons. Prominent among is certainly the process of democratization that appears to have gained tremendous salience in contemporary India with the involvement of the so-called peripheral sections of society in political processes. Judiciary is certainly a major player as some of its recent judgements demonstrate. One of the path-breaking judicial pronouncements happens to be the verdicts relating to the basic structure doctrine, which establishes beyond doubt the importance of some of the parts of the Constitution and critical democratic institutions in sustaining India's constitutional democracy. One needs to read and also understand the Puttaswamy judgement. Hence, it will not be an exaggeration to suggest that the arguments supportive of the right to privacy have their roots in the basic structure verdicts. For instance, the argument that fundamental rights are inviolable seems to have logically justified the point that the bench made in favour of making the right to privacy integral to the basic structure. Basic to the argument is, in other words, the idea that unwarranted interference by the state in individual life is contrary to the foundational principles on which the Constitution is based. At one level, this is an obvious contention because it draws on the 1791 Fourth Amendment Act of the US Constitution. It is distinctive, at another level, because the Puttaswamy judgement focusses on an area of individual concern that appears to have escaped the judiciary's attention so far. By arguing that the right to privacy is not independent of fundamental rights enshrined in Part III of the Constitution, the bench also upholds the view that it is an inalienable right which needs to be recognized as critically important for India's constitutional democracy. What is most striking is the distinction that the bench makes between 'positive' and 'negative' elements of privacy. While the former restrains the state from interference in individual without legal-judicial endorsement, the latter dwells on mechanism, whereby the state is made responsible to create legislative framework in which the right to privacy is privileged. Two important ideas are critical here: on the one hand, the state cannot be allowed to force the individuals to share their personal data under the AADHAR scheme as it contravenes the justiciable fundamental rights; the state is also, on the other, expected to develop an adequately strong legal framework to ward off designs that are likely to affect individuals' right to privacy.

To conclude, the 2017 Puttaswamy judgement is both a break and continuity with the past: it is a break because it has made the right to privacy a justiciable right, which was not so explicitly stated in the past. It is, at the same time, a continuity with the traditions since the Puttaswamy verdict is nothing but a forceful argument for defending liberal democracy in which the individual remains the core. On the whole, it is a pronouncement that reconfirms the dictum that constitutional democracy in India is far more deep-rooted than what is visible on the surface. This makes a powerful and also ideologically persuasive statement, suggesting that democracy in India is not merely 'a window dressing' as BR Ambedkar had apprehended, but an organically linked driving force which helps build a robust constitution in a country which defies the conventional conceptualization of democracy and democratic behaviour. Critical to the Puttaswamy pronouncement is also the idea that judiciary acts as a mirror in the sense that it reflects the politico-ideological views that seem important in contemporary India.

From the point of view of India's constitutional identity, the 2017 Puttaswamy judgement is a milestone for two significant reasons: on the one hand, it confirms that there are ample rooms in India's constitutional practices to be innovative and also accommodative of newer sociopolitical ideas supportive of the processes of democratization. In that sense, the Constitution is not merely a compilation of rules and regulations, but a directional document having the capacity to adapt to the rapidly changing social, economic and political milieu. The verdict thus represents, on the other, the aspirations and goals that citizenry considers appropriate for their well-being and also betterment. Seeking to address a present concern, the judgement is also a cornerstone for futuristic constitutional endeavour, tuned to democracy and democratic governance in India. Like any other Supreme Court judgements, this verdict will remain a mile stone in the sense that it re-establishes, rather firmly, the contention that India's constitutional identity is being constantly reinvented or reworked in response to the inputs from the grassroots sociopolitical campaigns for further democratization. At one level, this does not seem to be very striking as it is a characteristic of judicial pronouncement of being always attentive to an immediate issue; at a far more perceptive level which has far more significant theoretical implications, the Puttaswamy judgement reformulates the conventional (or rather clichéd) ideas in an expansive conceptual format. In other words, despite not being explicitly stated in the Constitution, the right to privacy was justified by the nine-judge judicial bench as clearly organic to the fundamental rights enshrined in Part III of the Constitution of India. Here lies its significance not merely as an important judgement, but as a pronouncement that reconfirms India's constitutional identity in conformity with those foundational principles of constitutional liberalism that the founding fathers so assiduously nurtured.

Decriminalizing homosexuality

Amendment to a Constitution can never be an exception because, to remain relevant to the changing socio-economic and political milieu, it is the only instrument. It is, in other words, a device for transformation since with amendment, a Constitution reformulates (and also adds) designs to address the newer concerns. As reinvention of the Constitution seems to be inevitable, its identity undergoes constant changes. This is a historical truth since without adapting the Constitution to the changing needs and requirements, it will just become an instrument without much substance; if that is not the case, the Constitution shall cease to be a living organism. This is the perspective in which the continuously changing constitutional identity needs to be understood and conceptualized.

The discussion of the above judgements has amply proved how judiciary plays a critical role in transforming India's constitutional identity. What is common in all the above judicial pronouncements is the fact that judges form their opinion by strictly adhering to the foundational principles from which the Indian Constitution draws its sustenance. In other words, the path-breaking verdicts are reflective of their concern for freedom, rights and equality. These are cardinal principles on which the founding fathers had reposed their faith and helped draft the 1950 Constitution, which was also politico-ideologically directional for future. The 2018 Supreme Court judgement recognizing the legitimate rights of the LGBTQ[24] community in India is another landmark decision reiterating its faith in the fundamental values of constitutional democracy that has flourished with the inauguration of the 1950 Constitution in India. As per the apex court, 'the right to live with dignity has been recognized. Sexual orientation is a natural phenomenon determined by biology and science. Any discrimination on this basis is unconstitutional'.[25] By decriminalizing the conventionally 'normal' sexual conduct and behaviour, India's Supreme Court struck down section 377 of Indian Penal Code which came into effect in 1861 and criminalized sexual 'intercourse against the order of nature' as punishable with imprisonment of between ten years and a life sentence, along with a fine. Not only it is contrary to those fundamental principles on which liberal constitutionalism is based, it is also an endeavour of debasing human beings as human beings. While delivering its judgement, the Supreme Court of India cited verdicts pronounced elsewhere to justify its own point of view. Referring to one of the judgements of the US Supreme Court, the division bench thus wrote that

> LGBT were entitled to respect for their private lives and that the State could not demean their existence or control their destiny by making their private sexual conduct a crime, because their right to liberty under the Due Process Clause gives them the full right to engage in their conduct without the intervention of the State.

Basic to the argument is the importance of recognizing 'the difference', which is instinctive of human beings. Different sexual conduct or behaviour should not be a hindrance in realizing one's potential as a human being. There are two important aspects to this argument: on the one hand, the court is very sensitive to the claim of LGBTQ community to be recognized with dignity at par with the rest of the society; by insisting on this, the court also seeks to, on the other, translate equality in its true form and application. For the court, dignity of individuals as human beings seems to be the most important; it is clear as it has elaborated its argument by reiterating the point with force and persuasion when it stated that

> the fundamental idea of dignity is regarded as inseparable facet of human personality. Dignity has been duly recognized as an important aspect of the right to life under Article 21 of the Constitution. In the international sphere, the right to live with dignity had been identified as a human right way back in 1948 with the introduction of the Universal Declaration of Human Rights. . . . Without the right to live with dignity, all other fundamental rights may not realize their complete meaning.

So, there is nothing unusual in adopting a course of action, which is complementary to the attainment of the fundamental democratic principles on which India's Constitution is based. This is a global concern as the court has aptly mentioned by referring to the Universal Declaration of Human Rights of 1948. That the judgement is an expansion of the universal human desire to be treated equally is evident when it was mentioned that 'our Constitution fosters and strengthens the spirit of equality and envisions a society where every person enjoys equal rights which enable him/her to grow and realize his/her potential as an individual'. By drawing on the fundamental aim that India's Constitution strives to attain, the court further argues that

> it is the duty of the courts to realize the constitutional vision of equal rights in consonance with the current demands and situations and not to

> read and interpret the same as per the standards of equality that existed decades ago. The judiciary cannot remain oblivious to the fact that the society is constantly evolving and many a variation may emerge with the changing times. There is a constant need to transform the constitutional idealism into reality by fostering respect for human rights, promoting inclusion of pluralism, bringing harmony, that is, unity among diversity, abandoning the idea of alienation or some unacceptable social notions built on medieval egos and establishing the cult of egalitarian liberalism founded on reasonable principles that can withstand scrutiny.

Critical here are three important points that need to be taken into account, as per the court, to realize the foundational values on which India's Constitution rests. First, the court allows reinterpretation of the provisions of legislative designs since the context in which they were adopted no longer exists; in other words, the court prefers a contextual interpretation of the provisions guiding human behaviour as appropriate or otherwise. Second, the judiciary cannot abdicate its responsibility of conceptualizing the legal instruments with reference to the rapidly changing social, economic and political milieu, which have a direct bearing on human behaviour. What it means is that whatever was apt in the past may not be so in the present. A fairly logical argument, this appears to have acted decisively in shaping the 2018 judicial response to the demands of equality by the LGBTQ community. Finally, this judgement is surely a break with the past as the past design is not only weird, but also inhuman in the changed environment when ideas of democracy and democratization are being understood more with their wider connotations and implications. Democracy is truly about the demos and, under no circumstances, it can be restricted by imposing guidelines for human behaviour, which are anything but democratic. The court's argument hinges on its concern for realizing equality in its true form and spirit. This is also a critical step towards fostering the much exalted idea of inclusive existence completely shunning discrimination of any kind. Being sensitive of its responsibility, the court thus further emphasizes that

> as the final arbiter of the Constitution, [it] has to keep in view the necessities of the needy and weaker sections. The role of the Court assumes further importance when the class or community whose rights are in question are those who have been the object of humiliation, discrimination, separation and violence by not only the State and the society at large but also at the hands of their very own family members.

The idea is very clear. For the judiciary, discrimination is contrary to the core values from which India's constitutional democracy draws its sustenance. Perturbed by the fact that despite having had a democratic Constitution and supportive institutions, the LGBTQ community continues to remain socially marginalized and suffer due to the seemingly universally acceptable ideas about their so-called weird behaviour. Being the custodian of the Constitution, it is the responsibility of the court to reverse the system by introducing laws to that effect which it articulated by stating that 'the development of law cannot be a mute spectator to the struggle for the realization and attainment of the rights of such members of the society'. Here, there is a resonance of what BR Ambedkar suggested in the Constituent Assembly while defending why India's Constitution was the bulkiest of all the constitutions. According to him, he did not want to leave any grey area in the Constitution in terms of values, principles and conceptualizations, since it would allow the future law makers to devise designs in conformity with their priorities which may run counter to the core constitutional values. As the Constitution is committed to attain aspired liberal goals – liberty, equality and fraternity, it was easier for the court to undertake such a step which, despite being odd to many, was perfectly in tune with what the founding father so assiduously upheld.

Along with securing legitimate rights of the LGBTQ community, the court has also touched upon two critical areas, which are useful to conceptualize India's constitutional identity in the changed socio-economic and political perspective. Integral to the idea of demosprudence in which the importance of demos outweighs the rest, the court, on the one hand, feels that India's constitutional identity needs to be conceptualized in the format of transformative constitutionalism. Dubbing the Preamble to the Constitution as 'a laser beam' in the sense that it helps identify the critical areas for democratic governance, the court, on the other, feels that the 'egalitarian democracy and its provisions can be comprehended only by a spacious, social science approach, not by pedantic, traditional legalism'. This is further justified by suggesting that

> the purpose of having a Constitution is to transform the society for the better and this objective is the fundamental pillar of transformative constitutionalism. . . . The Constitution would become a stale and a dead document without dynamic, vibrant and pragmatic interpretation. Constitutional provisions have to be construed and developed in such a manner that the real intent and existence percolates to all segments of society. That is the *raison d'etre* for the Constitution.

As suggested here, a Constitution is not just a compilation of rules and regulations, it is directional as well. There are fundamental ideas which sustain the Constitution though the actual provisions are likely to change in view of the circumstances in which it is expected to act. What is emphasized here is the dialectical interconnection between the constitutional provisions and the context; here perhaps lies the dynamism of a Constitution being an instrument of transformation. In other words, being a device for transformation, a Constitution provides enough room for change as and when it is needed; here the court has a critical role to play, as the judgement emphatically declares by saying that

> the principle of transformative constitutionalism also places upon the judicial arm of the State a duty to ensure and uphold the supremacy of the Constitution, while, at the same time ensuring that the sense of transformation is ushered in constantly and endlessly in the society by interpreting and enforcing the Constitution as well as other provisions of law in consonance with the avowed object. The idea is to steer the country and its institutions in a democratic egalitarian direction where there is increased protection of fundamental rights and other freedoms. It is in this way that transformative constitutionalism attains the status of an ideal model imbibing the philosophy and morals of constitutionalism and fostering greater respect for human rights. It ought to be remembered that the Constitution is not a mere parchment; it derives its strength from the ideals and values enshrined in it. However, it is only when we adhere to constitutionalism as the supreme creed and faith and develop a constitutional culture to protect the fundamental rights of an individual that we can preserve and strengthen the values of our compassionate Constitution.

There are three significant points that deserve attention to help conceptualize India's constitutional identity, which is being constantly reworked and reinvented. First, it has been made amply clear that the Constitution is not just a rule book; it provides specific directions to accomplish the avowed objective of making India an egalitarian society. Constitutional provisions are thus directional in the sense that they steer a specific course of action for the polity to adopt. Second, when the question of steering a specific path comes to the fore, the importance of the court is emphasized. 'The juridical arm of the State' is a critical player insofar as steering the state towards fulfilling the foundational principles of the Constitution. The court is, in other words, responsible for interpretation or reinterpretation of the provisions of the Constitution in accordance with those cardinal values without which it will lose its identity in the conceptual format of liberal constitutionalism. Finally, by accepting that the Constitution is an instrument for visible social, economic and political transformation, the court further stipulates that it cannot be oblivious of this responsibility. How can this be achieved? For the court, one needs to be extremely sensitive of (a) the philosophy and morals of constitutionalism fostering greater respect for human rights, (b) the organically developed constitutional culture supporting human dignity and respect, and (c) importance of the Constitution being an instrument and device for compassion and change.

In comprehending transformative constitutionalism, the court pays adequate attention to constitutional morality, which is not 'limited to the mere observance of the core principles of constitutionalism', but embraces 'within itself virtues of a wide magnitude such that ushering in a pluralistic and inclusive society, while, at the same time, adhering to the other principles of constitutionalism'. By defining constitutional morality as widely as possible, the court also expands its scope by including social morality though it is aware that in case of ascertaining justiciability of a law, constitutional morality is privileged. So, constitutional morality needs to be understood along with social morality, which does not seem to be always congruent with the former. The judgement makes this point by forcefully arguing that

> in the garb of social morality, the members of the LGBTQ community must not be outlawed or given step-motherly treatment of malefactor by the society. If this happens or if such a treatment to the LGBTQ community is allowed to persist, then the constitutional courts, which are under the obligation to protect the fundamental rights, would be failing in the discharge of their duty. A failure to do so would reduce the citizenry rights to a cipher.

Implicit here is the argument that constitutional morality should be immune from social morality since it is, in this context, contrary to the fundamental principles of democratic constitutionalism. As far as the 1950 Constitution is concerned, the values of liberty, equality and fraternity are always privileged. Because of well-entrenched prejudices against people with 'the socially unacceptable sexual behaviour and conduct', the LGBTQ community never received what they deserved as part of Indian citizenry. The court has thus a responsibility to ensure what has thus been denied to this community on the basis of well-entrenched prejudices, which are justified as social morality. Hence, by defining constitutional morality as inclusive of social morality, the court thus mentions that

> it is the concept of constitutional morality which strives and urges the organs of the State to maintain such a heterogeneous fibre in the society, not just in the limited sense, but also in multifarious ways. It is the responsibility of all the three organs of the State to curb any propensity or proclivity of popular sentiment or majoritarianism. Any attempt to push and shove a homogeneous, uniform, consistent and a standardized philosophy throughout the society would violate the principle of constitutional morality. Devotion and fidelity to constitutional morality must not be equated with the popular sentiment prevalent at a particular point of time.

Asymmetrical behaviour should not be a constraint in the fulfilment of the ideals of a democratic society. Individuals with 'a different sexual behaviour and conduct' have also the right to be treated at par with others in society. Lack of conformity with the majority's attitude and behaviour can never be a ground for denial of rights and freedom which are available to others. Given India's diverse social, economic and political texture, diversity is inherent to Indian self. The court upholds the view by stating that

> any asymmetrical attitude in the society, so long as it is within the legal and constitutional framework, must at least provide an environment

> in which it could be sustained, if not fostered. It is only when such an approach is adopted that the freedom of expression including that of choice would be allowed to prosper and flourish and if that is achieved, freedom and liberty which is the quintessence of constitutional morality, will be allowed to survive.

The LGBTQ may appear to be an exception or weird if it is conceptualized in a straitjacketed manner; it is not so since human beings are biologically different with different natural behaviours. A democratic polity meant to secure justice, liberty and equality for all ceases to be so if it allows discrimination on the basis of the socially defined 'peculiar' behaviour. This is a clear defiance of the fundamental values and principles of constitutional democracy, and, by seeking to establish a democratic polity, the founding fathers and those who presided over India's destiny following independence upheld them to fulfil their aspirations. Thus, the judgement ends with a poignant note which deserves to be quoted in full. As it took seventy years after independence to ensure that LGBTQ community is to be treated at par with the rest of the society, the court thus feels that

> history owes an apology to the members of this community and their families, for the delay in providing redressal for the ignominy and ostracism that they have suffered through the centuries. The members of this community were compelled to live a life full of fear of reprisal and persecution. This was on account of the ignorance of the majority to recognize that homosexuality is a completely natural condition, part of a range of human sexuality. The misconception of this provision denied them the Fundamental Right to equality guaranteed by Article 14. It infringed the Fundamental Right to non-discrimination under Article 15, and the Fundamental Right to live a life of dignity and privacy guaranteed under Article 21. The LGBT persons deserve to live a life unshackled from the shadow of being un-apprehended felons.

The 2018 judgement, by according recognition to the LGBTQ community as integral to India's constitutional democracy, can be said to have corrected a historical wrong which was perpetuated simply because of a well-entrenched prejudiced mind. Socially retrogressive, the attitudinal slur on those having a different sexual orientation was sustained despite challenges presumably because of the prevalent mindset supporting visible discrimination. Many battles were fought; in 2001, the Naz Foundation, a New Delhi-based non-governmental organization that works in the field of HIV/AIDS prevention, had challenged 377 section of the Indian Penal Code in the Delhi High Court which ruled in its favour saying that the law does not apply to consenting adults. The joy was short-lived because a Supreme Court bench, headed by Justice GS Singhvi, reversed the order in 2013 and declared homosexuality a criminal offence again. The court also told that it was beyond its authority to outlaw the section; it was the parliament which could, by following the legislative routes, replace the legally justified restriction. Given the long history of challenges and counter-challenges, the 2018 pronouncement is undoubtedly a revolutionary step in two major ways: on the one hand, it has translated into reality the founding fathers' concern for making India an egalitarian space for everybody regardless of gender, class, caste or ethnicity. By putting the sexual preference at the centre stage, the court again proves that it is a powerful instrument in pursuing the core constitutional goals that the founding fathers had set out for future India.

The court judgement is a revolutionary step undoubtedly though it was accomplished after a long-drawn struggle by those espousing the LGBTQ cause in which people from all walks of life participated. That the apex court was reluctant in 2013 to scrap the archaic law which was repealed almost everywhere is also a testimony to the role that the democratic struggle plays in shaping the judicial priorities. It was not possible for the judiciary to adopt the course that it had in 2018, which also suggests how a changed mindset was supportive of outlawing section 377 in a rather conducive environment. There is a conceptual point here: organs of the state do not seem to be exactly independent of the milieu in which they act and operate for the fulfilment of the constitutional values which are inviolable. In case of the 2018 judgement, it was hailed since it reaffirms the commitment of the state to the values that the founding fathers held so dear while preparing India for her journey as an independent polity. That the LGBTQ community has a legitimate claim to be treated as rightful citizens did not seem to have received adequate attention in the past presumably because of a well-entrenched mindset prejudicial to its existence. Change was visible but not accepted which was evident when India's Supreme Court was not inclined to discard the outlandish piece of legislative decision of 1861 in 2016. It took exactly two years for the apex court to outlaw the section since it is a fragrant violation of the basic principles which the Indian Constitution upholds.

In the light of the above discussion, one can safely conclude that transformative constitutionalism is an important aspect of India's constitutional identity, which is formed and also regularly reinvented in response to newer socio-economic and political demands arising out of democratic struggle being waged at grass roots and also at various walks of life. The 1950 Constitution is thus not a lifeless compilation of provisions, but is vibrant and organically connected with the prevalent social, economic and political reality which is evident by being accommodative of newer demands and views, provided they conform to the core values of India's constitutional democracy. The judgement may have been delivered to secure the rights and freedom of a particular section of society; nonetheless, it is also a testimony to the court being aware of larger changes and greater tolerance for diversity. In other words, the 2018 judgement may have a specific aim; it has the potential of

> fundamentally reshaping the jurisprudence around equality in India [because by discarding archaic laws] the Supreme Court's judgment

> could potentially give new meaning to the notion of equal protection of laws, protecting not just the LGBT community, but potentially every minority in a country of minorities.[26]

From the conceptual point of view, the judgement provides enough inputs to understand equality, freedom and justice in a different light. It has also taken into account the fact how contextual influences become a source of radical changes in our perception, which gets reflected in the judicial pronouncement. This is a valid point of significant importance if it is judged with reference to the fact that the same Supreme Court did not find any merit in the NAZ Foundation petition in 2016, which did not decriminalize homosexuality. It is therefore a remarkable piece of judgement because not only has it recognized the rights and freedom of the LGBTQ community, it has also undone its own decision that it took in 2016. By being accommodative of newer social, economic and political demands within the overall constitutional framework, the judgement further reconfirms that India's constitutional identity is hardly static, but is being constantly reinvented without, of course, undermining the fundamental principles on which it is built.

The story however remains incomplete without reference to another judgement of 2018 regarding the lifting of ban on the entry of women in the age of 10 and 50 years in the Sabrimala Ayyappa temple in Kerala. On the basis of its commitment to the core values of India's constitutional government and practices, the majority of the judges in the division bench held that the ban on women is a smear on their dignity and the consequence of hegemonic patriarchy, which are constitutionally unjustified. The point is very clear: more or less following the judgement securing justice for the LGBTQ community in 2018, the judges felt that it was perfectly in tune with their commitment to the principal values on which the 1950 Constitution rests. In other words, for the Supreme Court, the Sabrimala case is a test of constitutional morality, and the majority of the judges held the view that the forcible ban on women entry is violative of the equality principles of Articles 14, 15 and 17. By strictly applying the test of rationality and 'implicitly concluded that Swami Ayyapppa's vow of permanent celibacy was "too abstruse to compromise absolute principles of the Constitution"'.[27] There is a twist, however: in her dissenting note, Justice Indu Malhotra held the view that the court had no right to impose its rationality or morality on the form of worship of a deity. If it is done, it amounts, as she felt, to a negation of the freedom to practise one's own religion according to one's faith and beliefs. Though diametrically opposite, the judgement by the majority and the dissenting judgement by Justice Malhotra have valid points: while the former interprets the restriction in conformity with the constitutional rationality which should be uniform regardless of circumstances, the dissenting note by emphasizing individual rationality does not seem to be contradictory with the core principles of constitutional democracy that has flourished in India.

The latter also warns that by making the Constitution as sacrosanct and upholding constitutional morality as abiding, the majority judgement tends to accord 'the holy book status' to the Constitution, which is unwarranted because it is contrary to the fundamental democratic ethos of demos being supreme. It has thus been perceptively argued that

> constitutional morality is an important check on religious obscurantism but when carried to an extreme it can also be destructive of harmless variety and difference. There is a danger of reducing the Constitution itself to another unquestionable 'holy book', killing diversity in the name of countering discrimination.[28]

There is substance in this contention because the judgement is, argues an analyst, 'an act of social engineering and based on the belief that faith and custom must correspond to the diktats of modernity; it has mechanically directed radical change on a Hindu culture that is both eternal and constantly adaptive', which led some to believe that 'quite unwittingly, the Supreme Court may have set the stage for a hardening of attitudes'.[29] The idea is clear. Uniformity is not desirable because it strikes at the foundation of India being a diverse society which the nationalists and those who set out a democratic path for India by adopting constitutional democracy would never have approved. So, the debate unfolds with the concern whether constitutional morality is privileged even at the cost of losing India's well-entrenched diversity or otherwise. There could hardly be a conclusive answer though it will set in motion various new sets of arguments leading to newer conceptualization and understanding of India's constitutional identity.

Concluding observations

By analysing selective judgements of India's Supreme Court, the chapter reinforces the point that in the shaping of India's constitutional identity, the apex court plays a critical role by interpreting/reinterpreting or even discarding well-established legislative and judicial decisions. Implicit here are two important points: on the one hand, it directs our attention to the fact that constitutional provisions are neither sacrosanct nor inviolable and hence they can be modified, changed or even abdicated if they run out of their utility in the prevalent circumstances. There is, however, a cautionary note which brings to our attention, on the other, that the provisions can be altered or discarded, provided that does not affect the fundamental character of India's Constitution. One is here reminded of the basic structure doctrine which allows amendments to the extent they do not challenge the basic structure or those conceptual pillars and institution which are critical to India's constitutional identity as a constitutional democracy.[30] The moot point here is that revision in the constitutional provisions is permissible so long as the inner kernel of the Constitution or its identity remains unaltered.

Besides highlighting the critical role of the courts in determining politico-ideological priorities, these judgements also strengthen the argument that they are enmeshed with the political processes. This is also illustrative of the fact that courts do not form their opinion in a vacuum, but in a context in which multiple ideas keep on jostling for space in the public domain. What is argued here is the point that the courts decide on the basis of the inputs that they receive by being integrally connected with the prevalent socio-economic and political reality in which they are rooted. What it further means is that judgements are a testimony to the concern and also understanding that the courts develop while being engaged in both day-to-day struggle and the wider battle for substantial changes. The 2018 LGBTQ judgement shall exemplify the point very persuasively: in 2016, the apex court was not convinced and the LGBTQ community was denied what it has to be demanding for quite some time. By 2018, the situation seems to have undergone a sea change and the same court came out in clear terms that the denial is simply repugnant to the constitutional ethos that have so far been nurtured in India's constitutional democracy. The decision, however, did not come voluntarily; instead, it was an outcome of sustained struggle that the members of the LGBTQ community had undertaken for securing their legitimate rights as citizens of democratic India. In conceptual terms, it was a power struggle in which the LGBTQ claim for equality, freedom and justice gained precedence and with its endorsement the apex court took a position which, it felt, conformed to India's constitutional identity as a constitutional democracy.

There is one final point. By upholding the core principles of constitutionalism, India's Supreme Court not only interprets but also provides definite directions to future legislative designs. It has therefore a critical role in shaping India's constitutional identity which is also an outcome of an ideational struggle in which multiple actors coalesce to step out either for change or sustenance of the system. This also confirms the argument that for a persuasive discussion of India's constitutional identity, one needs to be sensitive to the dialectical interconnection between what the Constitution upholds as sacrosanct principles and their acceptance by the governed. In its role as an arbiter, a final arbiter strictly in the legal sense, the apex court intervenes when the views from the context do not match with the constitutional values. What it means is that constitutional identity evolves and is also designed out of an ideational battle in which, besides the organs of the state, the demos have also an important responsibility to discharge. It cannot however be conceptualized so neatly presumably because of the complex socio-economic and political circumstances in which this ideational battle takes place. Nonetheless, it can fairly be said that while acting as an arbiter, the courts cannot escape the contextual inputs based on newer social, economic and political demands emerging out of grass-roots struggles. Being the custodian of the Constitution, the court filters these inputs by ascertaining whether they are contrary or supportive of the core values on which the Constitution rests; only then they figure in their pronouncements. So, India's constitutional identity cannot be said to be exactly derivative, but is an outcome of a very complex interplay of ideas in an equally complex social, economic and political milieu.

Notes

1 www.dailyo.in/politics/triple-talaq-allahabad-high-court-islamic-law/story/1/14454.html, Allahabad High Court judgement, 2016, accessed on 28 April 2018.
2 ibid.
3 ibid.
4 The text of the judgement is drawn on www.thehindubusinessline.com/multimedia/archive/03194/Supreme_Court_judg_3194881a.pdf, Shayara Bano and others versus Union of India, Writ Petition (C) No. 118 of 2016, accessed on 29 April 2018.
5 Drawn in Shayara Bano and others versus Union of India, Writ Petition (C) No. 118 of 2016, available in www.thehindubusinessline.com/multimedia/archive/03194/Supreme_Court_judg_3194881a.pdf, accessed on 29 April 2018.
6 Salman Khurshid, *Triple Talaq: Examining Faith*, Oxford University Press, New Delhi, 2018, p. 32.
7 ibid, p. 124.
8 Cited from Shayara Bano and others versus Union of India, Writ Petition (C) No. 118 of 2016, available in www.thehindubusinessline.com/multimedia/archive/03194/Supreme_Court_judg_3194881a.pdf, accessed on 29 April 2018.
9 ibid.
10 Justice J Kurian's views are cited from Shayara Bano and others versus Union of India, Writ Petition (C) No. 118 of 2016, available in www.thehindubusinessline.com/multimedia/archive/03194/Supreme_Court_judg_3194881a.pdf, accessed on 29 April 2018.
11 ibid.
12 Justice JS Khehar's views are cited from Shayara Bano and others versus Union of India, Writ Petition (C) No. 118 of 2016, available in www.thehindubusinessline.com/multimedia/archive/03194/Supreme_Court_judg_3194881a.pdf, accessed on 29 April 2018.
13 Justice J Khanna's views are citied by Justice JS Khehar's in his judgement on Shayara Bano and others versus Union of India, Writ Petition (C) No. 118 of 2016, available in www.thehindubusinessline.com/multimedia/archive/03194/Supreme_Court_judg_3194881a.pdf, accessed on 29 April 2018.
14 ibid.
15 Salman Khurshid, *Triple Talaq: Examining Faith*, Oxford University Press, New Delhi, 2018, p. 135.
16 Salman Khurshid, 'Double jeopardy on Triple Talaq: why the Triple Talaq is not about empowerment of women at all', *The Times of India*, New Delhi, 23 January 2018.
17 The idea of intersectionality is drawn on Kimberle Williams Crenshaw, 'Mapping the margins: intersectionality, identity politics, and violence against women of colour', *Stanford Law Review*, Vol. 43, No. 6, July 1991, pp. 1241–1299. According to Crenshaw,

> Many women of colour are burdened by poverty, child-care responsibilities and the lack of job skills. These burdens, largely the consequence of gender and class oppression are then compounded by the racially discriminatory

employment and housing practices women of colour often face. . . . . These observations reveal how intersectionality shapes the experiences of many women of colour. Economic considerations-access to employment, housing and wealth confirm that class structures play an important part in defining the experience of women of colour vis-à-vis battering. But it would be a mistake to conclude from these observations that it is simply the fact of poverty that is at issue here. Rather, their experiences reveal how diverse structure intersect, since even the class dimension is independent from race and gender. (p. 1243)

18 Orini Shani, *How India Became Democratic: Citizenship and the Making of Universal Franchise*, Penguin, India, 2018, pp. 1–2.
19 Vivek Prahladan, 'Emergence of the Indian constitution: affirmative action and cultural fault lines', *Economic and Political Weekly*, 18 February 2012, p. 42.
20 James Madison, Item No. 49, Clinton Rossiter (ed.), *The Federalist Papers*, Mentor, New York, 1961, p. 314.
21 Gary Jeffrey Jacobsohn, 'Constitutional identity', *The Review of Politics*, Vol. 68, No. 3, 2006, p. 371.
22 Justice KS Puttaswamy (Retired) versus Union of India and others, 24 August 2017, available in http://indiakanoon.org/doc/91938676/, accessed on 13 July 2018. All the citations that follow are from the judgement.
23 The Fourth Amendment of the US Constitution states that

the right of the people to be secure in their persons, houses, papers and effects against unreasonable searches and seizures, shall not be violated, and no warrants shall issue, but upon probable cause, supported by Oath or affirmation, and particularly describing the place to be searched, and the persons or things to be seized.

24 LGBTQ – Lesbian, Gay, Bisexual, Transgender, Queer.
25 https://indiankanoon.org/doc/12376270/, All the citations that follow are from the Supreme Court judgement on Navtej Singh Johar and Others versus the Union of India, 6 September 2018 in response to the original Writ Petition (Criminal) No. 76 of 2016.
26 Alok Prasanna Kumar and Arghya Sengupta, 'Historic and necessary: by decriminalizing gays, SC ushers in new dawn for an inclusive society and country', *The Times of India*, New Delhi, 7 September 2018.
27 Swapan Dasgupta, 'Why Sabrimala verdict is an act of social engineering'. *The Times of India*, New Delhi, 7 October 2018.
28 R Jaganthan, 'A flawed Sabrimala verdict: don't kill religious diversity in the name of countering gender discrimination', *The Times of India*, New Delhi, 5 October 2018.
29 Swapan Dasgupta, 'Why Sabrimala verdict is an act of social engineering'. *The Times of India*, New Delhi, 7 October 2018.
30 I have elaborated this point in my *Constitutionalizing India: An Ideational Project*, Oxford University Press, New Delhi, 2018, Chapter 9.

Conclusion

There are many ways of conceptualizing constitutional identity. Legally one is reconciled with the idea of characterizing constitutional identity in terms of core legal principles on which a country's Constitution is based. Apparently, this is fair since a Constitution is primarily a compilation of legally articulated provisions, and a legal reading of these enactments reveals their nature and also texture. So, for legal-constitutionalists, it does not seem to be a hard task because an appropriate legal reading of the constitutional provisions is the best option to follow to conceptualize constitutional identity. This is legalistic and does not seem to be confusing since constitutional identity is conceptualized in terms of the letters of the Constitution. One of the serious limitations of such a conceptualization stems from the charges that exclusive legalistic understanding of a Constitution will hardly help us comprehend the true nature of a Constitution which is also interwoven with how it is politico-ideologically construed. As is commonly understood, a Constitution, despite being just a collection of rules and regulations, is also political in the sense that it evolves in a set of power-relationships which hardly remain static. And, that Constitution is the best that passes through the test of time which means that it adapts itself with the changing socio-economic and political milieu without compromising on the fundamental politico-ideological values, mores and principles from which it derives its sustenance. Significant here is a claim that for an appropriate understanding of constitutional identity, one needs to be sensitive to the context in which it evolves. It is a matter of common sense that liberal constitutionalism develops in a milieu in which constitutional liberalism is privileged. What it defends is the conceptualization that constitutional identity is primarily a context-driven phenomenon which further confirms that a mere legal articulation of the constitutional provisions can neither be illuminating nor ideologically perceptive for being highly restrictive, both in its nature and meaning. This is an obvious and logic-driven articulation of a conceptualization; there is no scope for confusion. Different circumstances, however, emerge if contrary positions are justified which is always the case if the constitutional values fail to make inroads in a society in which it evolves. Implicit here are two complementary arguments: on the one hand, it makes the point that mere codification of laws by drawing upon the Enlightenment values and principles does not, by itself, ensure their ready acceptance by the people; one needs to inculcate a mindset in their support which is a long-drawn process. There is also the point, on the other, that a mindset, once evolved, will automatically ensure the continuity of the Constitution based on the aspired politico-ideological preferences. What is required is also to create and consolidate a politico-cultural milieu to strengthen those priorities which are consciously chosen by the demos to fulfil what they deem appropriate for their future. Basic here is the point that constitutional identity does not emerge naturally, but is constructed keeping in view the exalted values and principles complementary to what a specific multitude of people considers appropriate for attaining specific politico-ideological goals.

As is argued above, constitutional identity needs to be understood with reference to the wider socio-economic and political context in which multiple politico-ideological forces, drawing on identical ideological predilections, jostle for creating legitimate spaces for themselves. There is therefore a constant struggle being waged for devising what is deemed to be the best option under particular circumstances. What is common among those battling for priorities is their commitment to an ideological priority: in case of India, or, for that matter, any liberal polity, it is constitutional liberalism that is the reigning ideal which can never be undermined under any circumstances. Basic here are two core points: on the one hand, privileging of constitutional liberalism stipulates a specific ideological path for a liberal polity; it is a deliberate preference that evolves out of sustained practices and gets consolidated as they gain acceptance at large; as the Constitution is also an ideological response, it is designed/or redesigned, on the other, in keeping with those ideological priorities which are taken as axiomatic at a particular historical juncture. Constitutional identity is thus a conceptualizing endeavour which unfolds in a historical perspective. The endeavour is not, at all, ideology-neutral since it is directed to privilege one ideology or a set of ideology over another. It is not thus surprising that the US Constitution-makers preferred the Enlightenment values while drafting the 1789 US Constitution. Similar is the case in India: the 1950 Constitution of India was the outcome of concerted efforts on the part of the founding fathers for designing a Constitution and creating a concomitant structure of governance for the future polity. In other words, it is a text-context dialectics that finally led to the making of the Constitution for independent India. Basic here is the point that constitutional identity is not a matter of chance, at all, in view of the contention that it evolves out of complex processes in which specific ideological priorities are privileged, which also confirms what appears to be a linear development does not seem so. Constitutional identity is not thus, to speak metaphorically, an icing on the cake, but the substance which makes it. Fundamental here is the point that for a fair understanding of constitutional identity as a conceptual phenomenon, one needs to go beyond what the legally enacted provisions stipulate to the wider politico-ideological environment in which they evolve and also derive their meaning and sustenance.

The story, as the text shows, is however incomplete unless one takes into account the efforts that the legislature, judiciary and others institutions of governance make in pursuing a specific kind of governance drawing on the fundamental ideological priorities that a polity upholds. As Jacobsohn argues, representing a mix of aspirations and commitments expressive of nation's past, constitutional identity also 'evolves in ongoing political and interpretive activities occurring in courts, legislatures, and other public and private domains'.[1] Stating that constitutional identity is hardly a fixed entity, he further confirms that it is being constantly redefined by many social and political institutions which are not, in classical sense, part of the institutionalized forms of public authority. This is a powerful, and also persuasive, conceptualization as it leaves a legitimate space for those inputs which may not have emerged out of the activities being undertaken by the recognized actors in the public domain. The trajectory of India's constitutional identity is illustrative here. As the nationalist campaign grew in importance, the British authority in India devised various constitutional designs to accommodate the Indians in governance. It was ideologically justified presumably because of the colonizers' faith, at least in principle, in constitutional liberalism. The journey that had begun out of compulsion set in motion a process which loomed large as history progressed, and it is thus not an overstretched assumption that constitutional democracy that India had adopted after the British withdrawal had its roots in the past. It was an uninterrupted journey: constitutional liberalism had emerged as integral to India's rise as a constitutional democracy. For the founding fathers, the choice was not a difficult one because liberal constitutionalism became, by then, organic to India's socio-political existence. The 1950 Constitution of India had to be the one that it finally became. What was set out in the past continues to remain so suggesting that Constitution has struck deep roots in Indian polity. In other words, by being attentive to the values of constitutional democracy, the institutions of governance, judiciary and legislature, in particular, complement the processes towards sustaining the design that, despite being a legacy of colonialism, became generic to India's socio-economic and political life. In conceptual terms, the trajectory of India's constitutional identity thus provides powerful inputs to theoretically articulate how it eventually created parallel socio-economic and political processes consolidating an urge for liberal constitutionalism as integral to the Indian mindset.

II

Constitutional identity is a historical construct: it evolves out of text-context dialectical interconnections. It is true that the founding fathers drafted the 1950 Constitution after having put almost three years of hard work. A perusal of the debates in the Assembly reveals that the discussion was intensive and always tuned to the concern of the participants for making independent a truly democratic polity. The debates also underline how consensus had emerged among the members despite not being entirely persuaded presumably because of an identical politico-ideological goal that they espoused. An interesting chapter of India's rise as a constitutional democracy, the long-drawn debates in the Constituent Assembly are very useful to understand how India's constitutional identity had evolved at a particular historical juncture. There is, however, substance in the argument that it drew on the colonial tradition; nonetheless, it was not a smooth sailing, as the proceedings in the Assembly confirm. In view of the majority endorsement of the system of constitutional democracy that flourished in colonial India, liberal constitutionalism was privileged though there were many members, especially the Gandhians, who not only challenged, but also offered an alternative Gandhian mode of democratic governance, village swaraj, for India.

So, there were multiple influences which informed the endeavour that the Assembly members had undertaken to evolve India's constitutional identity. The purpose here is to argue that constitutional identity, because it blossoms in a socio-economic and political context, cannot immune from the contextual influences. Furthermore, the framers while being involved in the drafting of the Constitution brought their knowledge of the prevalent constitutional systems to the discussions. This does not seem to be odd because, as history reveals, the drafting of a written Constitution also involves a process of adapting international standards to indigenous requirements. It is thus not surprising that 'close similarities exist between many Constitution, but each Constitution invariably acquires unique characteristics as it stretches to respond to local needs'.[2] This is a process leading to the assimilation of values borrowed from elsewhere. The idea is put most eloquently by Upendra Baxi who, while justifying assimilation being an obvious choice, thus argued that

> constitution-makers everywhere remain concerned with the best constitutional design; however, the 'best' consists in 'shopping' around available models and adapting these to their needs and aspirations. The eventual mix, or more picturesquely put, the 'bricolage' is constrained by history interlaced with future-looking aspirations for transformation. South Asian constitutions are no exceptions.[3]

Implicit here are two basic arguments which are useful to conceptualize India's constitutional identity: on the one, it has been emphasized that for drafting a Constitution, borrowing or 'shopping around', to quote Baxi, for an appropriate model is inevitable since the framers seem persuaded. This is however not a blind borrowing as Baxi further explains, on the other, that the 'bricolage', to survive, needs to be sensitive to the contextual requirements along with future-looking nationalist aspirational zeal. In other words, constitutional identity is a creative blending of both the borrowed and indigenous ideas which are justified in a particular historical context. This is not unusual as the past history of designing constitutions demonstrates. Beginning with the role played by Greek 'law-givers', who always drew on what they learnt while drafting 'set of laws' in another context, the tradition continues, as a cursory look at the city states' constitutions reveals.

An analytical account of the debates in the Constituent Assembly also reveals that the founding fathers were also seriously concerned with the making of a Constitution which was to fulfil the aspirations that the nation had upheld during its battle against colonialism. It was clear when the Constitution was being drafted that India was to become a constitutional democracy which also confirms how history shaped India's constitutional identity even when the existent regime was not, at all, democratic, for obvious reasons. In a very loose sense, the 1950 Constitution was thus not exactly a break with the past. Despite being aware of this, the framers did not seem to have been perturbed by this, as Jawaharlal Nehru candidly expressed when he stated that

> a constitution is something which should last a long time, which is built on a strong foundation, and which may of course be varied from time to time – it should not be rigid – nevertheless one should think of it as something which is going to last, which is not a transitory Constitution, a provisional Constitution.[4]

A full sense of this argument can be captured if it is read with the following comment that Nehru made in favour of a Constitution which should not either be rigid in character. Being aware that a rigid Constitution however good it was in terms of values was also not desirable, he thus emphatically argued that a Constitution was

> something which you are going to change from day to day, as something which has provisions for the next year or the year after next and so on and so forth. … After all, what is going to be done in the future will largely depend upon the sentiment of the people and future Assemblies and Parliaments that will meet.[5]

The argument can be conceptualized at two levels: at one, it was made clear the Constitution needed to be amended to keep pace with the rapidly changing social, economic and political realities; at a rather perceptive level, Nehru emphasized the critical role that the future parliamentarians were to play in shaping the constitutional provisions in response to the newer socio-economic and political demands and challenges. The point is very clear: constitutional identity needs to be reinvented, of course, within the broad, and widely accepted, politico-ideological priorities which are foundational in character. For instance, since the core of India's constitutional democracy is liberal constitutionalism, it can never be undermined as it is critical to her existence as a liberal democratic polity.

India's Constitution makers were particularly concerned with the retention of those values which remained integral to consolidation of liberal constitutionalism, which they seem to have instinctively imbibed largely due to their exposure to the Enlightenment ideas. For them, bereft of these ideas, their principal politico-ideological mission of imbuing India with the core liberal values remained elusive. It was most succinctly stated by BR Ambedkar when he, in the Assembly, insisted on the inclusion of the 'Directive' in the text of the Constitution. According to him,

> with regard to the word 'directive' I think, it is necessary and important that the word should be retained because it is to be understood that in enacting this part of the constitution, the Constituent Assembly ... is giving certain directions to the future legislature and future executive to show in what manner they are to exercise the legislative and executive power which they will have. If the word 'directive' is omitted I am afraid the intention of the Constituent Assembly in enacting this part will fail its purpose. Surely, as some have said, it is not the intention to introduce in this part these principles as mere pious declarations. It is the intention of this Assembly that in future both the legislature and the executive should not merely pay lip service to these principles enacted in the part, but they should be made the basis of all executive and legislative action that may be taken hereafter in the matter of the governance of the country. I therefore submit that the [word] ... 'directive' [is] necessary and should be retained.[6]

This is perhaps one of the most exhaustive description of what should constitute constitutional identity as a conceptual category in general and India's constitutional identity in particular. On a surface reading, one is inclined to endorse the claim that Ambedkar was favourably disposed to this idea to quell the Gandhians' attack on him when he dismissed their insistence on organizing India's governance around Gandhi's notion of village swaraj. It was therefore a strategic design with immediate gain. This appears to be superficial if one reads the above text in between lines. It is true that Babasaheb elaborated this point when the Assembly dealt with the Directive Principles of State Policy; so there was a *prima facie* justification to suggest that it was a tactical step. But a careful reading of the above statement reveals that the word 'directive' is directional in keeping with the basic thrust of the constitutional practices that the founding fathers desired to instil. In other words, the principles in Part IV (Directive Principles of State Policy) of the Constitution were not pious declarations but contained those concerns which the framers had espoused while challenging the alien authority. By insisting that these principles were crucial in governance, Babasaheb articulated a design of constitutional governance which was ideologically rooted in the rich tradition of constitutional liberalism; it was a tradition which, despite being clearly Western in origin, evolved organically in India for a variety of complex historical, political and ideological reasons.[7] That these principles should be made the basis of all executive and legislative action in future was a testimony to the claim that they were part and parcel of India's constitutional democracy. As shown in Chapter 3, the Directive Principles acted as determinants in the evolution of the Basic Structure doctrine, which was a significant development in India's constitutional history for, by upholding them it (a) reiterated the polity's faith in liberal constitutionalism, (b) redefined democracy by going beyond its political meaning to seek to capture its social and political dimensions as well and also (c) reaffirmed that India's constitutional identity is not static, but is being constantly reinvented.

According to Ambedkar, within the broad parameters of constitutional democracy, the Constitution is allowed to be accommodative of newer inputs which are reflective of newer demands and challenges. A democrat per excellence, he always insisted that under no circumstances, the view of people being sovereign could be wished away which he explained by saying that 'what should be the policy of the State and how the Society should be organized in its social and economic side are matters which must be decided by the people themselves according to time and circumstances'.[8] Implicit here was his concern for realizing democracy in both spirit and content, which was possible once demos reigned supreme and engaged in deciding what was most appropriate for them. Hence, he further warned that the future course of action

> cannot be laid down in the Constitution itself because that is destroying democracy altogether. If you state in the Constitution that the social organization of the State shall take a particular form, you are ... taking away the liberty of the people to decide what should be the social organization in which they wish to live.[9]

Here Ambedkar made two important points which are critical to India's constitutional identity: first, drawn on his faith in the Enlightenment values, he unambiguously defended the supremacy of the demos in so far as the system of governance was concerned. Second, for him, democracy was not just about the structure of government, but also offered a value perspective in which popular will was articulated; it was to be guided in accordance with the fundamental ideological preferences though the exact forms were to be decided by the people in response to the needs of the hour. What it means is the claim that changes in the constitutional format are allowed, provided that they are endorsed by the demos which further confirms India's constitutional identity as a liberal democracy remains in its place. In other words, the design may change, but within the broad foundational principles that the founding fathers had established at the dawn of India's political independence in 1947. This does not seem to be unusual as it is universally acknowledged. In the early twentieth century, US judge Billings Learned Hand articulated an identical concern when he stated that

> I often wonder whether we do not rest our hopes too much upon Constitutions, upon laws and upon courts. These are false hopes; believe me, these are false hopes. Liberty lies in the hearts of men and women; when it dies there, no Constitution, no law, no court can save it.[10]

At one level, the judge made no qualms to suggest that mere institutional guarantee was not, at all, adequate, to retain the democracy; what was required was an alert people, a vigilant people, who allowed no distortion in the system. At another far more perceptive level, he further argued that democracy survived in a context of free flow of ideas which he articulated by suggesting that 'the mutual confidence on which all else depends can be maintained only by an open mind and a brave reliance upon free discussion'.[11] By reiterating that shackle-free discussion was a vital requirement of democracy, he drew our attention to one of the fundamental principles of the Enlightenment philosophy, which could never be shunned, and being raised in an environment in the US in which liberal democracy was privileged, it perhaps came to him naturally. For him, the constitutional rules and regulations however noble did not survive unless they were adequately supported by evolving a complementary mindset. Democracy was about the critical importance of demos and their critical role in governance which was possible only in an environment of free and fair play of ideas; otherwise, it would be a facade with no substance, at all. The primary concern that Learned Hand had shown was for building a milieu in which discussion and contestations did not appear to be an anathema; instead, they were the driving forces. Two ideas are significant here: on the one hand, Hand reiterated an obvious statement, namely constitutionalizing constitutional values was possible in a supportive environment which, once dissected, also refers to the creation and also consolidation of a corresponding mindset. By drawing on the dialectical interaction between the former and the latter, Hand laid out, on the other, a powerful conceptual foundation for constitutional identity, which was not merely what was codified in the Constitution, but was articulated in popular ethos and values. Argued thus, constitutional identity was not just manifested in a set of justiciable rules, but in the spirit of defending them as integral to the politico-ideological vision supportive of an institutionalized form of governance.

Even at the risk of repeating, let me restate the point that I made at the outset. Drawn on the principle of constitutional liberalism, the founding fathers, while being engaged in drafting the Constitution, made their ideological preferences amply clear: they were convinced that constitutional democracy in the liberal mould was the only option for independent India. It is true that besides liberal constitutionalism, no other ideological alternative was seriously discussed in the Constituent Assembly; the most intensive debate that took place was over whether an individual or a village should be the basic unit of governance; there were passing reference to the Soviet model of state-led planned development though it seldom received the attention that it deserved presumably because the majority of the Assembly members had no inkling towards Marxism as an ideological option. So, constitutional liberalism was the only alternative that gained massive support. A perusal of how it became so brings us back to the well-entrenched constitutional identity that flourished during the course of colonial rule. Liberal democracy of the Western variety gradually, but steadily, sipped in the public mindset to the extent of being indispensable; the claim has a substance because when the founding fathers adopted constitutional democracy for independent India, there was hardly a murmur in the public domain; instead, it was accepted as given which reinforces the argument that liberal democracy, being integral to India's constitutional identity, was hardly unnatural in her rise as a democratic polity.

III

A careful scan of India's constitutional identity developed both during the British rule and its aftermath shows that it was constantly being reinvented. A fairly accepted argument, this also suggests that it will be theoretically restrictive if constitutional identity is conceived of as static. Implicit here are two significant points with massive theoretical implications: first, it dwells on how constitutional identity is forged which is certainly not preordained because the texture of constitutional rules and regulations undergo changes (through procedurally accepted amendments) to accommodate newer demands and inputs suggestive of newer aspirational ideals. Second, it also entails the point that the core of constitutional identity remains the same regardless of the changes in its text as a result of being accommodative of newer concerns. This is particularly significant in liberal democracies in which the Constitution remains as respected as in the past despite change of regimes largely due to the wider acceptance of the fundamental values from which it draws its sustenance. This is a major step in forging constitutional identity. Jacobsohn has captured this by drawing our attention to the constituents of constitutional identity and how it is created and consolidated by saying that

> a constitution is a large piece of nation's constitutional identity, but it is not coterminous with it. In most cases, it lays down key markers of that identity, then to be adapted to changing political and social realities in ways that modify, clarify, or reinforce it through dialogical engagement of various public and private sources of influence and power.[12]

There are thus three aspects which one needs to highlight to conceptualize constitutional identity: based on certain exalted ideological principles, constitutional identity is also adapted to the changing socio-economic and political reality, which is possible out of a dialogical engagement. This entails a process in which several institutions, both political and governmental, participate. In case of India, it is judiciary that played a very decisive role in shaping India's constitutional identity in its battle for retaining her constitutional democracy, a fabric which the founding fathers so assiduously built over long years of their struggle against colonialism. India's apex court rose to the occasion in 1973 while deciding whether parliamentary authority for amending the Constitution was absolute or not. In the famous Kesavananda Bharati case (1973), the Supreme Court of India developed the basic structure doctrine, suggesting that there were specific features of the Constitution which were deemed to be sufficiently fundamental to India's democratic-secular Constitution. The doctrine was never defined precisely because the judiciary felt that a precise definition was likely to restrict the concept which was clearly context-dependent. Nonetheless, there are some features in the Constitution which are recognized as critical to the doctrine. In a landmark judgement of 2016 that outlawed the appointment of National Judicial Appointment Commission, chief Justice JS Khehar identified some of the prominent features that cannot be overlooked while conceptualizing the basic structure doctrine. According to him,

> the 'basic structure' of the Constitution, presently inter alia includes the supremacy of the Constitution, the republican and democratic form of Government, the 'federal' character of distribution of power, secularism, 'separation of powers' between the legislature, the executive and the judiciary, and 'independence of the judiciary'. The [Supreme] Court, while carving out each of the above 'basic structure' placed reliance on one of more Articles of the Constitution (sometimes, in conjunction with the preamble of the Constitution). It goes without saying, that for carving out each of the 'core' or 'basic features/basic structure' of the Constitution, only the provisions of the Constitution are relied upon. It is therefore apparent, that the determination of the 'basic features' or the 'basic structure' is made exclusively from the provisions of the Constitution'. ... Clearly the 'basic structure' is truly a set of fundamental foundational principles, drawn from the provisions of the Constitution itself. These are not fanciful principles carved out by the judiciary, at its own. Therefore, if the conclusion is drawn that [a fundamental constitutional principle] has been violated, it is to be understood that the rule/principle collectively, or individually, emerging from the [well-defined] constitutional provisions, had been breached or ... had been transgressed.[13]

The doctrine had its root in German jurisprudence that insists that there are implied and enforceable limits to the constitutional change through the amendment process. This is corroborated by Khehar's detailed explanation in which he, more or less, clearly identified the features which can easily be specified as integral to the basic structure of the Constitution. In a nutshell, what is argued here is the point that the Constitution represents certain basic norms, values and principles that cannot be undermined under any circumstances. They are sacrosanct because on them depends the nature of the Constitution. As India has a liberal democratic Constitution, constitutional liberalism needs to be upheld since it provides the basic character to the polity. The Supreme Court of India was very clear that fundamentals of the fundamental are required to be upheld since they epitomize those core values on which the Constitution is based. Hence, the court argues that 'the expression, amendment, of this Constitution does not enable the Parliament to abrogate … the basic structure of the Constitution … to completely change the fundamental features of the Constitution so as to destroy its identity'.[14] One of the most perceptive judicial verdicts, the Kesavananda judgement of the majority of the judges in bench of thirteen of the Supreme Court judges did not exactly define the basic structure of the Constitution though they provided enough inputs to understand what it means. The concern was to uphold constitutional liberalism, which became part and parcel of India's existence as a constitutional democracy. For the court, it is the preamble to the Constitution which holds the substance of governance, a faith that was established when it was stated that 'it cannot be overlooked that the basic theory of our Constitution is that "Pouvoir Constituent" is vested in the people and was exercised, for and on other behalf by the Constituent Assembly for the purpose of framing the Constitution'.[15] The argument was further elaborated by emphasizing that

> the Preamble serves several important purposes. Firstly, it indicates the source from which the Constitution comes, viz., the people of India. Next, it contains the enacting clause which brings into force the Constitution. In the third place, it declares the great rights and freedoms which the people of India intended to secure to all citizens and the basic type of government and polity which was to be established.[16]

It was also made clear that the Preamble constitutes the nervous system of India's constitutional identity, which was eloquently argued by emphasizing that

> the Preamble to the Constitution which our founding fathers have, after the Constitution was framed finally settled to conform to the ideals and aspirations of the people embodied in that instrument, have in ringing tone declared the purposes and objectives which the Constitution was intended to subserve.[17]

Emphatic in its belief that constitutional identity which evolved historically could not be fiddled with, the apex court also underlined that amendment of the part of the Constitution known to hold the basic structure thus was suicidal. Hence, the court had reasons to believe that

> the people of India will not be rash enough to amend the glorious words of the Preamble; and as long as the Preamble is there the Governments will have to honour the Preamble and the Constitution will have to continue as a vehicle which would lead us to the goals.[18]

As shown in Chapter 5, the basic structure doctrine is both a culmination and also a beginning of a serious debate over the nature of India's constitutional identity: the idea was critical in many judgements that followed the Kesavananda Bharati verdict; this was also an idea which reinforces the point that Constitution reigns supreme, and the values from which it draws its sustenance cannot easily be abnegated. What is also striking is the fact that the doctrine privileges demos, since they constitute the primary source of power in a democracy; and the Constitution epitomizes that authority in no unclear terms. A perusal of the debates in the Constituent Assembly shows that regardless of their differences over the forms of government, both the Gandhians and their opponents supported the Objective Resolution that Jawaharlal Nehru moved in December 1946 in the Constituent Assembly since it corresponded with their commitment to make the demos the ultimate source of authority. Setting in motion a clearly defined ideological mission, the Resolution was also a testimony to the priorities that the founding fathers had accorded to popular sovereignty. Under no circumstances, these principles cannot be undermined; they are inviolable, as Justice JS Khehar, the former chief justice of India, most succinctly conveyed this by exhorting that

> the 'basic structure' of the Constitution is inviolable, and as such, the Constitution cannot be amended so as to negate any 'basic features' thereof, and so also, if a challenge is raised to an ordinary legislation based on one of the 'basic features' of the Constitution, it would be valid to do so. If such a challenge is accepted, on the ground of violation of the 'basic structure', it would mean that the bunch of Articles of the Constitution (including the preamble thereof, wherever relevant), which constitute the particular 'basic feature', had been violated.[19]

This is actually a reiteration of the point that is usually made while dealing with the nature of the basic structure doctrine which is integral to India's constitutional identity. If they are allowed to be abrogated at will by the executive, endorsed by legislative 'tyranny' due to excessive numerical strength in the legislature, the argument goes, India's distinctive constitutional identity shall not only be adversely affected, but will also lose its politico-ideological sanctity. That the idea that was articulated about five decades ago in the 1973 Kesavananda Bharati case continues to remain relevant today confirms the point that the basic structure doctrine has become organic to constitutional discourses in India. A well-entrenched and widely accepted constitutional intent, the basic structure doctrine can thus be said to have not only consolidated liberal constitutional democracy in India, it has also created a legitimate space in our collective mind primarily because it is complementary to her existence as a democratic polity. This has a very significant implication, since basic features are not merely reduced to a set of constitutional characteristics; it is very much a part and parcel of India's democratic political processes in which the role of the demons is immensely significant. So, despite its roots in juridical exercises, the basic structure doctrine has struck organic roots in India's socio-economic and cultural processes contributing to and also strengthening a specific kind of constitutional identity in support of constitutional democracy, largely in the liberal format. This further confirms that being a part of India's constitutional identity, basic structure doctrine, notwithstanding its origin in a judicial intervention, has now become integral to India's cultural ethos sharply questioning efforts towards undermining constitutional democracy and, at the same time, zealously supporting endeavours for the fulfilment of those politico-ideological goals which are complementary to India's constitutional democracy.

IV

Constitutional identity is a conceptual category. Hence, it is also a cerebral design in accordance with certain politico-ideological principles which can be indigenous in origin and also derivative in character. Being the repository of fundamentals of a fundamental document, the Constitution, constitutional identity ceases to be a mere conceptual category once it decisively acts in shaping the design of the Constitution and also its unfolding; it is not about a set of principles, but also denotes a set of directions for a constitutional polity in accordance with the former. A perusal of the processes that culminated in the articulation of the Enlightenment principles which later became integral to British constitutional practices shall illustrate the point. In the evolution of constitutional identity in Britain, one cannot gloss over the role of the 1688 Glorious revolution which, by overthrowing James II, established parliamentary sovereignty. Beginning with the 1648 Puritan Revolution, the processes had culminated in the Glorious Revolution once the monarchy was made subservient to the elected parliamentarians. Thomas Hobbes' *Leviathan* (1651) and later John Locke's *The Second Treatise of Civil Government* (1689), and of course, JS Mill's Representative Government (1861), besides supportive parliamentary legislations, endorsed those ideas which gradually became part of the constitutional discourses supportive of parliamentary democracy in Britain. Important here is the argument that the British constitutional identity, drawn on Enlightenment values, which were articulated by their ideologues, emerged out of specific historical processes. Similarly, in the construction of the US constitutional identity, the role of the British Enlightenment and its articulation in *The Federalist Papers* (1788) was immensely critical. Gradually, these inputs became part and parcel of constitutional identity in the US, which was always upheld to ascertain the constitutionality of legislative acts and executive deeds. What is emphasized here is the point about the historicity of a parameter which constitutionality of identity articulates. The story does not seem to be dissimilar in case of India. Drawn on their faith in constitutional liberalism, the founding fathers drafted a Constitution which was largely liberal in character. It was also felt that a liberal Constitution was vacuous unless it was complemented by constitutional morality, which Ambedkar defined as 'reverence' to the Constitution for being true to the core values and ethos of liberal constitutionalism. The idea was accepted and pursued enthusiastically in independent India as history progressed. This was also an offshoot of complementary socio-economic and political processes upholding India's liberal constitutional identity. As shown above, the judiciary also steadfastly held the view by striking down executive feats in undermining those constitutional features which are critical to liberal constitutionalism in India: they cannot be fiddled with to the detriment of what is defined as the basic structure of the Constitution. The argument is crystal clear: India is a liberal-democratic polity which is constitutionally protected; in conceptualizing her constitutional identity, the characterization of India being a liberal-constitutional-democratic polity thus remains a significant politico-ideological attribute that is required to be upheld under all circumstances for its sustenance. By implication, it also means that as soon as the fundamental principles on which India rests as a liberal compact are undermined, she ceases to be what she is now. So, constitutional identity is a construct which is also a politico-ideological marker for a polity at one level; at another, it is also deterrent in the sense that an attack on those defining principles will both cause irreparable damage to the ideological foundation on which they thrive and generate processes leading ultimately to its liquidation.

At the end, there is an epistemological query: being an articulation of the core constitutional-ideological principles and practices, constitutional identity is clearly directional, as its trajectory since its inauguration in 1950 confirms. There is an advantage by conceptualizing constitutional identity being a directional/or guiding device since it leaves a scope also to justify the point that the direction-driven constitutional identity needs to be adaptive to the context in which it develops organic roots. There are two implications if constitutional identity is conceptualized in such an epistemological format: on the one hand, it is clear that constitutional identity cannot be fixed; it is required to be regularly reinvented since the context is always in flux. With the acceptance of this kind of argument, one thus confronts, on the other, the point that if the fundamentals of the fundamental undergo changes, can they still be called fundamental! This is partly correct and partly false: partly correct because if fundamentals are discarded, what is left as constitutional identity; partly false because if it is not adaptive, constitutional identity shall be devoid of substance since it draws on 'principles' which are not contextually relevant. Here, Jacobsohns' conceptualization of constitutional identity seems appropriate. As per him, constitutional identity must be viewed as 'embodiments of unique histories and circumstances',[20] which undergo metamorphosis, and in order to remain relevant and also meaningful, it has to be adapted accordingly. The idea is drawn on Edmund Burke's famous definition of Constitution which, according to him, is 'made by peculiar circumstances, occasions, tempers, dispositions, and moral, civil and social habitudes of the people that disclose themselves only in a long space of time'.[21] So, there is substance when the claim is made by suggesting that India's constitutional identity evolved out of long-drawn historical processes leading to the privileging of liberal democracy over other competing ideological discourses. It was accepted by the framers of the Constitution after fierce debates on each and every aspect of constitutional democracy that India adopted after decolonization. So, India's liberal constitutional identity is historically ordained and also nurtured in circumstances in which it was also ideationally justified presumably because it matched with, what Bhikhu Parekh characterizes as 'the country's self-given identity'.[22] Important here is the point that India preferred constitutional liberalism because it came to her rather instinctively by being exposed to complementary politico-ideological influences during the British colonial rule. As a result, the ideas of equality, freedom and fraternity were readily upheld by the founding fathers when they met to draft the Constitution. These ideas remain sacrosanct though changes are also brought about as and when it was needed. In other words, in so far as constitutional identity is concerned, continuity and stability are as critical as a change. The evolution of the basic structure doctrine and also the judicial embargo on Triple Talaq are illustrative here. Similarly, by insisting that parliament, despite being an elected body, is bound by the Constitution, India's apex court by evolving the basic structure doctrine reinforced a familiar point that upholds that since Constitution epitomizes the *vox populi*, it can never be undermined even by the parliamentarians who get democratically elected. Here, freedom in its undiluted form is protected. In the same vein, the Triple Talaq judgement is also a serious attempt in expanding the idea of equality, which was severely restricted since the Muslim men were allowed to divorce their legally wedded wives instantaneously by resorting to Triple Talaq; it was a clear violation of constitutional guarantee of the right to freedom and equality. As shown above, the court upheld the plea and outlawed Triple Talaq. Not only was the judgement a serious attempt in seeking to realize equality and freedom in absolute terms, it was also a significant steps towards empowering Muslim women. The challenges notwithstanding by 'backward and misogynist Muslim men, backed by the opposition', with their legal victory, Muslim women 'are not likely to remain silent pawns';[23] and, with wider support from across the communities, the battle for equality and freedom was no longer confined to them only, but became one with wider concerns. Examples can be multiplied to substantiate the point that continuity and stability are critical to our conceptualization of constitutional identity and so is change. Hence, it has been argued most persuasively that

> identity in the constitutional domain, however elusive a concept it may be, is best comprehended within [the prevalent socio-economic and political context] in which all elements [of the political processes],

including identity itself, are modifiable through their engagement with one another.[24]

Constitutional identity is both sacrosanct and flexible in a specific sense: the fundamentals of the fundamental cannot be changed, but can be expanded in keeping with the former, since they constitute the core of constitutional identity. Ideationally, the inputs from the libertarian thinkers, both from India and elsewhere, remain relevant along with the context in which they are put to test both during the British rule and its aftermath. The 1950 Constitution of India can be said to be a carbon copy of the past constitutional designs though it can be persuasively argued that in so far as its foundational values are concerned, there are, of course, elements of continuity and stability. This however needs to be understood with reference to the contention that by being true to the fundamental values and principles, India's constitutional identity is not immune from transformation simply because it is being enmeshed in the rapidly changing prevalent socio-economic and political reality. There is therefore substance in the claim that at one level, India's constitutional identity is clearly 'sacred' and hence not to be fiddled with; at another perceptive level, it is receptive to change, provided, of course, it does not adversely affect the fundamentals of the fundamental.

There is one basic point that the book offers by suggesting that no discussion of India's constitutional identity shall be persuasive unless one draws attention to the creative blending of both derivative and nationalist-indigenous sources. This is now fairly accepted that the founding fathers readily accepted the liberal constitutionalism presumably because they were raised in an environment in which it was privileged. There is substance in the claim though the question why the Enlightenment values gain precedence in their approach remains unanswered. Let me problematize it further. According to Article 1 of the 1950 Constitution, 'India that is Bharat, shall be a union of states'. Why was Bharat included since the expression India was adequate to demarcate the territory? The inclusion of the term, Bharat, is illustrative of framers' concern for linking contemporary India with her past when the territory was known as Bharat which is not merely a marker for geography, but history, culture, society, economy, politics and so on and so forth. A perusal of the debates in the Constituent Assembly on Article 1 reveals that the participants were persuaded by the contention that the comprehension of India was not possible without understanding her past legacy when she was known as Bharat. In fact, claims were made quite forcefully to defend the point, raised during the course of the debate. Even BR Ambedkar, in his last speech in the Constituent Assembly on 25 November 1949 referred to the well-established democracies that flourished in ancient India. That he meant what he stated was evident when, despite being opposed to Gandhian village swaraj, he agreed to the incorporation of panchayati governance in Part IV of the Constitution (Directive Principles of State Policy). Perhaps owing to their organic roots in India's socio-political fabric, the discussion on village swaraj in the Assembly hovered around claims that democracy was not an alien idea, but was rooted in India's indigenous traditions. By referring to Henry Maine's text entitled *Village Republics of the East* which was, in his writings, signposted by Charles Metcalfe (1785–1846) in his defence for localizing governance, the framers seem to have further substantiated their claims that it was also recognized by the British ideologues. The adoption of the 1882 Rippon Resolution, which institutionalized local government in India, was a recognition of the idea of village swaraj; they further upheld in their intervention. In a similar vein, secularism as an idea appears to have been ingrained in the Gandhian notion of *Sarva Dharma Samabhava* (equal respect to all religions), which was also forcefully argued in the Assembly. There are solid reasons to believe that secularism evolved in India naturally presumably because of the well-entrenched social, economic and political diversities, being nurtured since time immemorial. One of the most persuasive expositions of this conceptual claim is the one that Swami Vivekananda offered in his famous 1893 Chicago speech before the Parliament of World Religions in which he unequivocally stated that

> I am proud to belong to a religion [Hinduism] which has taught the world both tolerance and universal acceptance. We believe not only in universal toleration, but we accept all religions as true. I am proud to belong to a nation which has sheltered the persecuted and the refugees of all nations of the earth. I am proud to tell you that we have gathered in our bosom the purest remnant of the Israelites, who came to southern India and took refuge with us is the very year in which their holy temple was shattered to pieces by Roman tyranny. I am proud to belong to the religion which has sheltered and is still fostering the remnant of the grand Zoroastrian nation.[25]

This was distinctive of the Indian tradition, Vivekananda stated, of being respectful of all religions. In his defence, he referred to specific Vedic hymns highlighting the fact that 'toleration' and 'universal acceptance' remained an important ingredient of India's well-entrenched cultural traditions. The aim was to put across the point that the Indians being tolerant and respectful of all religions was not inculcated, but evolved naturally by being nurtured in an environment in which it was always privileged. The idea was forcefully conveyed by the Swami when he questioned the assumption that 'unity of [people of different religions] will not come by the triumph of any of the religions and the destruction of the others'. Instead, he emphasized the idea of *Sarva Dharma Samabhava* by persuasively arguing that

> the Christian is not to become a Hindu or a Buddhist, nor a Hindu or a Buddhist to become Christian. But each must assimilate the spirit of the others and yet preserve his individuality and grow according to his own law of growth.[26]

So, one's religious denomination was just a nomenclature for oneself, which was not a deterrent to one being friendlier to the others, Vivekananda argued. In other words, for him, it was an important source of learning since each religious tradition had its own cultural packages, and by being receptive, the communities would come together around a spirit of well-being for everybody regardless of his/her religious or ethnic identities.

In defending the argument that India's constitutional identity is a creative admixture of both exogenous and indigenous influences, Vivekananda's Chicago speech provides a powerful justification. As the Swami had shown by reference to Vedic texts, what was identified as Enlightenment values and principles also had its roots in India's sociocultural traditions. In the light of this contention, it can now be fairly argued that the nationalists while pondering on issues of constitutionalism readily endorsed the colonial intervention as it corresponded with their sociocultural preferences, which they imbibed instinctively. There were, of course, political considerations, which may appear to have governed their choice if one understands the preference merely on the basis of a surface reading of the situation; an in-depth reading of why the choice was readily accepted (barring a few exceptions) by all, however, suggests that it had happened largely because the spirit of accommodation and consensus was not, at all, foreign to Indians, but was part and parcel of their being as Indians. To put it differently, being nurtured in a tradition of being accommodative and receptive to others, it was natural for the Indians to appreciate the spirit of *Vasudhaiva Kutumbakam* (the world being a family). It was reconfirmed in the Constituent Assembly when the participants notwithstanding their clear politico-ideological incompatibilities contributed to the making of the 1950 Constitution as one collectivity that submerged their differences for the sake of a common cause. This is a testimony to the fact that being together for a mission is also suggestive of how the spirit of togetherness which they imbibed instinctively cemented a bond instantaneously. Basic here is the argument that India's constitutional identity cannot be fully grasped without reference to the historical-civilizational perspective in which it has evolved and led to the creation and consolidation of a conducive sociocultural and political milieu in which constitutional-liberal-democracy emerged as a natural choice. *India's Constitutional Identity* is just a baby step towards unearthing those processes which culminated and also help sustain constitutional democracy in India despite occasional challenges and threats to her continuity.

Notes

1 Garry Jeffrey Jacobsohn, 'Constitutional identity', *The Review of Politics*, Vol. 68, 2006, p. 361.
2 Peter Leyland and Andrew Harding (eds.), *Constitutional Courts: A Comparative Study*, Wildy, Simmonds and Hill, London, 2009, p. 3.
3 Upendra Baxi, 'Modelling 'optimal' constitutional design for government structures: some debutant remarks', in Sunil Khilnani, Vikram Raghavan and Arun

K Thiruvengadam (eds.), *Comparative Constitutionalism in South Asia*, Oxford University Press, New Delhi, 2013, p. 23.

4 Jawaharlal Nehru, Constituent Assembly, 25 November 1948, *Constituent Assembly Debates*, Book No. 2, pp. 588–589.

5 ibid., pp. 589–590.

6 BR Ambedkar, Constituent Assembly, 19 November 1948, *Constituent Assembly Debates*, Book No. 2, p. 476.

7 I have dealt with how constitutional liberalism triumphed in India, both during colonialism and its aftermath, in my *Constitutionalizing India: An Ideational Project*, Oxford University Press, New Delhi, 2018.

8 BR Ambedkar, Constituent Assembly, 15 November 1948, *Constituent Assembly Debates*, Book No. 2, p. 413.

9 BR Ambedkar, Constituent Assembly, 4 November 1948, *Constituent Assembly Debates*, Book No. 2, p. 39.

10 http://digitalcommons.law.yale.edu/fss_papers/4099, *cited in* Jerome N Frank, "Some reflections on judge learned hand" (1957). Faculty Scholarship Series. Paper 4099, p. 669.

11 ibid., p. 671.

12 Gary Jeffrey Jacobsohn, 'Constitutional identity', in Sujit Chowdhury, Madhav Khosla and Pratap Bhanu Mehta (eds.), *The Oxford Handbook of the Indian Constitution*, Oxford University Press, New Delhi, 2016, p. 124.

13 https://indiankanoon.org/doc/66970168/, The Supreme Court of India versus the Union of India, October 2015, chief justice, JS Khehar's pronouncement (paragraph 220), accessed on 1 May 2018.

14 https://indiankanoon.org/doc/257876/, Kesavananda Bharati versus the State of Kerala, 1973, accessed on 27 April 2018, p. 1565.

15 ibid., p. 1178.

16 ibid., p. 1038.

17 ibid., p. 1106.

18 ibid., p. 1121.

19 https://indiankanoon.org/doc/66970168/, The Supreme Court of India versus the Union of India, October 2015, chief justice, JS Khehar's pronouncement (paragraph 221), accessed on 1 May 2018.

20 Garry Jeffrey Jacobsohn, 'Constitutional identity', *The Review of Politics*, Vol. 68, 2006, p. 372.

21 Edmund Burke, 'Speech on a motion made in the House of Commons, 7 May 1782, for a committee to inquire into the state of representation of the commons in parliament', cited in Garry Jeffrey Jacobsohn, 'Constitutional identity', *The Review of Politics*, Vol. 68, 2006, p. 372.

22 Bhikhu Parekh, 'The constitution as a statement of Indian identity', in Rajeev Bhargava (ed.), *Politics and Ethics of the Indian Constitution*, Oxford University Press, New Delhi, 2008, p. 46.

23 Jyoti Punwani, 'Triple Talaq judgment and after', *Economic and Political Weekly*, 28 April, 2018, p. 15.

24 Garry Jeffrey Jacobsohn, 'Constitutional identity', *The Review of Politics*, Vol. 68, 2006, p. 395.

25 *Swami Vivekananda's Addresses at the World's Parliament of Religions*, Chicago, 1893, Advaita Ashrama, Calcutta, 1993, p. 26.

26 ibid., p. 52.

Bibliography

A bibliography is always directional in character in the sense that it provides research-directions to those seeking to explore the theme further. Hence, a bibliography can never be an exhaustive list of books or texts. It is always selective since it is prepared by the author with reference to his/her intellectual inclinations and priorities. However, given the fact that there are some texts which are conceptually fundamental, no bibliography can ignore them. And, also, there are books which are distinctive by being distinctive in their approaches, and these generally find places in most of the bibliographies. As these are widely known, I have not included some of them, which, however, does not mean that they are not important; instead, by not putting them in the bibliography, I put across the point that they are assumed to have been read by the scholars seeking to explore the untrodden aspects of India's rise and growth as a constitutional democracy.

Three important criteria seem to have gone in preparing this bibliography: first, it contains books, articles and other relevant texts which are obviously helpful in substantiating the argument and illuminating the theme; this further means that I am extremely selective which also keeps space for argument that no bibliography can be absolutely exact. Second, the book is about an idea, and not, about a conventional theme. My purpose is to comprehend India's constitutional identity on the basis of ideas, values and ethos that go in its making. One therefore needs to be sensitive to the historical conceptualization of India's constitutional past at the behest of colonialism since the colonial interventions also had a visible impact on its articulation during the British rule and its immediate aftermath. Hence, the bibliography has space for authors who dwelled on this aspect of India's constitutionalizing processes. Finally, in a similar vein, the bibliography also takes into account the important contribution of the nationalists in steering India's constitutional identity in a specific fashion. This is evident if one looks at how constitutionalism and constitutional practices have evolved in India, particularly after decolonization. There are many books, essays and media texts which, by focussing on the gradual transformation of India's constitutional identity, reveal how nuanced the processes are. This is obvious since a Constitution, unless it is adapted to the changing socio-economic and political realities, ceases to be a living organism, and, in consequence, cannot be effective in creating an acceptable template for governance. With the inclusion of these texts, the bibliography seeks to support the contention that without being receptive to the newer genre of thinking no research is worthwhile.

There is a note of caution. Bibliographies which authors prepare for their monographs are essentially tilted towards their academic preferences. Titles are included accordingly. Hence, they are an outcome of authors' unambiguous choice for those preferred texts which are considered relevant, if not appropriate, for specific kinds of arguments. The following bibliography is not an exception because the list of texts follows the same criterion which helps find a direction in accordance with the argument, set out at the outset. I don't claim to have put in the public domain an exhaustive bibliography since it is simply impossible on counts which I have just mentioned. Nonetheless, the following list of texts is pertinent for further research on constitutionalization, constitutionalism and constitutional practices in India, which, *inter alia*, help build useful resources for future endeavours at exploring how constitutional democracy flourishes in circumstances which the classical theorists characterized as not so conducive! This enhances the utility of this bibliography further because it provides meaningful inputs for evolving alternative conceptualizations and ideas which are distantly possible by being confined to the established domains of knowledge. In this respect, this bibliography is not merely directional, but also potentially a big push towards developing a new genre of thinking by drawing attention to those aspects of constitutionalization, constitutionalism and constitutional practices which have not received, so far, as much attention as is required.

The national documents

The Constitutional Proposals of the Sapru Committee, 1945, reproduced in B Shiva Rao (ed.), *The Framing of India's Constitution*, Vol. 1, Universal Law Publishing House, New Delhi, 1967.

The Motilal Nehru Committee Report, 1928, reproduced in B Shiva Rao (ed.), *The Framing of India's Constitution*, Vol. 1, Universal Law Publishing House, New Delhi, 1967.

Books and published articles

Adeney, Katharine and Lawrence Saez, *Coalition Politics and Hindu Nationalism*, Routledge, Oxford and New York, 2005.

Austin, Granville, *The Indian Constitution: The Cornerstone of a Nation*, Oxford University Press, New Delhi, 1966.

Austin, Granville, *Working a Democratic Constitution: A History of the Indian Experience*, Oxford University Press, New Delhi, 1999.

Bajpai, Rochana, 'Constituent Assembly Debates and minority rights', *Economic and Political Weekly*, Vol. 35, No. 21–22, 27 May 2000.

Bajpai, Rochana, *Debating Difference: Group Rights and Liberal Democracy in India*, Oxford University Press, New Delhi, 2011.

Basrur, Rajesh M (ed.), *Challenges to Democracy in India*, Oxford University Press, New Delhi, 2009.

Basu, Durga Das, *Introduction to the Constitution of India*, LexisNexis, Gurgaon, 2015.

Berlin, Isaiah, *Four Essays on Liberty*, Oxford University Press, New York, 1969.

Bernstein, James, *Dawning of the Raj: The Life and Trials of Warren Hastings*, Ivan R. Dee, Chicago, 2000.

Bhagwati, Jagdish and Arvind Panagariya, *India's Tryst with Destiny: Debunking Myths That Undermine Progress and Addressing New Challenges*, Collins Business, Noida, 2012.

Bhargava, Rajeev (ed.), *Politics and Ethics of the Indian Constitution*, Oxford University Press, New Delhi, 2008.

Bhatia, Gautam, *Offend, Shock or Disturb: Free Speech under the Indian Constitution*, Oxford University Press, New Delhi, 2016.

Bombwall, KR, *Indian Constitution and Administration*, Modern Publication, Ambala Cantt, 1978.

Bose, Sumantra, *Transforming India: Challenges to the World's Largest Democracy*, Picador India, New Delhi, 2013.

Brass, Paul, *Language, Religion and Politics in North India*, Cambridge University Press, Cambridge, 1974.

Brass, Paul, *The Politics of India since Independence*, Cambridge University Press, Cambridge, 1994.

Chakrabarty, Bidyut, 'BR Ambedkar and the history of constitutionalizing India', *Contemporary South Asia*, Vol. 24, No. 2, 2016, pp. 133–148.

Chakrabarty, Bidyut, 'BR Ambedkar: a "rebel" liberal in the Gandhian universe', *Indian Historical Review*, Sage, Vol. 23, No. 2, 2016, pp. 221–240.

Chakrabarty, Dipesh, *Provincializing Europe: Postcolonial Thought and Historical Difference*, Oxford University Press, New Delhi, 2000.

Chaube, Shibanikinkar, *Constituent Assembly of India: Springboard of Revolution*, Manohar, New Delhi, 2000.

Chaube, Shibanikinkar, *The Making and Working of the Indian Constitution*, National Book Trust, New Delhi, 2009.

Chiriyankandath, James, 'Creating a secular state in a religious country: the debate in the Indian Constituent Assembly', *Commonwealth and Comparative Politics*, Vol. 38, No. 2, 2000, pp. 1–24.

Chopra, Pran (ed.), *The Supreme Court Versus the Constitution: A Challenge to Federalism*, Sage, New Delhi, 2006.

Chowdhruy, Sujit, Madhav Khosla and Pratap Bhanu Mehta (eds.), *The Oxford Handbook of the Indian Constitution*, Oxford University Press, New Delhi, 2016.

Conniff, James, 'Burke and India: the failure of the theory of trusteeship', *Political Research Quarterly*, Vol. 46, No. 1, 1993, p. 257.

Dasgupta, Jyotirindra, *Language, Conflict and National Development*, University of California Press, Berkeley, 1970.

Dasgupta, Sandipto, 'A language which is foreign to us: continuities and anxieties in the making of the Indian Constitution', *Comparative Studies of South Asia, Africa and the Middle East*, Vol. 34, No. 2, 2014, pp. 228–242.

Dirks, Nicholas, *Castes of Mind: Colonialism and the Making of Modern India*, Princeton University Press, Princeton, 2001.

Doniger, Wendy and Martha C Nusbaum (eds.), *Pluralism and Democracy in India: Debating the Hindu Right*, Oxford University Press, New York, 2015.

Dworkin, Ronald, *A Matter of Principle*, Harvard University Press, Cambridge, 1986.

Dworkin, Ronald, *Freedom's Law*, Harvard University Press, Cambridge, 1986.

Dworkin, Ronald, *Law's Empire*, Harvard University Press, Cambridge, 1986.

Dworkin, Ronald, *Taking Rights Seriously*, Universal Law Publishing House, New Delhi, 1999.

Elangovan, Arvind, 'Constitutionalism, political exclusion, and implications for Indian Constitutional history: the case of Montague-Chelmsford reforms (1919)', *South Asian History and Culture*, Vol. 7, No. 3, 2016, pp. 271–288.

Elangovan, Arvind, 'Provincial autonomy, Sir Benegal Narsing Rau, and an improbable imagination of constitutionalism in India, 1935–38', *Comparative Studies of South Asia, Africa and the Middle East*, Vol. 36, No. 1, 2016, pp. 66–82.

Elangovan, Arvind, 'The making of the Indian Constitution: a case for a non-nationalist approach', *History Compass*, Vol. 12, No. 1, 2014, pp. 1–10.

Elangovan, Arvind, '"The road not taken": Sir Benegal Narsing Rau and the Indian constitution' in Sekhar Bandyopadhyay (ed.), *Decolonization and the Politics of Transition in South Asia*, Orient Blackswan, New Delhi, 2016, pp. 331–343.

Gajendragadkar, PB, *Law, Liberty and Social Justice*, New Age Printing Press, Bombay, 1965.

Galanter, Marc, *Competing Equalities: Law and the Backward Classes in India*, Oxford University Press, New Delhi, 1984.

Galanter, Marc, *Law and Society in Modern India*, Oxford University Press, New Delhi, 1997.

Galanter, Marc, 'Who are the backward classes?', *Economic and Political Weekly*, Vol. 13, No. 43–44, 28 October 1978, pp. 1152–1160.

Gudavarthy, Ajay, *Maoism, Democracy and Globalization: Cross-Currents in Indian Politics*, Sage, New Delhi, 2014.

Guha, Ranajit, *Dominance Without Hegemony: History and Power in Colonial India*, Oxford University Press, New Delhi, 1998.

Hansen, Thomas Blom, *The Saffron Wave: Democracy and Hindu Nationalism in Modern India*, Oxford University Press, New Delhi, 1999.

Hansen, Thomas Blom and Christophe Jaffrelot (eds.), *The BJP and the Compulsions of Politics in India*, Oxford University Press, New Delhi, 1998.

Hasan, Zoya, *Politics of Inclusion: Castes, Minorities and Affirmative Action*, Oxford University Press, New Delhi, 2009.

Hasan, Zoya, Eswaran Sridharan and R Sudarshan (eds.), *India's Living Constitution: Ideas, Practices, Controversies*, Permanent Black, Ranikhet, 2002.

Hayek, Friedrich A, *The Constitution of Liberty*, University of Chicago Press, Chicago, 1978.

Indian Round Table Conference (1931), *Indian Round Table Conference 12 November, 1930–19 January, 1931*, Proceedings, HM Stationary Office, London, 1931.

Jacobsohn, Gary Jeffrey, 'Constitutional identity', *The Review of Politics*, Vol. 68, No. 3, 2006, pp. 361–397.

Jaffrelot, Christophe, *Dr. Ambedkar and Untouchability: Analysing and Fighting Caste*, Permanent Black, Ranikhet, 2005.

Jaffrelot, Christophe, *India's Silent Revolution: The Rise of the Low Castes in North Indian Politics*, Permanent Black, Ranikhet, 2003.

Jaffrelot, Christophe, *The Hindu Nationalist Movement in India*, Viking, New Delhi, 1993.

Jayal, Niraja gopal, *Citizenship and Its Discontents: An Indian History*, Permament Black, Ranikhet, 2013.

Kalekar Commission (1956), *Report of the Backward Classes Commission*, Government of India, New Delhi, 1956.

Kashyap, Subhash C, *Our Constitution: An Introduction to India's Constitution and Constitutional Law*, National Book Trust, New Delhi, 2015 (reprint).

Kashyap, Subhash C, *The Indian Constitution: Conflicts and Controversies*, Vitasta Publications, New Delhi, 2010.

Khilnani, Sunil, *The Idea of India*, Hamish Hamilton, London, 1997.

Khosla, Madhav, *The Indian Constitution*, Oxford University Press, New Delhi, 2012.

King, Robert D, *Nehru and the Language Politics of India*, Oxford University Press, New Delhi, 1997.

Krishnaswami, Sudhir, *Democracy and Constitutionalism in India: A Study of the Basic Structure Doctrine*, Oxford University Press, New Delhi, 2009.

Kumar, Aishwary, *Radical Equality: Ambedkar, Gandhi and the Risk of Democracy*, Stanford University Press, Stanford, 2015.

Kumar, Ravinder, 'Gandhi, Ambedkar and Poona Pact, 1932', *South Asia: Journal of South Asian Studies*, Vol. 8, No. 1, 1985, pp. 132–143.

Kymlicka, Will, *Multicultural Citizenship: A Liberal Theory of Minority Rights*, Clarendon Press, Oxford, 1995.

Kymlicka, Will, *Politics in the Vernacular*, Oxford University Press, Oxford, 2001.

Larson, Gerald, 'Mandal, Mandir, Masjid: the citizen as an endangered species in independent India' in Robert D Baird (ed.), *Religion and Law in Independent India*, Manohar, New Delhi, 1993, pp. 31–43.

Larson, Gerald, *Religion and Personal Law in Secular India: A Call to Judgment*, Indiana University Press, Bloomington, 2001.

Legg, Stephen, 'Dyarchy: democracy, autocracy and the scalar sovereignty of interwar India', *Comparative Studies of South Asia, Africa and the Middle East*, Vol. 36, No. 1, 2016, pp. 28–41.

Mahajan, Gurpreet, *Identities and Rights: Aspects of Liberal Politics in India*, Oxford University Press, New Delhi, 1998.

Mehrotra, SR and Dinyar Patel (eds.), *Dadabhai Naoroji: Selected Private Papers*, Oxford University Press, New Delhi, 2016.

Mehta, Uday Singh, *Liberalism and Empire: India in British Liberal Thought*, Oxford University Press, New Delhi, 1999.

Metcalf, Thomas R, *Ideologies of the Raj*, Cambridge University Press, Cambridge, 1998.

Mukherjee, Mithi, 'Justice, war and imperium: India and Britain in Edmund Burke's prosecutorial speeches in the impeachment trial of Warren Hastings', *Law and History Review*, Vol. 23, No. 3, Fall 2005, pp. 589–630.

Mukherjee, Ramkrishna, *The Rise and Fall of the East India Company*, Monthly Review Press, New York, 1974.

Naoroji, Dadabhai, *Poverty and Un-British Rule in India*, S. Sonnenschein, London, 1901.

Nehru, Jawaharlal, *An Autobiography*, John Lane the Bodley Head, London, 1941.

Nehru, Jawaharlal, *The Discovery of India*, Oxford University Press, New Delhi, 1989 (reprint).

Noorani, Abdul Gafoor, *Constitutional Questions in India: The President, Parliament and the States*, Oxford University Press, New Delhi, 2000.

O'Hanlon, Rosalind, *Caste, Conflict and Ideology: Mahatma Jotirao Phule and Low Caste Protest in Nineteenth-Century Western India*, Cambridge University Press, Cambridge, 1985.

Omvedt, Gail, *Cultural Revolt in a Colonial Society: The Non-Brahmin Movement in Western India, 1873–1930*, Scientific Socialist Educational Trust, Bombay, 1976.

Omvedt, Gail, *Dalits and the Democratic Revolution: Dr Ambedkar and Dalit Movement in Colonial India*, Sage, New Delhi, 1994.

Outlines of a New Constitution, 1946, by Benegal Narsing Rau, reproduced in B Shiva Rao (ed.), *The Framing of India's Constitution*, Vol. 1, Universal Law Publishing House, New Delhi, 1967.

Parekh, Bhikhu, *Debating India: Essays on Political Discourse*, Oxford University Press, New Delhi, 2015.

Petit, Philip, *Republicanism: A Theory of Freedom and Government*, Oxford University Press, Oxford, 1999.

Philips, Anne, *The Politics of Presence*, Clarendon Press, Oxford, 1995.

Philips, Cyril Henry, *The East India Company, 1784–1834*, Manchester University Press, Manchester, 1961.

Prasad, Ganesh, 'Whiggism in India', *Political Science Quarterly*, Vol. 86, 1966, pp. 11–19.

Pylee, MV, *Constitutional Government in India*, Asia Publishing House, London, 1965.

Ramnath, Kalyani, 'We the people: seamless webs and social revolution in India's Constituent Assembly Debates', *South Asia Research*, Vol. 32, No. 1, 2012, pp. 81–93.

Rao, Shiva, *The Framing of India's Constitution*, 5 Vols, Universal Law Publishing Company, New Delhi, 1968.

Rathore, Akash Singh, *Indian Political Theory: Laying the Ground Work for Svaraj*, Routledge, Oxford and New York, 2017.

Rege, Sharmila (selected and introduced), *Against the Madness of Manu: BR Ambedkar's Writings on Brahmanical Patriarchy*, Navayana Publishing Pvt Ltd., New Delhi, 2013.

Roover, Jakob De, *Europe, India and the Limits of Secularism*, Oxford University Press, New Delhi, 2015.

Rosenfeld, Michel, *Affirmative Action and Justice: A Philosophical and Constitutional Enquiry*, Yale University Press, New Haven, 1991.

Roy, Anupama, *Citizenship in India*, Oxford University Press, New Delhi, 2016.

Roy, Anupama, *Mapping Citizenship in India*, Oxford University Press, New Delhi, 2010.

Roy, Srirupa, *Beyond Belief: India and the Politics of Postcolonial Nationalism*, Duke University Press, Durham, 2007.

Rudolph, Lloyd and Susanne Hoeber Rudolph, *The Realm of the Public Sphere: Identity and Policy*, Oxford University Press, New Delhi, 2008.

Saez, Lawrennce, *Federalism with a Centre*, Sage, New Delhi, 2002.

Saxena, Rekha, *Situating Federalism: Mechanisms of Intergovernmental Relations in Canada and India*, Manohar, New Delhi, 2006.

Sen, Amartya, *Collective Choice and Social Welfare*, Penguin, New Delhi, 2017 (reprint).

Sen, Amartya, *Development as Freedom*, Oxford University Press, New Delhi, 1999.

Sen, Amartya, *Identity and Violence: The Illusion of Destiny*, Allen Lane, London, 2006.

Sen, Amartya, *The Argumentative Indian: Writings on Indian History, Culture and Identity*, Picador, New York, 2005.

Sen, Amartya, *The Idea of Justice*, Allen Lane, New York, 2009.

Sen, Sarbani, *The Constitution of India: Popular Sovereignty and Democratic Transformations*, Oxford University Press, New Delhi, 2007.

Seth, Sanjay, 'Rewriting histories of nationalism: the politics of "moderate nationalism" in India, 1870–1905', *American Historical Review*, Vol. 104, No. 1, February 1999, pp. 95–116.

Sharma, Brij Kishore, *Introduction to the Constitution of India*, Prentice Hall of India, New Delhi, 2005.

Smith, Donald Eugene, *Nehru and Democracy: The Political Thought of an Asian Democrat*, Orient Longman, Calcutta, 1958.

Somanathan, Rohini, 'Assumptions and arithmetic of caste-based reservations', *Economic and Political Weekly*, Vol. 41, No. 24, 17 June 2006, pp. 917–921.

Sowell, Thomas, *Affirmative Action around the World: An Empirical Study*, Yale University Press, New Haven, 2004.

Stokes, Eric, *The English Utilitarians and India*, Cambridge University Press, Cambridge, 1959.

Sutherland, Lucy, *The East India Company in Eighteenth-century Politics*, Clarendon Press, Oxford, 1962.

Tilly, Charles, *Durable Inequality*, California University Press, Berkeley, 2002.

Topdar, Sudipa, 'Duties of a "good citizen": colonial secondary school textbook policies in late nineteenth-century India', *South Asian History and Culture*, Vol. 6, No. 3, 2015 (Annual Issue), pp. 417–439.

Tripathi, PK, 'Free speech in the Indian constitution: background and prospect', *Yale Law Journal*, Vol. 67, No. 3, 1958, pp. 191–201.

Upadhyaha, Prakash Chandra, 'The politics of Indian secularism', *Modern Asian Studies*, Vol. 26, No. 4, 1992, pp. 815–853.

Varshney, Ashutosh, 'Contested meanings: India's national identity, Hindu nationalism and the politics of anxiety', *Daedalus*, Vol. 122, No. 3, 1993, pp. 227–261.

Varshney, Ashutosh, *Ethnic Conflict and Civic Life: Hindus and Muslims in India*, Yale University Press, New Haven, 2002.

Venkatesan, Venkatasubramanian, *Constitutional Conundrums: Challenges to India's Democratic Process*, LexisNexis, Haryana, 2014.

Verma, Vidhu, *Non-discrimination and Equality in India: Contesting Boundaries of Social Justice*, Routledge, Oxford and New York, 2012.

Weiner, Myron, 'The political consequences of preferential policies: a comparative perspective', *Comparative Politics*, Vol. 16, No. 1, 1983, pp. 35–52.

Weiner, Myron, 'The struggle for equality: caste in Indian politics', in Atul Kohli (ed.), *The Success of India's Democracy*, Cambridge University Press, Cambridge, pp. 193–225.

Williams, Melissa, *Votes, Trust and Memory: Marginalised Groups and the Failings of Liberal Representation*, Princeton University Press, Princeton, 1998.

Willinson, Steven, *Votes and Violence: Electoral Competition and Ethnic Riots in India*, Cambridge University Press, Cambridge, 2004.

Zachariah, Benjamin, *Developing India: An Intellectual and Social History, c. 1930–50*, Oxford University Press, New Delhi, 2005.

Zeillot, Eleanor, *From Untouchable to Dalit: Essays on the Ambedkar Movement*, Manohar, New Delhi, 1996.

Unpublished PhD dissertation

Dasgupta, Sandipto, *Localizing the Revolution*, Unpublished PhD dissertation, Columbia University, 2014.

Elangovan, Arvind, *A Constitutional Imagination of India: Sir Benegal Narsing Rau Amidst the Retreat of Liberal Idealism (1919–1950)*, Unpublished PhD dissertation, University of Chicago, 2012.

Index

Note: Page numbers followed by "n" denote endnotes.